Dabrowski's Theory of Positive Disintegration

Sal Mendaglio, Ph.D., Editor

Great Potential Press, Inc.™

Copy editing: Jennifer Ault
Interior design: The Printed Page
Cover design: Hutchison-Frey/The Printed Page
Cover photo: Russ Huett Photography

Published by Great Potential Press, Inc.
P.O. Box 5057
Scottsdale, AZ 85261

Printed on recycled paper

11 10 09 08 07 5 4 3 2 1

Library of Congress Cataloging-in-Publication Data

Dabrowski's theory of positive disintegration / Sal Mendaglio, editor.
p. cm.
Includes bibliographical references and index.
ISBN-13: 978-0-910707-84-8
ISBN-10: 0-910707-84-7
1. Gifted children—Education. 2. Personality development. 3. Dabrowski, Kazimierz. I. Mendaglio, Sal, 1946-
LC3993.2.D23 2008
155.2'5—dc22
2007036813

ISBN 10 0-910707-84-7
ISBN 13 978-0-910707-84-8

Dedication

To Barbara, my wife, for her devotion to me and this project,
and to Bill Tillier, my friend, for his devotion
to Kazimierz Dabrowski and his theory.

Acknowledgments

I wish to express my appreciation to several people. My heartfelt thanks go to Barbara, my wife, who not only supported me materially throughout this journey, but also provided me with food for thought through her comments and questions in our conversations about the theory.

Bill Tillier provided the impetus for the book. Bill is a preeminent advocate for the theory of positive disintegration. In numerous conversations over the years, he helped me navigate my way through Dabrowski's idiosyncratic use of language. Bill was not only generous with his time and sharing of his first-hand knowledge, but also by providing me with a wealth of original material that was indispensable for my understanding of the theory.

I thank the contributors for their enthusiastic response to my invitation. They also endured graciously my suggestions regarding their chapters.

Finally, I thank Jim Webb and Janet Gore of Great Potential Press for their commitment to the project. I particularly appreciated Jim's support toward the end of the process, when his knowledge of personality theory and research, his professionalism, and his enthusiasm were very helpful to me.

Table of Contents

List of Tables and Figures

Preface

Why the Book?

I wonder how many times authors or editors have declared: "This book must be done." Well, I add my name to that list: "This book begged to be done!" Here is my case for the assertion. The theory of positive disintegration has been an influential force in gifted education for the past 20 years. It is difficult to search databases using "gifted" and "social" or "emotional" without finding numerous citations to Kazimierz Dabrowski's theory. Publications and conference sessions on aspects of the theory have occurred frequently over the years. But for all of the intense interest evident in the field of gifted education, there is no resource representing the full breadth and depth of the theory of positive disintegration. Yes, many publications discuss various components, aspects, and applications of the theory, but there is no single volume to represent the theory. A book is needed because people are likely to know only some portions of the theory, not realizing that their knowledge is incomplete.

Another reason for this book is that, despite the theory's popularity in gifted education, positive disintegration is virtually unknown in the field of psychology where I believe it should be situated. Positive disintegration is Dabrowski's theory of personality and, as such, should find its rightful place in personology, along with other important personality theories such as Freud's, Adler's, and Rogers.' This book is aimed at readers interested in both gifted education and psychology.

My idea to do an edited book on the theory began with an intuition regarding why Dabrowski's theory was not more widely known within psychology. It struck me that the most well-known theories seemed to have one thing in common—secondary sources: Freud's psychoanalysis had

Ernest Jones, Adler's individual psychology had Heinze Ansbacher, and Piaget's cognitive developmental theory had David Elkind. Authors of secondary sources made the original presentations of the theories accessible to readers (as anyone who has read Piaget in the original knows first hand).

Of course, a person could argue that these theories became popular because of their intrinsic conceptual value, which then led to their having secondary sources. But Dabrowski's theory also had been recognized in his day by prominent psychologists; Aronson, Mowrer, and Maslow, for example, praised the quality and uniqueness of Dabrowski's theory. This line of thinking convinced me that the theory needed secondary sources to help others become aware of Dabrowski's unique contributions.

Though I felt I had a solid grounding in the theory and a high level of motivation, I decided that the secondary sources should include individuals who had worked more intensely and longer with the theory than I had. At the Biennial Conference on Dabrowski's Theory, June 2004 (co-sponsored by the Centre for Gifted Education, University of Calgary), I sought potential contributors' responses to my idea. I talked first with Andrew Kawczak, a collaborator of Dabrowski's, who was very supportive of the idea. Encouraged by Andrew's endorsement, I spoke with other appropriate symposium participants, who also supported the need for such a book.

The Authors and the Organization of the Book

The authors are individuals who worked closely with Dabrowski and those who have had a long-standing interest in the theory, many of whom are recognized scholars in the field of gifted education. Authors' chapters are organized into three parts of the book.

Part I discusses the theory itself, with references to Dabrowski the person. William (Bill) Tillier, who wrote the biographical sketch of the theorist, was the last of Dabrowski's graduate students at the University of Alberta. In the ensuing years, Bill created, and still maintains, a Dabrowski archive that contains not only his original works, but also related publications. Bill also created and oversees a website dedicated to the theory.

My chapter presents an overview and argues that positive disintegration is a personality theory particularly meaningful for this century and for counseling applications of the theory. In my overview, I attempt to provide a faithful rendition of Dabrowski's presentation of the theory as expressed in his major English-language books. However, as with any other theories represented in secondary sources, the chapter is my interpretation of the theory.

Michael Piechowski is a unique contributor. For years, he was a close collaborator of Dabrowski, and Michael is largely responsible for introducing the theory to the field of gifted education. In his chapter, Michael presents a personalized account of his work with Dabrowski and the theory.

Marlene Rankel worked closely with Dabrowski on his research and collaborated with him on some as-yet-unpublished manuscripts. Her chapter, representing Dabrowski's application of his theory to education, is based on one of their unpublished manuscripts.

Bill Tillier's second contribution deals with the philosophical underpinnings of positive disintegration. Dabrowski himself cited some of the philosophical influences in his writing. Bill supplements this with his personal communication on the subject with the man himself.

Dexter Amend, another of Dabrowski's students, also worked closely with him. Dexter assisted Dabrowski both in developing a neurological examination that he used with patients and in planning conferences with him. Dexter's chapter explores the concept of creativity as evidenced in both Dabrowski the person and his theory.

Elizabeth Mika's chapter examines Dabrowski's view of mental health as it is represented in one of Dabrowski's Polish-language books. Because of her fluency in the language, Elizabeth is able to glean insights expressed in his first language.

Part II focuses on the application of positive disintegration to gifted education. Linda Silverman provides an overview of the topic and includes the story of how she became involved with Dabrowski's theory. Linda, along with Michael Piechowski, has been instrumental in dissemination of the theory through her efforts in research, numerous publications, and conference presentations on the subject.

Michael Pyryt's chapter represents an overview of research on the theory in gifted education. Michael has had a long-standing interest in the theory and its application to gifted individuals. He and I have collaborated on our work in this area on numerous occasions.

Frank Falk is a well-established researcher focusing primarily on Dabrowski's concept of overexcitability. In his chapter, Frank and his colleagues Buket Yakamaci-Guzel, Alice (Hsin-Jen) Chang, Raquel Pardo de Santayana Sanz, and Rosa Aurora Chavez-Eakle present the findings of a study assessing overexcitability across cultures.

Part III explores the theory from different perspectives. Laurence Nixon contrasts Dabrowski's work with literature relating to mysticism. Laurence was introduced to the theory through his work with Andrew Kowczak, now a retired professor of philosophy. Laurence has had a long-standing interest in positive disintegration and spirituality.

Nancy Miller, a frequent collaborator with Piechowski, Silverman, and Falk, discusses the theory within her discipline, sociology. Her analysis includes references to classic works such as George H. Mead and symbolic interactionism.

In my second contribution, I contrast positive disintegration with three other approaches to personality. Such comparisons highlight the uniqueness of Dabrowski's work.

At this point, Dabrowski's theory does not have its Ernest Jones or Heinze Ansbacher. Until one emerges, I think that the authors' contributions to this volume will enable readers to gain an appreciation for the uniqueness and complexity of the theory of positive disintegration.

SM
Calgary, Alberta

Part I

The Theory of Positive Disintegration

Chapter 1
Kazimierz Dabrowski: The Man

William Tillier, M.Sc.[1]

I feel privileged to provide a biography of Kazimierz Dabrowski, as he had a profound affect on my life. I was just beginning my master's program in Edmonton when one of his colleagues, Marlene Rankel, picked me out of a crowd and said, "I have a book for you to read and someone for you to meet." Reading the book (Dabrowski, 1972) gave me a unique perspective and insight into my personality and life history that I had never had before, and I couldn't wait to meet him. I certainly wasn't disappointed, and it was my privilege to be his student and later, to receive his unpublished papers.

Over the years that I knew him, I developed a tremendous appreciation for many aspects of Dr. Dabrowski, but two particularly stand out. First, in my life experience, he was a unique human being. He had a tremendous energy about him, an animation, a twinkle in his eye, and yet he also had a tremendous sense of calm about him. He was extremely gracious and one of the most humble people I've ever met. Above all, Dabrowski had a remarkable sense of compassion and an ability to look you in the eye and deeply connect with you. On one occasion, I recall asking him about my anxiety, and he put his hand on my shoulder and said, "Ah yes, but this is not so negative." You couldn't help but feel better after just sitting beside him.

My second appreciation was academic. Dabrowski, a truly Renaissance man, had an astounding command of world cultures, the arts, philosophy, medicine, neurology, and of course, psychiatry and psychology. His theory is a complete system of thought. The more one tries to dissect it,

1 Bill Tillier, M.Sc., Psychologist (Retired), Department of Solicitor General and Public Security, Government of Alberta, Canada.

the more its comprehensiveness and integration become obvious. My appreciation for his body of work has grown over the years as I have come to know it more intimately.

One of my proudest moments came when Dabrowski, late in his life, asked me to keep his theory alive after his passing. I have honored his request through my Dabrowski website (http://members.shaw.ca/positivedisintegration) and the dissemination of his original writings. In the process, over the last 20 years, I have had the privilege of being friends with his daughter, Joanna (also a psychologist). There is no question that Dabrowski left a tremendous legacy, both in terms of his family and in the theory he gave us. In reflecting back on Dabrowski, it seems so obvious that he was a human being who lived his theory. He strove to meet his own high standards and acted as an exemplar by action; whatever the peril, you could sense he always chose the higher path in his life.

Dabrowski's Early Life

Kazimierz Dabrowski was born in September 1, 1902, in Klarowo, Lublin, Poland. Dabrowski's father, Antoni, was an agricultural administrator. Kazimierz was one of four children; he had an older brother and a younger brother and sister. Reflecting on the early death of his sister, Dabrowski said:

> *I learned about death very early in my life. Death appeared to me not just something threatening and incomprehensible, but as something that one must experience emotionally and cognitively at a close range. When I was six, my little three-year-old sister died of meningitis.* (1975, p. 233)

One of the most significant early influences on Dabrowski was his first-hand experience of World War I. He spoke of being particularly affected by observing the aftermath of a major battle that occurred near his hometown. As he walked among the dead soldiers laying in his former playfield, Dabrowski was fascinated by the various positions their bodies took and the different expressions frozen on their faces. Some seemed calm and peaceful, while others appeared horrified and frightened (K. Dabrowski, personal communication, 1977). Again, Dabrowski was forced to confront death, while also trying to make sense of the war and its brutality.

Dabrowski's early education took place in Lublin, where Catholic priests and pastors schooled him and he had a rich family exposure to books and music. His education continued in Lublin, attending university where he studied psychology, philosophy, and literature. He went to Warsaw in 1924 to study and completed an M.A. at Poznan. During his studies, his best friend and classmate inexplicably committed suicide. At the time, Dabrowski was contemplating becoming a professional musician. After his friend's suicide, he decided to enter medicine and study human behavior (M. Rankel, personal communication, January 2007).

Dabrowski was given a grant from the Polish National Culture Foundation to study psychology and education in Geneva in 1928-29 under neurologist/child psychologist Édouard Claparède (1873-1940) and philosopher/psychologist Jean Piaget (1896-1980) (Aronson, 1964). Dabrowski received his medical degree from the University of Geneva in 1929, completing a thesis on the conditions of suicide entitled "Les Conditions Psycholopique du Suicide" ["The Psychological Conditions of Suicide"] (1929). Dabrowski's curriculum vitae[2] indicates that in 1929 he also received a *Certificat de Pedagogie* [Teaching Certificate] from the University of Geneva. In 1930, Dabrowski studied psychoanalysis in Vienna under fellow Pole, Wilhelm Stekel (1868-1940) (Aronson, 1964).[3] During this time, he attended psychoanalytic meetings and "met most of the great psychoanalytic personalities, including Sigmund Freud" (K. Dabrowski, personal communication, 1977).

In 1931, Dabrowski studied child psychiatry in Paris under George Heuyer (1884-1977), a pioneer of child psychiatry in France, and he also attended lectures given by the prominent French neurologist and psychologist, Pierre Janet (1859-1947) (Aronson, 1964). Dabrowski's curriculum vitae lists a Ph.D. in psychology, University of Poznan, 1931, focused on self-mutilation and supervised by S. Blachowski.[4] Dabrowski's curriculum vitae also lists a second M.D. degree from the University of Poznan, 1931.

2 Dabrowski's curriculum vitae is available to us as he submitted it as part of his supporting documentation to several Canada Council grant applications; 1970, 1971-1972, 1972-1975, and 1973-1975.

3 Dabrowski's curriculum vitae indicates "Certificate of Psychoanalytic Studies, Vienna (under Wilhelm Stekel), 1931." It is not clear if a certificate was given or not.

4 There is some confusion over this degree. Aronson (1964, p. x) indicates that it was in "experimental psychology" and was granted by the University of Poznan in 1932.

In 1933, by invitation of the Rockefeller Foundation, Dabrowski and his first wife went to Harvard University to study public health.[5] From 1933 to 1934, Dabrowski studied under C. Macfie Campbell, Director of the Boston Psychopathic Hospital, and William Healy, first Director of the Judge Baker Foundation (Aronson, 1964). In 1934, Dabrowski returned to Switzerland and was made a *Privat Docent* [Lecturer] in child psychiatry at the University of Geneva under Édouard Claparède (Aronson, 1964).

Dabrowski returned to Poland to organize mental health services and, with financial support from the Rockefeller Foundation, established the Polish State Mental Hygiene Institute in Warsaw, which opened in 1935. From 1935 to 1948, except for the interruption of the German occupation, Dabrowski was the director of the Institute (Aronson, 1964).

Meanwhile, Dabrowski embarked on his prolific writing career—for example, publishing works on behaviorism (1934a), self-torture (1934b), and in 1935, a major work, *The Nervousness of Children and Youth*. In 1937, the first signs of the theory of positive disintegration could be clearly seen in Dabrowski's initial exposure to a North American audience in the English monograph "Psychological Bases of Self-Mutilation" (1937), published with the assistance of C. M. Campbell (who also provided a preface). Dabrowski followed up with another Polish article, with the English-language title "Types of Increased Psychic Excitability" (1938).

In the late 1930s, Dabrowski was involved with an anthroposophy association[6] dedicated to the work of Rudolf Steiner (1861-1925) in England, run by Alice Baily of Cambridge Wells, Kent. Dabrowski studied Steiner, a polymath best known for developing anthroposophy (a spiritual science) and Waldorf education. Parapsychology and Eastern studies also interested Dabrowski, and he practiced meditation daily.

5 Dabrowski's curriculum vitae indicates a "Certificate of School of Public Health," Harvard University, 1934. However, Battaglia (2002, p. 67) indicates that Dabrowski did not meet the criteria, and no certificate was given.

6 Anthroposophy, also called spiritual science, is a spiritual philosophy based on the teachings of Rudolph Steiner. It states that anyone who "conscientiously cultivates sense-free thinking" can attain experience of and insights into the spiritual world. Steiner attempted to develop anthroposophy as a non-materialistic application of science, a course of inquiry the majority of contemporary scientists reject. Anthroposophical ideas have been applied in areas such as Waldorf education, curative education, biodynamic agriculture, anthoposophical medicine, and eurythmy or dance therapy.

World War II and the Post-War Years: Humanitarianism and Imprisonment

The details of Dabrowski's life during the war years are sketchy, but there is no doubt that they were very difficult. Aronson indicated that "of the 400 Polish psychiatrists practicing before the war...only thirty-eight survived" (1964, p. x). Dabrowski's younger brother was killed in 1941, and his older brother was captured in the Warsaw Insurrection and sent to a concentration camp. In 1939, the Germans closed the Institute of Mental Health in Warsaw, and Dabrowski shifted his operations to a second institute in Zagórze. Dabrowski had apparently foreseen the disruption of the approaching war and had organized a "secret institute" for pedagogical work, disguised as an Institute for Tuberculosis. The Institute, where Dabrowski spent much of his time from 1942 to 1945, provided services for some 200 children and youth in the forests near Zagórze, and Dabrowski's Institute sheltered and saved many war orphans, priests, Polish soldiers, members of the resistance, and Jewish children (Battaglia, 2002).

In 1942, the Nazis imprisoned Dabrowski for several months on suspicion that he was involved with the Polish underground.[7] His second wife, Eugenia (whom he married in 1940, his first wife having passed away of tuberculosis), eventually negotiated his release, and Dabrowski resumed his former position of director of the Institute of Mental Health in Warsaw. Dabrowski said that during his wartime experiences, he saw examples of both the lowest possible inhuman behavior, as well as acts of the highest human character.

Dabrowski obtained his specialty as a psychiatrist in June 1948 from Wroclaw University (Battaglia, 2002). Dabrowski's curriculum vitae indicates: "Habilitation in Psychiatry, University of Wroclaw, 1948." Also in 1948, he founded and became president of the Polish Society of Mental Hygiene. In December 1948, Dabrowski received a Ford Foundation Fellowship, and he returned to the United States, where he studied mental health, neuropsychiatry, and child psychiatry (Battaglia, 2002).

---

7 My understanding is that Dabrowski was never held in a concentration camp *per se*; rather, he spent his several incarcerations in the Nazi prison system (including at Montelupich prison located in Kraków).

Imprisonment Under Stalin

In 1949, the Polish Government, under Stalin, closed the Warsaw Institute and declared Dabrowski a *persona non grata*; he and Eugenia attempted to flee. The Polish communists imprisoned Dabrowski in 1950 for some 18 months, and Eugenia was briefly imprisoned as well. When he was released, Dabrowski's activities were kept under strict control, and he was assigned work in Kobierzyn and Rabia resorts, apparently as a tuberculosis physician. Eventually, he was declared "rehabilitated" and was again allowed to teach, securing a professorship at the Catholic University of Lublin, and he again organized mental health services in Poland. He was also allowed to travel, and through the support of the Ford Foundation, he attended several international psychiatry congresses (e.g., in Spain, France, England). Dabrowski's curriculum vitae indicates: "Professorship in Experimental Psychology, Academy of Catholic Theology, Warsaw, 1956" and "Professorship in the Polish Academy of Sciences since 1958."

The Sixties: Dabrowski Establishes Roots in North America

In the early 1960s, Jason Aronson, editor of the *International Journal of Psychiatry*, traveled behind the iron curtain to invite psychiatrists to submit articles for his journal, and he met Dabrowski in Poland. Dabrowski later visited Brandeis University, where he was invited to give a lecture and where he met Abraham Maslow (1908-1970). The two had lengthy discussions and became friends.

Even though Maslow's (1970) conceptualization of self-actualization does emphasize developing autonomy, Dabrowski rejected it because it lacked a multilevel perspective and did not differentiate between lower versus higher aspects of the self. Maslow's self was to be actualized as is, with an acceptance of its shortcomings, even its lower-level animalistic impulses. "The self-actualized person sees reality more clearly: our subjects see human nature as it *is* and not as they would prefer it to be" (Maslow, 1970, p. 156). Dabrowski emphasized that development required the differentiation of higher versus lower aspects of the self and the consequent inhibition of lower features. In spite of their differences, Maslow endorsed Dabrowski's book, *Mental Growth through Positive Disintegration*, saying:

> *I consider this to be one of the most important contributions to psychological and psychiatric theory in this whole decade. There is*

> *little question in my mind that this book will be read for another decade or two, and very widely. It digs very deep and comes up with extremely important conclusions that will certainly change the course of psychological theorizing and the practice of psychotherapy for some time to come.* (Dabrowski, 1970, back cover)

In 1964, Dabrowski and Aronson spent two months translating material (Dabrowski, 1964a; 1964b) that became Dabrowski's first major book in English, *Positive Disintegration*, to which Aronson contributed an introduction. Aronson subsequently published the first chapters of this book in his journal (Dabrowski, 1966).

My understanding is that Dabrowski declined an offer of a position at Brandeis University to work with Maslow because he refused to renounce his Polish citizenship, a requirement for American citizenship (a stipulation of the offer). He instead accepted a position at a hospital in Montréal, Canada, in 1964, where dual citizenship was not an issue. While there, he met Andrew Kawczak, a Polish lawyer and subsequent philosopher, who became an important collaborator.

In 1965, Dabrowski secured a visiting professorship at the University of Alberta and moved his family to Edmonton. He also held a visiting professorship at Université Laval (Laval University), Quebec City. Dabrowski's second major English publication, *Personality-Shaping through Positive Disintegration* grew out of discussions with Kawczak and some of Kawczak's graduate students (Dabrowski, 1967). An introduction to this book was written by American learning theorist O. Horbart Mowrer (1907-1982). Another core group of students formed in Edmonton, and several went on to become Dabrowski's co-authors including Dexter Amend, Michael M. Piechowski, and Marlene Rankel.

The Seventies: A Final Flurry of Activity

Dabrowski spent his last years teaching, writing, and dividing his time between Alberta, Quebec, and Poland. Several Polish and English publications were the result of this last flurry of activity, including *Mental Growth though Positive Disintegration* (1970), *Psychoneurosis Is Not an Illness* (1972), *The Dynamics of Concepts* (1973), and the two-volume *Multilevelness of Emotional and Instinctive Functions* (Dabrowski, 1996a; Dabrowski & Piechowski, 1996).

It should be noted that English was Dabrowski's last learned language. The majority of his Polish publications (numbering in the hundreds) remain untranslated; however, many of his 20 or so major Polish books were also published in French and Spanish (in addition to his English works, referenced here). Major Dabrowski centers were developed in Spain and in Lima, Peru, where Sister Alvarez Calderon taught the work.

In 1979, Dabrowski had a serious heart attack in Edmonton but was resolute that he would not die on what he considered foreign soil. Kazimierz Dabrowski returned to Poland and died in Warsaw on November 26, 1980. At his request, he was buried beside his friend, Piotr Radlo, in the forest near the Institute at Zagórze. His wife, Eugenia, and two daughters, Joanna and Anna, survived him.

Dissemination of Dabrowski's Legacy

In November 1982, a memorial conference was held in Edmonton. By then, I was a psychologist working with the Government of Alberta; however, over the years, a priority of mine was to keep Dabrowski's theory alive by maintaining an archive containing his original writings, along with collections of publications related to his theory. With the development of the World Wide Web, I established and continue to maintain the Dabrowski website (http://members.shaw.ca/positivedisintegration). My efforts at disseminating his legacy have included making his original writings available to interested parties and participating in and hosting conferences on the theory.

Over the years, many Dabrowski-related workshops have been held, as well as a number of major conferences, including: Université Laval [Laval University], Quebec City, QC (1970), Loyola College, Montreal, QC (1972), Miami, FL (1980), Warsaw, Poland (1987), Keystone, CO (1994), Kananaskis, AB (1996), Kendall College, Evanston, IL (1998), Mont-Tremblant, QC (2000), Fort Lauderdale, FL (2002), and Calgary, AB (2004 and 2006). An important part of continuing Dabrowski's legacy has been maintaining friendships with former students of his, who have contributed to the dissemination of the theory in their own ways.

One area where Dabrowski's theory is alive and well is in the study of giftedness and gifted education. In Dabrowski's earlier Polish research (1967, 1972), he conducted comprehensive examinations and testing of children who displayed superior abilities. He found that every child displayed characteristics suggestive of positive disintegration. Piechowski (1979a; 1991) subsequently introduced Dabrowski's concept of overexcitability, a component of developmental potential, to the field of gifted education, and over the past 25 years, many research projects and papers have addressed the topic (see Mendaglio & Tillier, 2006).

I consider my participation in this book another way of keeping my promise to Dr. Dabrowski.

Chapter 2

Dabrowski's Theory of Positive Disintegration: A Personality Theory for the 21st Century

Sal Mendaglio, Ph.D.[1]

Why should a relatively obscure theory of personality, known only in North America in the fields of giftedness and gifted education and whose development began in the 1930s, be proclaimed a theory for the 21st century? In fact, I selected the title for two specific reasons. First, Dabrowski's theory of positive disintegration (TPD) places emotions in a central role, relegating intelligence to a secondary position of influence on personality development. Dabrowski's theory does not only state that emotions influence personality development, but it also specifies how this is accomplished. This emphasis on emotion and its relationship to personality, articulated some 60 to 70 years ago, reflects the emphasis on emotions that we have seen in psychology in the 1990s and continue to see in the 2000s. While emotions have always been an important consideration in personality theories, TPD is unique because it assigns an essential role to emotions in personality *development*, something that is now acknowledged in the field (e.g., Izard & Ackerman, 2000).

Second, some believe that there is a decline in interest in theories of personality (Walters, 2004). Dabrowski's theory, with its unique approach to

1 Sal Mendaglio, Ph.D., Associate Professor, Division of Teacher Preparation, Graduate Division of Educational Research and Research Associate, Centre for Gifted Education, Faculty of Education, University of Calgary, Calgary, Alberta, Canada.

personality, may serve to re-invigorate the field. At first glance, this may seem ambitious; however, Dabrowski's theory has a track record in vitalizing a field of study. Dabrowski's theory, after its introduction to the North American study of giftedness by Michael Piechowski (1979a), has significantly influenced research on the social and emotional aspects of giftedness (e.g., Baum, Olenchak, & Owen, 1998; Colangelo & Ogburn, 1989; Fiedler, 1998; Hazell, 1999; Mendaglio, 1998; Morrissey 1996; Piechowski, 1997; Schiever, 1985). For the past 20 years, the theory of positive disintegration has been *the* driving force in this area of study.

In this chapter, I provide an overview of the assumptions and key concepts of the theory of positive disintegration. I have tried to represent accurately Dabrowski's ideas, though what follows is, of course, my interpretation of the theory. Those familiar with the theory know of its evocative quality; TPD triggers strong emotional reactions when people are first introduced to it. Because of this quality of the theory, I begin with my initial exposure to it and my reactions.

I was introduced to TPD by Piechowski (1979a) in a book on counseling gifted individuals (Colangelo & Zaffran, 1979), and my reaction was not very positive. The theory was filled with strange language (e.g., positive disintegration, overexcitability) and unusual use of common terms.

However, given my interest in counseling gifted individuals, I found that I could not avoid the theory. I kept bumping into Dabrowski's theory in the counseling literature on giftedness and gifted education. TPD was becoming an influential force in the field, as evidenced by publications (e.g., Miller, Silverman & Falk, 1994; Piechowski, 1986; Silverman, 1993) and an increasing number of presentations at conferences such as the National Association for Gifted Children and the Council for Exceptional Children. In essence, I was forced to take a second look at the theory, and as I did, I became an enthusiastic student of TPD.

As I explain elsewhere (Mendaglio, 1999), one reason for my attitude change was that TPD provided a cogent explanation for a question that had arisen during my graduate student days: How can some intelligent, highly educated individuals be mean-spirited and hold negative attitudes, such as racism? My graduate school days coincided with several well-publicized American events—the Civil Rights movement, the Vietnam War, and the Watergate scandal. In addition, the question arose from some experiences in my daily life.

TPD provided an answer that no other theory that I had encountered provided—intelligence is not a sufficient condition for human development, because development is not equated with academic or material success in life. In TPD, development is equated with becoming truly human, a state accomplished by individuals who struggle to make sense of themselves and society. In the process, they transform themselves from self-serving human animals to altruistic human beings.

Delving further into TPD, I focused on another feature of the theory that was quite relevant to my work in counseling and psychotherapy—emotions. While teaching and practicing counseling, well before I had heard of TPD, I knew that emotions are critical to the practice of counseling and psychotherapy. Responding effectively to clients' emotions is a mainstay of effective counselling practice, especially for those professionals of the humanistic persuasion (e.g., Rogers, 1980). I had also noted that regardless of presenting problems (e.g., relationship issues, academic underachievement, parenting issues), the reason clients sought my services, and perhaps the services of other helping professionals, was because of their inability to cope with intense negative emotions. That determining factor most often tipped the scales for deciding to seek professional help. To capture this reasoning, my slogan became, "It's all about negative emotions"—negative, because clients do not seek counseling because of positive emotions. Implementing this in counseling, I had a twofold objective: (1) to help clients understand and accept their negative emotions, and (2) to reduce, if not eliminate, the distress experienced by my clients.

Dabrowski similarly focused on helping his patients understand and accept their negative emotions; however, his rationale for doing so was very different from mine. In TPD, experience of negative emotions is essential for advanced psychological development. Therefore, the goal of therapy is not to eliminate negative emotions, because when individuals are on the path of development, negative emotions are essential companions. Dabrowski taught his patients TPD concepts to help them understand the necessity of emotions in development. In essence, he taught his patients that their experiencing of intense negative emotions was a sign of their development—something to celebrate, not remediate. Specifically, patients were taught to reframe commonly held beliefs about negative emotions and to move from the view that they are symptoms to be eliminated, instead seeing the negative emotions as harbingers of growth and development. Such conceptual reframing is a hallmark of TPD.

The importance of emotions in TPD extends beyond helping patients understand that emotions trigger psychological growth and development. Emotions are essential for personality development. Although Dabrowski conceived of personality in a unique manner, TPD is surprisingly consistent with current views of the role of emotion in personality development. In the early years of the 21st century, researchers in fields of emotions (Brandstatter & Eliaz, 2001; Izard & Ackerman, 2000) and personality (Eisenberg, Fabes, Guthrie, & Reiser, 2002; Magnavita, 2002) generally agreed that emotions influence the development of personality. Izard (1971, 1977), who was well known for his research on emotion, investigating it when it was not popular to do so, said unequivocally, "That emotions affect the development of personality is a truism..." (Izard & Ackerman, 2000, p. 260).

What I find remarkable is that Dabrowski said this in his English-language books in the 1960s (1964a; 1967) and earlier in his Polish-language articles and books. Emotion, with a few notable exceptions, was not a popular field of study in the 1960s and 1970s in North American psychology. It was not until the 1990s that interest in emotion burst forth. Although there was some interest in the 1980s [for example, Howard Gardner's multiple intelligences, (1983)], the 1990s saw the emergence of emotional intelligence (Salovey & Mayer, 1990; Goleman, 1995). Emotional Quotient (EQ) was said to be as important, if not more important, than intelligence quotient (IQ) for success (e.g., Lynn, 2002).

The year 2000 saw the first issue of the American Psychological Association journal *Emotion* and a plethora of research investigations. Psychology had rediscovered emotions after years of neglect, even though their importance had been noted more than a century earlier by Darwin (1965/ 1872) and James (1990/1890).

In this history, it is striking that Dabrowski predated the current interest in emotions and their connection to personality. His first English-language publication appeared 70 years ago (1937). Though he did not use the term EQ, Dabrowski noted that intelligence was not as important as the emotional domain. Emotions were not a hindrance; they were a powerful influence on daily living, more so than intelligence. One example of this is his unpublished manuscript on his philosophy of education (Dabrowski, n.d. 1).

In spite of such historical contribution, TPD remains virtually unknown in North American education and psychology. However, there is one notable exception: TPD is very well known in the fields of giftedness and gifted education. Dabrowski's theory, with particular emphasis on certain of its elements, has been an influential force in these fields of study. TPD, with its emphasis on emotions, has been proposed as a theory to explain the emotional development of gifted individuals and a wide range of issues related to giftedness. The power of the theory has been demonstrated by its significant influence in the multi-disciplinary field of giftedness, in which TPD is used to understand and study a wide range of issues (see Mendaglio & Tillier, 2006).

From a rather unceremonious introduction, TPD has become a mainstay of my own theorizing about personality and counseling, as well as broadening my understanding of giftedness. I believe that psychologists in general will find TPD useful. Whether their interest lies in giftedness, personality theory, counseling and psychotherapy, or research, psychologists will find in TPD a conceptual framework that will spur them to examine their current assumptions about human functioning and possibly spark new, creative approaches.

In presenting the theory, I begin with a synopsis of TPD. Italicized words will be explained in the presentation of the assumptions and key concepts sections.

A Synopsis of TPD: A Grand Theory of Personality

The theory of positive disintegration is in the tradition of grand theories of personality such as Freud's psychoanalysis and Sullivan's interpersonal theory. Grand theories have similarities; they are ambitious attempts aimed at explaining phenomena such as personality development, human functioning, and psychopathology. The grand theories are complex and coherent. Each has a high level of internal consistency, and key concepts are logically anchored to the assumptions of the theories. A final similarity is the language of grand theories, which tends to be rich in meaning but bereft of specificity. The language theorists use to convey their ideas challenges students of such theories, and there are few operational definitions of concepts in these theories. The theorists' language and choice of labels for their concepts sometimes act as a barrier to their acceptance. For example, at one time, Freud's (1970/1924) psychoanalytic terms, such as *ego, id*, and *superego*, were novel and strange; they are now familiar throughout our culture. Sullivan (1953), in his interpersonal theory, created neologisms to convey his concepts—for example, *prototaxic, parataxic*, and *syntaxic* modes of experiencing—to depict a growing and maturing of experiencing reality. Dabrowski, too, introduced some new words in the presentation of his theory—for example, *overexcitability*; but his theory presents another type of challenge with respect to language. In Dabrowski's theory of positive disintegration, common psychological terms, such as *personality*, *disintegration*, *adjustment*, and *development*, are used in idiosyncratic ways. In reading my synopsis of the theory, readers should bear in mind my comments regarding grand theories, especially those to do with language. The words that are in italics are key terms that are defined more fully in a subsequent section.

In Dabrowski's theory, *personality* is not a fixed, universal attribute; personality must be shaped—created—by an individual to reflect his or her own unique character. *Positive disintegration*, the process by which personality is achieved, is a twofold process of: (1) disintegration of a primitive mental organization aimed at gratifying biological needs and mindlessly conforming to societal norms, and (2) re-integration at a higher level of functioning, in which the individual transcends biological determinism and becomes autonomous. Personality, shaped by positive disintegration, develops primarily as a result of the action of *developmental potential*, which is a constitutional endowment that includes *overexcitability*—a high level of reactivity of the central nervous system, and *dynamisms*—autonomous inner forces, assumed to be normally distributed in the population. Human development is depicted not by stages, but rather by a *multilevel*—hierarchical—continuum; it is a progression from a lower, primitive level to a higher, advanced level. Favorable developmental potential produces crises, characterized by *psychoneuroses*—strong anxieties and depressions—sparking disintegration of an individual's mental organization, the first phase of positive disintegration and the development of personality.

The second phase of positive disintegration—the beginnings of re-integration—includes an individual's creation of a *hierarchy of values*, viewed as a vertical arrangement of his or her *emotional reactions*, which is critical to the development of an individual's personality and *autonomy*. An individual's emotional reactions guide him or her in the creation of an individualized *personality ideal*, an autonomous standard that becomes the goal of an individual's development. Using that personality ideal, an individual examines his or her essence and makes existential choices that emphasize those aspects of essence that are "more myself" and inhibit those aspects that are "less myself." In this way, individuals achieve personality and become integrated at a high level of human functioning; they become truly human.

Assumptions

Four assumptions underlying TPD are key: multilevelness, conflict, psychopathology, and emotions.

Multilevelness: A Hierarchical View of Phenomena

The theme of hierarchy pervades the theory of positive disintegration. As the word suggests, Dabrowski believed that human development and experience can be arranged in a hierarchical manner, which he termed *multilevelness*. Human development, including neurological development, is assumed to proceed from lower, simple structures to higher, complex ones. In addition to general developmental processes, multilevelness applies to specific concepts including instincts, emotions, and conflict. A multilevel view of instincts applies to individual instincts as well as to classes of instincts. Dabrowski believed that higher instincts, such as the instincts of creativity and self-perfection, are uniquely human. Humans share lower ones like self-preservation and sexual instincts with animals.

Dabrowski also viewed each instinct in a multilevel manner. Self-preservation, for example, may exist in a lower form expressed by aggressively protecting one's physical well-being, or self-preservation may be transformed into a higher form, such as the action of preserving one's identity as a unique human being (Dabrowski, 1973).

Similarly, emotions are multilevel in nature, as characterized by concrete or increasingly abstract referents. For example, joy, at its lowest level, is associated with physical well-being from satisfying one's needs, such as having a great meal, and from satisfying wishes, such as watching one's favorite sports team win an important game. At a higher level, joy loses its physiological anchors, becomes more abstract, and is associated with, for example, successes in one's development.

Conflict also is considered in a hierarchical manner. Conflict produced by frustration of basic needs is primitive. Conflict resulting from an individual's failure to live up to his or her values is more advanced.

TPD assumes that there are "empirically verifiable differences between levels of all mental functions comparable to the difference between levels of intelligence" (Kawczak, 1970, p. 2) observed in individuals. Levels of mental functioning are seen hierarchically; therefore, mental development proceeds from lower to higher levels. A developmental view of empathy can illustrate this view. In its most primitive form, empathy is a process of emotion contagion; a child in a nursery cries, then all children cry. This initial form evolves into a more conscious, vicarious experiencing of others' feelings; a child sees another person in distress and feels that person's suffering as if it were his or her own. Finally, a more mature form of empathy enables an individual to become attuned to others and to appreciate their perspectives, including their thoughts and emotions.

Conflict and Psychopathology: Essential for Development

TPD assumes that individuals can only make the transition from lower levels of mental functioning to higher levels by experiencing inner conflict. Emanating from this assumption is the belief that many disorders found in the current edition of *Diagnostic and Statistical Manual of Mental Disorders* (American Psychiatric Association, 1994), several of which Dabrowski termed *psychoneuroses*, are essential for advanced psychological development. Dabrowski proclaimed in *Psychoneurosis Is Not an Illness* (1972) that symptoms associated with psychoneuroses, and even some psychoses, serve the transition from lower to higher development by generating the disintegration process.

Integration and Disintegration: Negative and Positive

In TPD, harmony and peacefulness are associated with the notion of integration, which consists of two types: primitive or primary, and secondary (Kawczak, 1970). The harmony associated with primary integration is characterized by the lack of multilevel inner conflict; individuals are simply motivated by basic instincts, drives, and conformity to social norms. These persons are so integrated mentally that they are in a semi-conscious state, responding to life with little or no reflection.

At the other extreme—secondary integration—harmony and peacefulness stem from the achievement of personality. The individual is accepting of self and others, autonomous, authentic, and has a daily life directed by a hierarchy of values.

It is the primary or primitive integration that psychoneurotic symptoms act upon. These symptoms emerge with the growing awareness by individuals of a discrepancy between how they ought to be and how they actually are. Such experiencing extends to society; individuals are distressed by the difference between the way the world should be and the reality.

Without such experiencing and the ensuing disintegration of the primary integrated level of mental functioning, development cannot occur.

Emotions: Directing Forces of Development

A final assumption, apparent in the above discussion, is that emotions are essential elements in the process of a transition from lower to higher mental functioning. Inner conflict or psychoneuroses include the experience of emotions such as anxiety, shame, guilt, and despair, and moods such as depression. It appears that, in this regard, Dabrowski was influenced by the theorizing of Mazurkiewicz, a renowned Polish psychiatrist, who conceived of emotions as "directing forces" (Aronson, 1964, p. xii) of development. Intense negative emotions and moods, typically regarded as impediments to growth and development, actually set the stage for advanced development by their disintegrating power. Intensely negative affective experiences begin the process of loosening a tightly integrated mental organization. Though painful for individuals, negative emotions—a hallmark of inner conflict—allow people to achieve a more advanced level of human development.

Components of the Theory of Positive Disintegration

The main components of TPD are subsumed under the headings of personality, factors of development, integration, disintegration, dynamisms, and levels of development.

Personality

O. Hobart Mowrer noted that Dabrowski proposed an "extraordinary" (Mowrer, 1967, p. xxvi) conception of personality. Dabrowski disagreed with "the generally accepted view [that] personality is a structure or organization of mental functions characteristic of every individual" (Dabrowski, 1973, p. 108). Though not cited, he may have been referring to Allport's definition: "Personality is the dynamic organization within the individual of those psychophysical systems that determined his unique adjustments to his environment" (Allport, 1937, p. 48). It is safe to say that Dabrowski would disagree with virtually any subsequent definition of personality as well for two reasons. First, he viewed personality as an achievement, not a universal attribute of individuals. Second, in his view, personality is not a neutral construct; it is value laden. In TPD, personality is the product of an individual's struggle to move upward toward an ideal

(Mowrer, 1967). Personality is equated with the highest level of human development:

> *Personality, in the context of this work, is a name given to an individual fully developed, both with respect to the scope and level of the most essential positive human qualities, an individual in whom all the aspects form a coherent and harmonized whole, and who possesses, in a high degree, the capability for insight into his own self, his own structure, his aspirations and aims (self-consciousness), who is convinced that his attitude is right, that his aims are of essential and lasting value (self-affirmation), and who is conscious that his development is not yet complete and therefore is working internally on his own improvement and education (self-education).* (Dabrowski, 1967, p. 5)

That personality includes knowing that one's attitudes are right and that one's aims are valued reflect the value-laden quality of Dabrowski's definition. Behaviors of individuals who have achieved personality are driven by their positive value systems. Values are categorized into universal human and individual values. Universal human values are positive characteristics that have been recognized by society over time. These include personal and social responsibility and a sense of justice, courage, honesty, religiosity, and discipline. Individual values include the acquisition of personally meaningful interests and capabilities that are deemed essential by the individual, enduring emotional bonds of love and friendship, and spirituality that pervades one's daily life.

Values, for Dabrowski, were equated with emotional experiencing; affective reactions to society and to oneself thus guide the creation of a hierarchy of values. Whether one's personality emerges depends on, among other things, an individual's hierarchy of values drawing on both universal and individual values. Personality, then, is neither a given nor neutral; it is an achievement and value laden.

Factors of Development

To fully appreciate Dabrowski's factors of development, it is important to consider how Dabrowski viewed development. He identified three types of development: (1) biologically determined, (2) autonomous mental, and (3) one-sided (Dabrowski, 1970). Biologically determined development, as the phrase suggests, is associated with the biological life cycle directed by the universal laws of physical development of the human species. This development shows a gradual integration of functions and a progression through the stages of birth, infancy, childhood, adolescence, adulthood, and death. In addition, biologically determined development includes conformity to the social environment. Adjustment is a theme in biologically determined development; individuals regulate their behaviors in accordance with their biological drives, and social norms control their drive gratification.

In autonomous mental development, individuals' inner mental forces combine with positive values to direct development. This type of development transcends the dictates of biology and society. Autonomous development is typified by frequent disintegration of functions and subsequent reintegration at a higher level. Positive maladjustment is a theme in this type of development; individuals regulate their behaviors by conforming to their personal values, which often conflict with commonly accepted social norms. This form of maladjustment is positive, because individuals reject being driven by basic drives and social norms that contradict universal positive values (Dabrowski, 1972).

In one-sided development, mental functions and structures are integrated in an egocentric and antisocial way. This type of development is manifested in mental states such as paranoia and behaviors such as criminality. Negative maladjustment is a theme in this type of development; individuals regulate their behaviors by the fulfillment of their own ends, regardless of the cost to others. This maladjustment is negative, because the reason for rejecting societal values is the gratification of primitive drives and egocentric needs (Dabrowski, 1972).

For Dabrowski, advanced human development was not simply successfully going through the biological life cycle. Nor was development equated with material success in life, such as high academic achievement, amassing vast amounts of money, or becoming a famous world figure. Development means transcending biological instincts and drives and the need to conform unconsciously to societal norms. A developed human being is characterized by such traits as autonomy, authenticity, and altruism.

Developmental Instinct and Developmental Potential

Within this view of development, Dabrowski identified three factors of development. The first factor consists of two related, hereditary, constitutional elements: developmental *instinct* and developmental *potential.* The developmental instinct is the "mother instinct" (Dabrowski, 1970, p. 27), the source of all developmental forces. Individuals inherit varying levels of the developmental instinct. Ironically, the developmental instinct, anchored to the biological makeup of an individual, though "not reducible to it" (Dabrowski, 1970, p. 27), is ultimately *the* force responsible for the transcendence of biological drives, such as self-preservation. The specific forces of development identified in TPD spring from this primordial instinct.

Developmental potential of individuals is a constitutional element that is different from the developmental instinct. TPD emphasizes the role of various instincts and constitutional elements, which Mowrer attributed to Dabrowski's lack of acquaintance with learning theory (Mowrer, 1967). The implication is that if Dabrowski had been familiar with learning theory, he would rely less on instincts in TPD. However, it is more likely that the focus on instinct reflects the importance Dabrowski placed on constitutional endowment as a major determiner of human development.

Dabrowski postulated that the developmental instinct manifested in developmental potential casts a powerful influence in mental growth; it is the "constitutional endowment which determines the character and the extent of mental growth possible for a given individual" (Dabrowski, 1972, p. 303). Developmental potential is seen primarily in a quality he termed *overexcitability*, a property of the central nervous system. Overexcitability is a higher than average responsiveness to stimuli due to heightened sensitivity of nervous system receptors (Dabrowski, 1972). Because overexcitability is an expression of developmental potential, it is also differentiated from the developmental instinct; whether overexcitability is part of an individual's makeup is ultimately determined by individuals' hereditary endowment. Some individuals' central nervous systems will be excitable, but not overly so. Overexcitability, then, influences how individuals experience internal and external reality. Individuals who are endowed with overexcitability perceive reality in a different, more intense, multifaceted manner than those not so endowed. They are likely to experience surprise and puzzlement at events in their daily lives.

Dabrowski identified five forms of overexcitability: psychomotor, sensual, imaginational, intellectual, and emotional. Psychomotorically overexcitable individuals tend to be high-energy, curious, have difficulty sitting still, need constant change of scenery, and are generally restless. Sensually overexcitable individuals are generally highly sensitive to sensory perceptions such as sights, smells, tastes, and tactile stimulation. Imaginationally overexcitable individuals are inclined to be daydreamers, have a rich fantasy life, and are often creative. Intellectually overexcitable individuals manifest abilities of analysis and synthesis, ask probing questions, and love learning for its own sake. Emotionally overexcitable individuals are sensitive individuals who experience emotions intensely, tending to take things to heart. They are empathic toward others and feel a strong need for exclusive relationships. Individuals may inherit some, all, or none of the five forms of overexcitability. In TPD, the presence of intellectual, imaginational, and emotional forms (sometimes referred to as "the big three") are deemed essential for advanced psychological development.

The forms of overexcitability are manifested in special interests and abilities, the seeds of which can be observed during early childhood. For example, intellectual overexcitability can be seen in children's sophisticated approach to formulating questions as they attempt to understand events or concepts. Perceptiveness with respect to the world around them and early mathematical ability are other special abilities that are associated with this form of overexcitability. Children with strong imaginational overexcitability show distinct interests in creative pursuits such as poetry, dance, and painting.

Autonomous inner forces are also part of developmental potential. It appears that Dabrowski was influenced by Jan Mazurkiewicz, with whose theory Dabrowski was familiar (see Dabrowski, 1964a, 1967). Mazurkiewicz postulated the existence, in both animals and human beings, of "*own* forces" (emphasis in original, Aronson, 1964, p. xii). These forces stem from within an organism, rather than being responses to external stimuli. Mazurkiewicz proposed that own forces are most operational in human beings. Dabrowski called this type of force *dynamism* and defined it as a "biological or mental force controlling behavior and its development. Instincts, drives, and intellectual processes combined with emotions are dynamisms" (1972, p. 294).

Social Environment

The social environment is the second factor of development in TPD. The effects of the social environment on individual development depend on the amount of endowed developmental potential. If an individual's developmental potential is particularly strong, then the quality of the social environment is of secondary importance. Such individuals are innately resilient and largely impervious to their social environment.

At the other extreme, when developmental potential is very weak, development—in the Dabrowskian sense—will not occur, even if the social environment is highly nurturing. The quality of the social environment is an important factor when developmental potential lies in between these extremes. In those cases, a nurturing social environment will have a beneficial effect and a negative social environment will have a negative effect on individuals' development.

Third Factor Dynamism

The third factor of development, so named by Dabrowski, is a special type of dynamism. The third factor is a particularly important dynamism that appears only after other dynamisms are activated. Admittedly a difficult concept to define (Dabrowski, 1973), it is described as the force by which individuals become more self-determined, controlling their behaviors through their inner voices and values. Once the third factor is activated, individuals are no longer at the mercy of biological needs or under the control of societal conventions. Individuals so characterized lead lives consciously and deliberately, selecting courses of action based on values that they have selected. Their approach to daily life is highly moral in nature. At this high level of development, individuals also increasingly engage in self-education and self-help.

Integrations and Disintegrations

Dabrowski described two types of integration—primary and secondary—and four types of disintegration—positive, negative, partial, and global.

Dabrowski equated rigidly integrated mental structures with automatic responses, which are associated with lower levels of functioning; Dabrowski called this state *primary integration.* In contrast, the less organized, volitional behaviors associated with higher levels of functioning are associated with *secondary integration.*

Primary integration characterizes individuals who are largely under the influence of the first factor (biology) and the second factor (environment). These individuals experience the human life cycle and may become very successful in societal terms, but they are not fully developed human beings. Persons characterized by secondary integration are influenced primarily by the third factor; they are inner directed and values driven. As fully human, they live life autonomously, authentically, and altruistically. Biological drives are sublimated into higher modes of expression. Conformity and nonconformity to societal norms are principled. Movement from primary to secondary integration arises from positive disintegration.

Positive disintegration is a twofold process: (1) dissolution of lower mental structures and functions, and (2) creation of higher forms (Dabrowski, 1970). During the dissolution part of the process, individuals experience intense external and internal conflicts that generate intense negative emotions. Such experiencing may be initially triggered by developmental milestones, such as puberty, or crises, such as the death of a loved one. As a result, individuals become increasingly conscious of self and the world. They become more and more distressed as they perceive a discrepancy between the way the world ought to be and the way it is, which Dabrowski called the "psychoneurotic conflict" (1973, p. 2). With the onset of awareness of this discrepancy, conflicts and negative experiences become more internally focused. Such experiencing destroys an individual's pre-existing mental organization which guided his or her daily behaviors.

In a sense, the first part of positive disintegration creates a state of ambiguity. Primary integration is a highly structured state that requires little, if any, reflection on the part of individuals. With the dissolution of one's mental organization, a state of high anxiety ensues that can be reduced only by creating some other organization. Higher-level mental organization arises from such forces as self-awareness, self-direction and autonomy, and the selection of values by which one will live his or her life. These and other related forces create a new, higher-level form of integrated mental organization and thus resolve the inner conflict and anxiety created by the dissolving part of the process. When both parts of the process occur, Dabrowski called it positive disintegration or global disintegration.

Dabrowski identified other types of disintegration—negative and partial. Negative disintegration occurs when individuals experience only part of positive disintegration: the dissolving part. That is, individuals are in a sense trapped in the dissolution state, experiencing conflicts and negative emotions with no resolution in sight, yet they are unable to return to their previous state of integration. Chronic psychotic illnesses and suicide are likely expressions of negative disintegration. Partial disintegrations do not have such dramatic outcomes. This type of disintegration may result in several outcomes: a return to the lower level of functioning, a partial re-integration at a higher level, or a transformation into global disintegration.

Genetic endowment, according to Dabrowski, plays an important role in integration and disintegration. Very favorable hereditary endowment is necessary for positive disintegration. Partial disintegration and negative disintegration come from "limited hereditary endowment"

(Dabrowski, 1970, p. 166). Dabrowski suggested that, in the case of a very favorable hereditary endowment, the quality of the social environment is not a critical factor; the biological substrate is sufficient to propel an individual toward secondary integration. However, for both partial and negative disintegration, the quality of the social environment is an important factor contributing significantly to the individual's experience. Individuals who remain in a primary integrated state do not have a sufficiently favorable genetic endowment to fuel the disintegration process. A favorable genetic endowment contains the nuclei of inner forces, which are not only essential for disintegration, but also define the process.

Inner Psychic Milieu

Dabrowski extended the idea of inner milieu—the internal physical and physiological environment of individuals—to inner psychic milieu, the internal mental environment (Dabrowski, Kawczak, & Piechowski, 1970). Inner milieu is the internal physical environment where a collection of processes and forces regulate various bodily functions, such as body temperature. Inner *psychic* milieu is the internal mental environment where cognitive forces, when activated, regulate development—for example, moving from an other-directed to a self-directed approach to life. While the inner milieu is given, the psychic environment is constructed.

The inner mental environment originates from a lack of balance between the parasympathetic and sympathetic nervous systems. Such imbalances create a disturbance in an individual's internal sensations, and he or she becomes aware of what Dabrowski called organismic "noise" (1972, p. 103). For example, disruption of a sense of well-being may be indicated by difficulties with sleeping, digestion, or energy level; the accompanying pain and anxiety then begin to affect the development of the internal mental environment by turning the individual's attention inward. Remaining at this rudimentary level results in a primitive form of mental environment where conscious activities are temporarily or permanently under the direction of basic drives (sexual, self-preservation, etc.), with little or no consciousness of a distinct self.

The type of mental environment that Dabrowski associated with positive disintegration is one that encompasses the totality of mental forces that create disintegration of mental structures and functions, forging a personality—the highest mental organization for individuals (1970, p. 64). Forces of the inner psychic milieu are initially disorganized and antagonistic; at times, one force may predominate, only to be replaced by another in a spontaneous manner. Conflict with the internal and external environments results due to the opposing aims of the forces and to the needs of internal and demands of external environments. As development progresses, the inner psychic milieu—the totality of forces—is transformed by the individual into a hierarchically organized complex of forces that are under the control of the individual's inner self and that result in self-directed behavior free of conflict. Dabrowski called the mental forces of the inner psychic milieu *dynamisms.*

Dynamisms

Dynamisms are autonomous inner forces, which are either biological or mental in nature, controlling individuals' behaviors and development. As noted earlier, Dabrowski described dynamisms as constellations of "instincts, drives, and intellectual processes combined with emotions" (1972, p. 294).

There are two general categories of dynamisms—dissolving and developmental—which correspond to the two-part process of positive disintegration. Dissolving dynamisms weaken, disrupt, and ultimately destroy primary integration. Among the first set of dynamisms that start the dissolving process are ambivalence and ambitendency. Ambivalence refers to changeable feelings of dislike or like, simultaneous feelings of inferiority and superiority, fluctuations of moods, and approach-avoidance conflicts. Ambitendencies include conflicting courses of action, indecision, and desiring incompatible goals or things. Experiencing such matters as fluctuation of moods and approach-avoidance conflicts, not previously experienced, begins to disrupt the mental balance. Inner forces such as ambivalences and ambitendencies can produce only temporary loosening of mental organization, resulting in a return to primary integration unless accompanied by other dynamisms.

The dynamisms responsible for the ultimate destruction of primary integration are autonomous inner forces that create a discontent with oneself and with society at large. This discontent intensifies as these dynamisms emerge in the person's interactions with the social environment. There are several dissolving dynamisms: astonishment with oneself, disquietude with oneself, feelings of inferiority toward oneself, dissatisfaction with oneself, feelings of shame and guilt, creativity and positive maladjustment.

Astonishment with oneself refers to the feeling that one's own cognitive qualities are unexpected and surprising. This signals the beginning of the individual's becoming an object of his of her awareness. Disquietude with oneself marks the beginning of negative attitudes toward self. To astonishment with oneself, which is largely cognitive in nature, disquietude with oneself adds an emotional component—negative feelings associated with a self-critical attitude. Feelings of inferiority toward oneself refers to the negative emotions one experiences as a result of increased awareness of the discrepancy between where one is and the higher level to which he or she aspires, i.e., between where one is and where one ought to be. This dynamism contributes significantly to the creation of an individual's hierarchy of values.

Dissatisfaction with oneself, one of the strongest dynamisms of this category, is a negative attitude toward oneself that includes not only disapproval and dislike of self, but also self-aggression and attempts to escape oneself. This dynamism produces experiences of intense anxiety and depression. Feelings of shame and guilt reflect an individual's response to external and internal opinions of self. Both shame and guilt result from dissatisfaction with oneself. Shame, a sense of embarrassment and distressful self-consciousness, is connected with others' perceptions of self, whether real or imagined. Blushing and increased pulse rate may be signs of shame. With guilt, the feelings are internalized. Embarrassment is experienced not only in relation to others, but also to oneself and one's ideals. There is an ownership of responsibility for one's own shortcomings or imperfections. Creative instinct, also influenced by dissatisfaction with self, refers to the individual's search for new experiences that are qualitatively different from current ones.

The last dynamism in the dissolving category requires special attention. Positive maladjustment is the rejection of primitive values held by one's social group or society at large. This is similar to Kierkegaard's belief that individuals need to reject anchoring their behaviors on common values. The rejection is conscious and selective, and it reflects an individual's hierarchy of values, created based on the way things ought to be rather than how they are.

In Dabrowski's view, there are both positive and negative forms of adjustment and maladjustment. Negative adjustment is shown by automatic and subservient behavior conforming to the demands of society. Negative maladjustment is reflected in criminal or pathological behaviors. The positive maladjustment dynamism propels the individual past automatic conformity. Positive adjustment is associated with advanced development, reflected in an individual's behavior influenced by a consciously constructed hierarchy of values.

Because of the dissolving dynamisms, individuals experience internal and external conflict characterized by persistent, intense, negative emotions, often described by Dabrowski by using Kierkegaard's phrase of "fear and trembling." Another classic phrase that comes to mind is G. Stanley Hall's "storm and stress" (Smith, 1993, p. 137), which he used to characterize adolescence.

Developmental dynamisms, which create a new mental organization, include self-awareness and self-control; subject and object in oneself; syntony (sympathy and resonance to others), identification, and empathy; the third factor; inner psychic transformation; education of oneself; and autopsychotherapy. Self-awareness and self-control include awareness of one's mental and behavioral activities, personal identity and uniqueness, and differential stability of personal characteristics. Self-awareness and self-control also include the realization that some personality traits are not only more stable than others, but some are more important. The awareness enables the individual to engage in self-control.

Subject and object in oneself refers to the process of self-observation and examination for the purpose of furthering one's mental development. Through active, constant self-exploration, the individual comprehends the essential elements of one's inner life. Ultimately, through this dynamism, an individual experiences his or her own essence, what he or she truly is.

Syntony, identification, and empathy are progressively more complex modes of relating to other individuals. Syntony refers to spontaneously feeling what others feel, a sympathetic reaction, and a social interest, analogous to what we now call "emotional contagion" (Singer, 2006, p. 859). Identification is more a cognitive and somewhat more conscious form that refers to understanding others. Empathy denotes gaining insight into others' experiences and their emotions, combined with an altruistic attitude toward others.

The third factor is the agent of conscious choice of development, seen as the inner self that coordinates an individual's mental life. This dynamism discriminates among functions and events according to their value for enhancing development; if they are not growth-promoting, they are rejected. Inner psychic transformation sublimates instincts and drives into elements that gradually become incorporated into one's personality. Impulses are not only consciously rejected, but also are transformed. Education of oneself and autopsychotherapy refer to the actualization of personal ideals by engaging in self-improvement, as required, guided by an individual's hierarchy of values. Autopsychotherapy also is the process of educating and guiding oneself during experiences of stress—the ability to cope with distress, whether it originates in external or internal environments. For Dabrowski, individuals who reach the higher levels of functioning literally become their own teachers and psychotherapists.

Dynamisms associated with the highest level of development include: responsibility for oneself and for others, autonomy, authentism, disposing and directing center, and personality ideal. Responsibility for oneself and for others refers to taking responsibility for one's own actions, thinking, and desires as seen in the context of one's life and in relationships with others. Others are not seen as objects but as subjects; individuals develop an I-thou relationship with other people. The sense of responsibility—that is, the need to take ownership of and improve one's shortcomings—extends to helping others who wish to improve.

Autonomy is the dynamism by which individuals consciously free themselves from lower drives and from aspects of the social environment that contradict positive values. Authentism, based on self-awareness, is the expression of one's emotions, cognitions, and attitudes. It refers to being consistent with one's hierarchy of values. Disposing and directing center determines immediate behavior of an individual, as well as his or her long range planning. At the highest level, this center emerges as a distinct dynamism that works toward harmonizing the unity of personality. The disposing and directing center becomes integrated into the personality ideal. Personality ideal is a standard against which an individual evaluates his or her actual personality. It eventually becomes the highest dynamism that shapes one's personality.

Many of terms that Dabrowski used to denote dynamisms are encountered in the fields of psychology and psychiatry. There is, however, a significant difference in the interpretation given to them. For example, *autonomy*, *authentic*, *empathy*, and *self-awareness* are encountered in other personality theories, particularly those of the humanistic tradition (Maslow, 1970; Rogers, 1951). However, Dabrowski did not simply use these concepts as descriptors of personality; he perceived them as forces allowing for and guiding personality development. A more dramatic illustration of the difference is found in the dissolving dynamisms. For example, *feelings of guilt and shame* and *dissatisfaction with oneself* are likely to be viewed as symptoms, but Dabrowski considered them to be forces essential for personality development. This perspective is emblematic of how Dabrowski viewed psychopathology.

Psychopathology

Dabrowski's view of mental health was anchored to positive disintegration and the development of personality. Being on the path of personality development—with all of the negative emotional experiences and conflicts—signified mental health. Lack of mental health was associated with lack of development of personality and with the complacency and automatic living associated with primary integration (Dabrowski, 1964a).

Dabrowski reframed individuals' experiences that are normally considered symptomatic of mental illness. In effect, he proposed that experiences deemed symptoms of disorders are in fact essential for human psychological growth and development (Dabrowski, 1972). This point of view was not restricted to psychoneuroses, but he also extended it to psychoses as well. He cautioned against the automatic assumption that such symptoms as delusions, anxiety, phobias, and depression are signs of mental illness, because they may be in fact signs of an individual's development (Dabrowski, 1964a).

Of course, Dabrowski believed that, at times, symptoms traditionally associated with severe psychopathology could, in fact, be signs of mental illness. However, he believed that symptoms associated with psychoneuroses are positive, because they indicate, at the very least, an individual's potential for advanced development.

Dabrowski distinguished between neuroses and psychoneuroses. Neuroses, he believed, are rooted in psychophysiological or psychosomatic disorders, i.e, in bodily organs or systems that do not show any sign of physical malfunction. Psychoneuroses, on the other hand, depict syndromes and processes that are expressions of individuals' internal and external conflict. Dissolving dynamisms, such as dissatisfaction with oneself, guilt feelings, feelings of inferiority, and positive maladjustment are examples of such psychoneurotic processes. Far from being mental disorders that need remediation, psychoneuroses are considered "basic constituent[s]" of the process of positive disintegration (Dabrowski, 1973, p. 149).

An important function served by psychoneurotic conflict is the creation of a hierarchy of values that directs an individual's behavior (Dabrowski, 1972). Emotions play a critical role in this process. Negative emotions of psychoneurotic conflict create a state of distress that is resolved by the activation of dynamisms such as empathy that lead to the experiencing of higher-level emotions. Individuals' experiencing of negative emotions signals that there is something morally wrong with their current attitudes and behaviors. Negative emotions arise from the awareness of discrepancy between the way such individuals believe they ought to be and the way they actually are. They are then motivated to reduce the distress produced by the discrepancy by moving toward their ideal. As individuals succeed in reducing the discrepancy, they experience higher-level emotions—emotions that flow from the movement toward an ideal—rather than the gratification of a biological need. In essence, it is the experience of higher-level emotions that links emotions to values in TPD and to the creation of a hierarchy of values. For example, if an individual who experiences psychoneurotic conflict *feels good* when helping other people, then helping others is added to his or her set of values. Dabrowski believed that psychoneuroses play a vital role in propelling individuals toward higher levels of human development.

Levels of Development

The phrase *levels of development* differs conceptually from *stages of development* used in other theories. Stages of development are often sequential, age-related, and universal. For example, in Erikson's (1950) theory, development progresses sequentially from trust vs. mistrust (associated with infancy) to ego integrity vs. despair (associated with old age), and this model is applicable to all individuals. In TPD, development does not occur in a lock-step fashion, in which an individual completes the criteria for one stage and then moves on to the next one. Individuals may be at one level of development for certain aspects and at a different level with respect to other areas. There are no age-related criteria associated with each level; individuals at a young age may manifest advanced development associated with the higher levels. Levels of development are not universal; individuals who reach the highest level of development are rare.

Consistent with his conceptualization of personality, Dabrowski's levels are imbued with moral dimensions. The five levels of development are modes of being in the world analogous to Kierkegaard's view of development. [Apparently Kierkegaard was one of Dabrowski's favorite writers (Kawczak, 1970), and the influence of the father of religious existentialism can be seen throughout Dabrowski's writings (e.g., numerous references to Kierkegaard's "fear and trembling").] Kierkegaard believed that love, particularly love of God, is the cornerstone of faith. Faith was the cornerstone of the highest of three "existential positions" (Carlisle, 2005, p. 93), also known as stages (McPherson, 2001).

Kierkegaard proposed three stages of development: aesthetic, ethical, and religious. Aestheticism, the lowest form, was characterized by hedonism. At this stage, individuals are motivated by satisfaction of basic instincts or drives and conforming to societal standards. Individuals can only progress to the ethical stage by becoming dissatisfied with the sense of self associated with gratification of impulses and conformity. They then choose to create a new self. The old self equated with hedonism is consciously rejected. The newly created self chooses to be ruled by a societal code of ethics. In the religious stage, individuals are neither bound by hedonism nor conventional ethics. Instead, the self is driven by faith in and love of God. Individuals who choose to make the transition from the ethical to the religious do so in fear and trembling. Once the transition is accomplished, their daily behaviors are motivated by their faith in God.

Kierkegaard also emphasized autonomy and authenticity. He believed that individuals create a self through the choices they make in the course of their existence, but the ability to make choices is a double-edged phenomenon. Having the ability to choose creates freedom; however, the ability to choose also leads to anxiety and dread. Such experiences are necessary components of becoming an authentic and personally responsible individual.

The influence of Kierkegaard's modes of being can be seen in Dabrowski's levels, which describe development as a progression from an initial primitive integrated mode of experiencing, followed by three forms of disintegration, and culminating in a re-integrated mode of experiencing that includes the attainment of personality. The five levels of development represent a movement from an egocentric to an altruistic mode—from behavior being motivated by basic drives and conformity to being motivated by values and autonomy.

Level I: Primary Integration

Primary integration is a cohesive mental organization dedicated to gratifying an individual's biological instincts, drives, and needs, including social needs. Attributes of the individual, such as intelligence, focus on self-interest and self-gratification. Behavioral responses are generally automatic, and there is little, or simply transient, self-consciousness. Little inner conflict is associated with this level of development; instead, conflict typically focuses on the external world and reflects a frustration of drives or needs or a lack of social approval. Primary integrated individuals experience crises and challenges associated with the life cycle, but they are not transformed by them.

Dabrowski noted that some individuals at this level are under the influence of the second factor of development, the social environment. In other words, some individuals characterized by primary integration are overly socialized; their way of being in the world is highly socially conforming. Such individuals may be, for example, primarily driven by a high need for approval from others. They may be "the salt of the earth" and successful materially.

In contrast, there is a second subgroup under the influence of the first factor of development (biology) that is sociopathic. Such individuals are motivated primarily by gratification of their needs and use others for that end. This subgroup includes those engaged in criminal activity. Though both of these subgroups represent a rigidly integrated mental organization, Dabrowski depicted primary integration as existing in varying degrees in individuals. One characteristic of primary integration is clear in TPD: it is antithetical to mental health:

> *The state of primary integration is a state contrary to mental health. A fairly high degree of primary integration is present in the average person; a very high degree of primary integration is present in the psychopath. The more cohesive the structure of primary integration is, the less the possibility of development; the greater the strength of automatic functioning, stereotypy, and habitual activity, the lower the level of mental health.* (Dabrowski, 1964a, p. 121)

Level I for Dabrowski did not represent psychological development. Development requires disintegration of the mental organization of primary integration.

Level II: Unilevel Disintegration

This level represents the first instance of disintegration, hence the first indication that development is occurring. The disintegration process is triggered by the onset of conflict, which is caused by developmental milestones such as puberty and menopause, and crises such as failures in school, work, or relationships. Experiencing such events creates intense negative emotions such as frustration, anxiety, and despair. Such intense emotions lead to uncertainty. The dynamisms of ambivalence and ambitendencies arise, and mental integration is loosened. Manifestations of Level II include identity confusion and moodiness.

Level II is a transition phase from integration to disintegration and is not sustainable: "Prolongation of unilevel disintegration often leads to reintegration on a lower level, to suicidal tendencies, or to psychosis" (Dabrowski, 1964a, p. 7). In the absence of mental structures to deal with the conflict, the individual either regresses to the primary integrated state, experiences further disintegration, or suffers some very drastic consequences.

Individuals have no readily available means of dealing effectively with the intense emotions associated with the novel experience of conflict. Some individuals cope with these experiences by turning to self-medication using alcohol, drugs, or in extreme cases, suicide. Other individuals become motivated to find more effective solutions to the distress caused by events that are not under their control. Such motivation places them on the path of further disintegration and the possibility for advanced development. The outcomes of Level II—regression to a lower level or further disintegration—depend on the interplay of the three factors of development: constitutional endowment, quality of the social environment, and the third factor.

Crises cannot be addressed by drawing upon what individuals have learned in the socialization process. As individuals try to deal with their conflicts by drawing upon previous learning, they come to realize that nothing appears applicable or helpful. Social norms and values that they were exposed to are questioned and ultimately rejected. Behaviors automatically motivated by one's biological drives and needs are also scrutinised and questioned. Consequently, the experience of distress increases. Dabrowski postulated that when crises have the effect of loosening the integrated mental organization of individuals, they have limited choices. Individuals either return to previous integrated state, or they move to the next level. Remaining in Level II may lead to dire consequences such as psychoses or suicide.

Level III: Spontaneous Multilevel Disintegration

Dabrowski noted that the transition from a unilevel to a multilevel phase of development is both crucial for advanced development and unexpected as an event in human development (1996a). In other words, movement from Level II to Level III is not a smooth transition; rather, it is a quantum leap with a multilevel experiencing of reality that cannot be predicted from a unilevel mode. To illustrate this point, Dabrowski posed the question: "[H]ow is a butterfly logically implied in the larva?" (1996a, p. 26). His response: The potential for the butterfly already exists in the larva. Analogously, the potential for multilevelness must be present in the individual's constitutional endowment—i.e., developmental potential—and specifically in the presence of a high level of overexcitability and the existence of the third factor.

The loosening of primary integration begun in Level II is transformed into a spontaneous and involuntary examination of beliefs, attitudes, and emotions, followed by a repudiation of those deemed lower in value by the individual. Various forms of negative emotions and self-critical attitudes, exemplified in the dissolving dynamisms (e.g., feelings of shame, dissatisfaction with self) begin the process of creating an inner psychic milieu, increasing an individual's awareness of self. These dynamisms represent intense negative emotions, which serve the processes of disintegration and promote an increasing awareness of self-as-object. Inner conflict arises from the individual's growing awareness that the way personal and social phenomena ought to be is discrepant with the way they are. This ideal-real discrepancy intensifies as the individual becomes increasingly self-aware and aware of societal values.

The emergence of multilevelness results in a revolution in how individuals perceive themselves and the world. Individuals are no longer content with meeting biological needs and automatically adhering to societal norms. Self-critical attitudes follow when individuals perceive themselves, for example, succumbing to gratification and self-interest in their relations with others. They have begun the process of transcending their biological bases and conformity, and they develop autonomy and authenticity in their dealings with themselves and others. In essence, they have begun creating a hierarchy of values and using it to gauge their mental states, behaviors, and approaches to other people.

Level IV: Organized Multilevel Disintegration

The main feature of this level is the individual's conscious control of the course of development; individuals become self-organizing. Whereas Level III is dominated by disintegrating dynamisms, Level IV sees the rise of developmental dynamisms such as autonomy, authenticity, self-education and autopsychotherapy, and the third factor. Under the direction of the third factor, individuals deliberately select higher values and courses of action, abandoning lower ones. In addition, individuals develop a strong sense of responsibility for self and others. A sense of social justice and empathic connection with others characterize individuals' interactions with others.

Level IV is the beginning of secondary integration as the individual becomes a self-educating and self-correcting person. He or she becomes aware of areas where learning is needed and seeks that information. When crises occur, he or she can help him- or herself, literally becoming his or her own therapist. The hierarchy of values is clearly entrenched and guides daily behavior.

Level V: Secondary Integration

At the apex of human development, personality is achieved. Individuals experience harmony and are at peace with themselves. They conduct their lives by enacting the personality ideal, whereby behavior is directed by their constructed hierarchy of values. Virtually no inner conflict is experienced, since the lower forms of motivations have been destroyed and replaced by the higher forms of empathy, autonomy, and authenticity.

Emotions, Development, and Personality

Dabrowski would undoubtedly agree with Izard and Ackerman's truism that emotions drive the process of development that culminates in the achievement of personality. However, Dabrowski would disagree with their contention that the process by which this occurs is not obvious (Izard & Ackerman, 2000). Emotions influence and direct personality development by their disintegrating and reintegrating power—by directing the process of positive disintegration. The disintegrating power of emotions is seen in general by the central role in TPD played by conflict, with its frustration, anxiety, and other intense emotions. Specific directing power of emotions can be seen in the disintegrating dynamisms, which are intense emotional reactions. The reintegrating power is seen in the creation of a hierarchy of values that lead individuals to behaviors resulting in the experience of higher emotions. Positive disintegration, the process responsible for personality achievement, is anchored to emotions.

Conclusion

For Dabrowski, personality is constructed through the process of positive disintegration. Emotions are forces that direct the process. The theory of positive disintegration not only places emotions in a central role in personality development, TPD specifies how emotions accomplish this. When Mowrer used the word "extraordinary" with reference to TPD, he was commenting on the uniqueness of Dabrowski's conception of personality. As things have evolved relative to the place of emotions in psychology, Mowrer's comment can be used in another way; it is extraordinary that a theory with origins in the 1930s could reflect thinking about personality development in the 2000s. For those who agree that emotions influence personality development, TPD is a personality theory for the 21st century.

Chapter 3
Discovering Dabrowski's Theory

Michael M. Piechowski, Ph.D.[1]

I started working with Dabrowski in the winter of 1967, soon after taking a faculty position at the University of Alberta in Edmonton. I had previously heard from an Italian friend about Dabrowski's theory that psychoneurosis should be treated not as an illness but rather as a process of emotional growth. This intrigued me. At 64, Dabrowski made a strong impression with his goatee, intense eyes, animation, lively gesticulation, friendly smile, and vibrant voice. I asked for something of his to read. Besides books published in Poland, he had several chapters in English in manuscript form. They seemed garbled. I realized that whoever did the translation did not understand what Dabrowski was saying. Unlike his French, Dabrowski's English was too limited to check the translation, although it was quite adequate in conversation and his seminars.

Dabrowski suggested that we meet on Sunday afternoons to go over these fractured texts. Sentence by sentence, I asked what he meant, and he explained. Dabrowski had the tendency to write a sentence where a paragraph was needed, so I kept asking for elaboration. Bit by bit, his theory emerged. Dabrowski talked passionately about the inner psychic milieu, the processes of positive disintegration, multilevelness (often coupled in one breath with multidimensional diagnosis), and the dynamisms. The thrust of his thinking was directed toward multilevel disintegration, and it was about this time that the conception of levels IV and V began to take its final form (see Table 3.1).

---

1 Michael M. Piechowski, Ph.D., Northland College (Emeritus); Senior Fellow, Institute for Educational Advancement, South Pasadena, California/Madison, Wisconsin.

Table 3.1: The Evolution of Dabrowski's Theory

Dabrowski's theory took many years to evolve to its final form in 1972. There are clear beginnings in his 1938 monograph on *Psychological Bases of Self-Mutilation.* World War II interrupted his work, and the rupture was compounded by communist takeover of Poland and his imprisonment for two years. When after Stalin's death in 1953 things relented politically to some degree, Dabrowski managed to publish *On Positive Disintegration* in 1956, which was later largely incorporated into the English translation as *Personality-Shaping through Positive Disintegration* in 1967. The structure of levels was not yet fully defined, and the main emphasis was on distinguishing unilevel from multilevel growth process.

Dynamisms of Positive Disintegration in Successive Versions of Dabrowski's Theory

	1964	1967	1970	1972/74/77		
Personality Ideal	+	+	+	+		and DDC on a high level
Autonomy			+	+	V	
Authentism			+	+		
Responsibility			+	+		
Education of Oneself			+	+		
Autopsychotherapy			+	+		
Self-Control			+	+		
Self-Awareness			+	+		
Inner Psychic Transformation			+	+	IV	shaping, organizing
Third Factor	+	+	+	+		
Subject-Object in Oneself	+	+	+	+		
Hierarchization			(+)			
Positive Maladjustment	—	—	+	+		
Guilt	++	+	+	+		
Shame	+	+	+	+	III	spontaneous multilevel
Astonishment with Oneself	(+)	(+)	+	+		
Disquietude with Oneself	+	+	+	+		
Inferiority toward Oneself	++	+	+	+		
Dissatisfaction with Oneself	+	+	+	+		
Second Factor	—	—	+	+		
Ambivalences	+	+	+	+	II	unilevel
Ambitendencies	+	+	+	+		
Creative Instinct			+	+		
Empathy			+	+		a group of dynamisms that extend through more than one level
Identification			+	+		
Inner Conflict			+	+		
Temperamental Syntony			+	+		
Disposing & Directing Center	+	+	+	+		

+ indicates inclusion and description; ++ indicates stronger emphasis on the dynamism; (+) indicates a mention without description. Dynamisms of Level IV prepare Level V.

Note. In 1964, 1967, and 1970, levels were not described as I, II, III, etc. This appears for the first time in 1972.

The result of these sessions were chapters in *Mental Growth through Positive Disintegration,* a work that owes a very significant part to Andrzej Kawczak, a philosopher at Loyola University of Montreal, who worked with Dabrowski for a number of years. Prior to the book's publication in London in 1970, Dabrowski had two pieces of our collaboration translated into French and published in *Annales Médico-Psychologiques.* The first, on the inner psychic milieu, contained my initial attempt to create a visual picture of the dynamisms of the theory that would place them in the order that Dabrowski felt they tended to emerge (Dabrowski, 1968). He must have thought the drawing an adequate visual approximation to his conception of his theory (Figure 3.1, page 44). He used to say that in his mind, he saw the dynamisms as if on stage, certainly a more animated and dramatic vision than my two-dimensional imitation of Moorish arches.

The second piece was on higher emotions and values, in which Dabrowski argued for an objectively based, universal hierarchy of values (Dabrowski & Piechowski, 1969). As a neurologist, he firmly believed that as a person achieves higher levels of development, corresponding changes take place in the nervous system. He relied on a neurological exam of his own design as an initial assessment of the person's developmental level.

The first concept for me to grasp was the inner psychic milieu, defined as the totality of dynamisms emerging in Level III. Dabrowski believed that multilevel disintegration was indispensable for development. Little significant inner life exists in Levels I (primary integration) and II (unilevel disintegration). For Dabrowski, inner life begins with multilevel processes of introspection, self-examination, and self-evaluation. The varieties of inner conflict between higher and lower in oneself are represented by the dynamisms of Level III.

Figure 3.1. Dynamisms of Positive Disintegration (Dabrowski, Kawczak, & Piechowski, 1970)

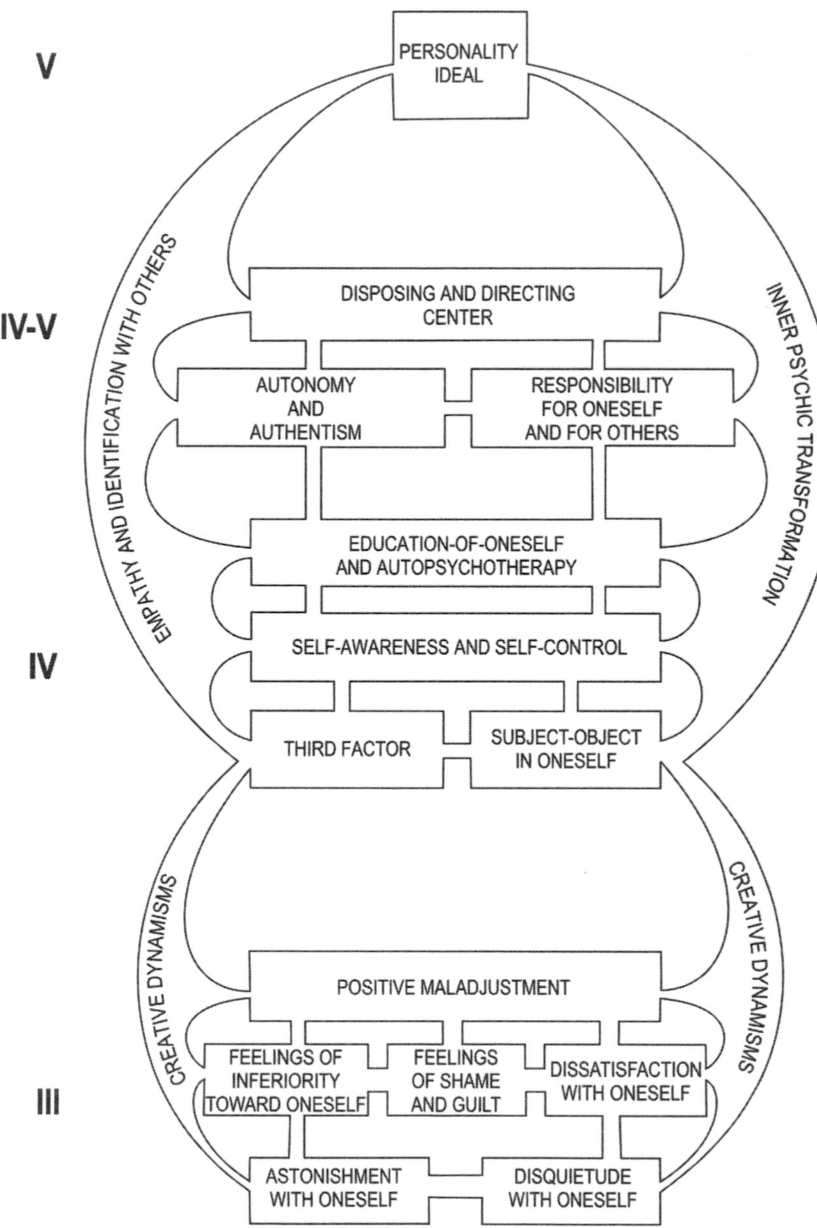

In the summer of 1968, Dabrowski was invited to the Esalen Institute in Big Sur, California to give a weeklong workshop. The invitation came through his contact with Abraham Maslow, who saw great promise in Dabrowski's theory as one that emphasized human potential (Maslow, 1968). Dabrowski asked me to come along to help him present the theory. We traveled in a large group—his wife and their two teenage daughters, and Andrzej Kawczak and his wife. Looking back, I can say that I did not fully grasp his theory at the time. My exposition was based entirely on the discussions and the writing that we labored over. Yet it went well. Being at Esalen was an unforgettable experience. The Esalen founders, Dick Price and Michael Murphy, were warmhearted hosts. The presence of Fritz Perls added color and frisson to the experience. True to type of makers of theories, Dabrowski and Perls did not have much to say to each other.

The Multilevelness Research Project

Dabrowski was trying hard to get funding for an institute where he could demonstrate his clinical methods. Because of the generally held view in those days that emotions are primitive undifferentiated energizers of behavior, any attempt to distinguish levels of emotional functioning was deemed unrealistic. And because of widely held views that emotions are more primitive than cognition and that values are relative and culturally determined, the attempt to differentiate levels of valuation as levels of emotional functioning was looked upon as quixotic.

Eventually, Canada Council gave Dabrowski a three-year research grant to showcase his theory through a multifaceted analysis of case examples. The idea was to ask volunteers to write autobiographies and open-ended responses to Verbal Stimuli, take an intelligence test, and take a neurological exam. A clinical-diagnostic interview collected essential information about the person. Dabrowski's principal research assistants in this project were Marlene King (now Rankel) and Dexter R. Amend. Marlene King was in charge of the enormous task of collecting the material and keeping track of subjects, their appointments, and their testing. Dexter R. Amend worked with Dabrowski on the description and final form of the neurological exam.

As the project was getting off the ground, I left the University of Alberta in January of 1970 to become once again a graduate student at the University of Wisconsin, this time in counseling. My departure did not make Dabrowski happy. However, our close collaboration continued until

1975. The years 1970 and 1971 were spent working together on his book *Psychoneurosis Is Not an Illness* (1972). Pages with clarifications, elaborations, inclusion of new clinical examples, and successive revisions grew to a stack one foot high. As Dabrowski tended to grossly underestimate the amount of work needed, I was tempted to send my stack of pages to him as concrete evidence of the amount of labor involved. At one time, I told him that I was sure it would have been easier to be his patient than to work with him. He agreed. Still, his sense of urgency about the work made the whole atmosphere around him charged with excitement.

In the meantime, his research team screened hundreds of subjects by means of an inventory. In the end, 81 subjects completed the autobiography and open-ended Verbal Stimuli, for which the instructions were "to describe freely in relation to each word listed your emotional association and experiences." The stimuli were: great sadness, great joy, death, uncertainty, solitude and loneliness, suicide, nervousness, inhibition, inner conflict, ideal, success, and immortality. Dabrowski and his team sifted through the accumulated material searching for cases representative of each level of development.

The initial plan was to develop measures roughly defining the level of emotional development for a given individual. But emotional development is complex. Every individual has a developmental "center of gravity" or dominant level at which he or she functions emotionally and intellectually. Leaning away from this "center"—now toward a lower level, now toward a higher one—is to be expected. In every profile, there will be residues of previous developmental levels, as well as precursors of higher levels—those toward which the individual is moving. Consequently, one cannot hope to find individuals narrowly confined to only one level. Furthermore, not all dynamisms are activated uniformly. Some advance and some lag behind, while others may never be brought into play. No cross section of development can represent only one level (unless it be Level I). A new method of analyzing autobiographical material was needed.

Dabrowski's way of reading the material was to look for key emotional events to assess the type and level of development. He used to designate the level of an identified dynamism or emotional experience as, say, II or III. But he also made intermediate designations, for instance II/III (more II and less III) or III/II (more III and less II). Now this is subtle! Not infrequently, he would give a dynamism a different name. I was beginning to see that some order must be introduced here—the theoretical terms ought to be consistent. And this is how the final structure of the levels became fixed. In order for an analysis to be possible, the dynamisms had to be defined and their list closed to stave off any of Dabrowski's further inventions.

Devising a Method of Analysis

The autobiographies and Verbal Stimuli so selected were sent to me for analysis. It was up to me to figure out how to analyze them for dynamisms and telling signs of developmental level. Since no single case qualified as representing Level IV, Dabrowski decided on Antoine de Saint-Exupéry, the French aviator and author of the *Little Prince*, *Night Flight*, and *Citadel*, who perished on a reconnaissance mission over the Mediterranean in 1944. He was 44 years old. His notebooks and letters had adequate material for a developmental analysis.

The question of method was simply this: how to read the text to identify all of the indicators of developmental level in a consistent way so that the qualitative process of identifying the terms of the theory could produce quantitative results for comparisons. At this point, I had no training in psychological research. I was trained first as a plant physiologist and then as a molecular biologist. I knew that scientific inquiry begins with a question and observation and that observations can be counted. I needed units of analysis. The Greeks conceived of *atomos* as something so small that it cannot be cut any further, the ultimate uncuttable unit. I decided to cut the text into the smallest swatches of text that remained coherent and could be understood if read apart from the rest of the text. I called these units "response units." They varied in size, just as analysis by paragraphs would have units of varied size. I learned later that what I did was to prepare the text for content analysis.

The task was to tie the terms of the theory to personal expressions of experience. On the first reading of each unit, I tried to decide whether, in what was being expressed, one could identify a dynamism or any other telling sign of a level. This was tedium of the first degree. I tried to determine the developmental level of the expression. Incipient and weak expressions of dynamisms were designated as "precursors." After reading all of the units for dynamisms, I then tried to discern whether any of the "functions" were represented. This was tedium of the second degree, and the more bothersome of the two. Then, I noticed that people describing their experiences were also showing overexcitability. I found it virtually impossible to rate the units simultaneously for dynamisms and overexcitabilities. These terms are conceptually very different and require a different mental set. Consequently, they had to be rated in separate readings of the material.

Why wasn't there a second independent rater, one may ask. The answer to this is simply that I was alone with the task, 1,437 miles away from Edmonton, and I was developing the method as I went along. But even one rater can be checked for reliability, as I explain later.

In the end, six cases were completed plus Antoine de Saint-Exupéry. Because each response unit was a sampling event to fish out the theoretical terms, the number of response units, rather than the number of subjects, constituted the proper N here. The final N was 866 response units. Table 3.2 shows the age, intelligence, the number of response units, and the number of ratings for each subject (Piechowski, 1975b).

Table 3.2: Subject Data (Piechowski, 1975b)

Subject	Age & Sex	IQ	Number of response units	Number of ratings
no. 1	23, M	115+	46	53
no. 2	23, F	129	96	117
no. 3	44, F	117	112	194
no. 4	17, M	120	162	325
no. 5	20, M	108	155	294
no. 6	34, F	140	182	346
Saint-Exupéry	44, M	not known	113	261
			866	1590

Each response unit was rated as follows. First, I attempted to establish whether the expressed content was a manifestation of one of the developmental dynamisms. Sometimes more than one dynamism was identified. If none was identified, then I tried to identify what aspect of behavior could be discerned—e.g., sadness, joy, anger, fear, etc. These expressions of behavior Dabrowski called "functions." Next, I assigned a level to the response unit. The level rating has nine possible values: five full levels—I, II, III, IV, and V—and four midlevels—I-II, II-III, III-IV, and IV-V. When this was done, I read the material over again for the presence of forms of overexcitability.

Converting Dabrowski's large conceptions of levels—rich structures made of many dynamisms—into a numerical expression raises the question: Where does a level begin and where does it end? The Roman numerals for levels needed to be converted into the range of values obtained from averaging all of the sampling events for a given subject. Therefore, values 2.0, 3.0, and 4.0 are the modal values for the three levels. The range of values for Level II would have to be from 1.6 to 2.5, for Level III from 2.6 to 3.5, for Level IV from 3.6 to 4.5. Level I is left with 1.0–1.5, and Level V with 4.6–5.0.

I made a graph of the distribution of dynamisms in the material of each subject (see Figure 3.2, page). Each instance of a dynamism was represented by a dot, which was placed in a slot reserved for that dynamism. The vertical scale held the dynamism slots, the horizontal scale the actual number of instances a given dynamism was counted. Stacking the graphs showed that, moving from the lower- to the higher-level subjects, the appropriate dynamisms of higher level become more frequent, while those of lower levels diminish in frequency.

Figure 3.2. Dynamisms of Positive Disintegration in Six Subjects and Antoine de Saint-Exupéry

Each dot represents a single occurrence of a given dynamism. II, III, and IV refer to developmental levels. C is a group of dynamisms that extend through more than one level. (Piechowski, 1975b).

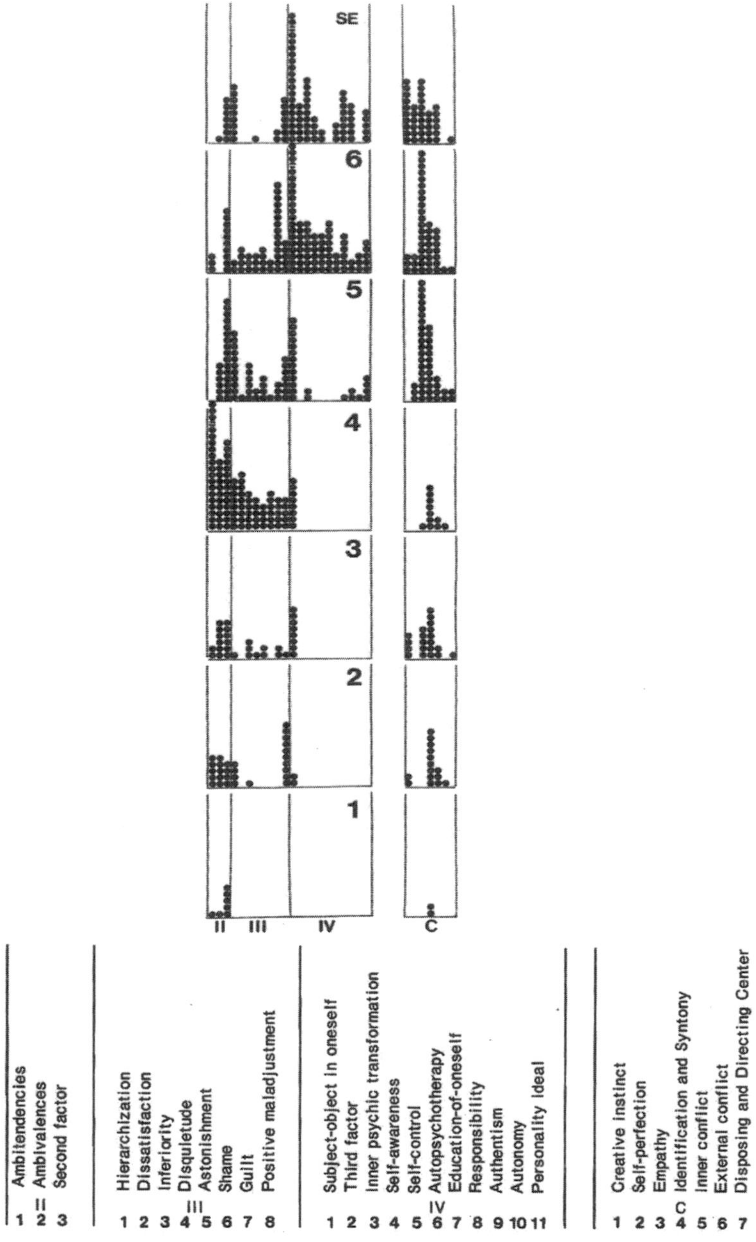

It occurred to me that one could compare Dabrowski's intuitive, clinical assessment of the developmental potential (DP) of each subject with the values obtained from the equation DP = d + oe (read on for an explanation of this). The subjects' DP values were then placed on an arbitrary metric scale extending from 0 to 50. Dabrowski's values were placed on the opposite side of the scale. The agreement was fairly good (Piechowski, 1975b).

Furthermore, Dabrowski's neurological examination is composed of 14 items. Each item produces one level designation. The sum divided by 14 showed close agreement with the level index obtained from autobiographies. The agreement of the neurological level index for each subject with the value obtained from Verbal Stimuli was again quite close, except for no. 6 (Table 3.3).

Table 3.3: Level Index from Neurological Examination, Autobiography, and Verbal Stimuli (Dabrowski and Piechowski, 1977)

Subject	Neurological Examination	Autobiography	Verbal Stimuli
no. 1	1.27	1.31	1.33
no. 2	2.18	2.29	2.28
no. 3	2.40	2.42	2.43
no. 4	2.33	2.22	2.30
no. 5	2.62	2.66	2.92
no. 6	2.79	3.21	3.41

Post Facto Empirical Tests of the Theory

So what was finally accomplished? The detailed, atomistic content analysis of the autobiographies and Verbal Stimuli made possible three empirical tests of Dabrowski's theory. The possibility of such tests did not present itself until after the ratings were done.

The dynamism ratings from each subject did form a cluster. Each cluster corresponded to part of the overall spectrum of dynamisms from Level II to V. The material from each subject provided a developmental cross-section. These cross-sections overlapped and together reproduced the complete spectrum. This made one empirical test of the theory.

The second empirical test was provided by checking the constancy of DP. DP was calculated by adding the frequencies of dynamisms (d) and overexcitabilities (oe): DP = d + oe. The relative frequencies varied, but the sum was expected to remain constant. When the material from a chronologically written autobiography was divided into two halves—early and later portions of life—the DP value was very close for the two halves. However, between the first and the second half, the balance of dynamisms and overexcitabilities changed dramatically.[2]

The third empirical test compared clinical intuitive estimates of DP for each subject made by Dabrowski with the calculated values obtained from the content analysis. These two sets of values showed reasonable agreement (Piechowski, 1975b). The close three-way agreement between the level index obtained from the neurological examination with the indices obtained from autobiography and Verbal Stimuli serves as an additional test.

No doubt, the question exists whether all of these values and comparisons are completely independent from each other. Since there was no possibility of carrying out a blind analysis, I made every effort to be meticulous about dissecting the material as consistently as possible—and the correlations for split halves showed that it was—in order to be able to arrive at a reasonable pool of quantitative data from which to reconstruct the patterns predicted by the theory and test some of its basic assumptions.

---

2 *Test of Internal Consistency* (from Piechowski, 1975b). There were four rating categories: dynamisms (D), dynamism precursors (P), functions (F), and overexcitabilities (OE). For a given subject, the total number of ratings was b = D + P + F + OE. A unit may have zero, one, or more ratings. The total number of units for a subject was a. The ratio b/a was called the yield (Y). The ratio Y was useful as one test of the internal consistency of the rating process of the one rater, myself. Calculated from each half of the material from each subject—thus 14 pairs—it gave the not-so-shabby .97 as the correlation for these pairs.

Another test of internal consistency was the computation of the value for developmental potential from DP = d+ oe [as above], where d is the frequency of expressions of dynamisms in a subject's material and oe is the frequency of expressions of overexcitability. The material from each subject was divided into two halves. The DP was then computed from each half independently. The correlation between these 14 pairs of values was .94.

As development advances, expressions of dynamisms increase in frequency, while expressions of overexcitability decrease. One could speculate that the raw material of overexcitabilities is being transformed into specific intrapsychic agents of inner transformation. One of the autobiographies (no. 6) showed this trend, as it had a consistent chronological order. I divided it into two parts, from age 3 to 15, and from 16 to 35. In the first part, the proportion of expressions of overexcitabilities was 46% and of dynamisms 38%. In the second part, the overexcitability portion was 17% and the dynamisms portion was 61%. The sums were, respectively, 84 and 78, which is pretty close. One could conclude from this that developmental potential remains constant.

The Good Form of Dabrowski's Theory

From this detailed effort grew my understanding of the nature of the dynamisms and of the structure of the theory. I learned that to gain the working knowledge of a theory, much labor goes into understanding it. The process of trying to recognize the expression of a dynamism, an overexcitability, or a "function" in the varied ways people described their feelings and experiences was, in a way, my field experience. I gained more respect for other theories when, years later, I taught theories of personality, because I knew that I had not lived with each theory as I did with the theory of positive disintegration.

As a proposal for my dissertation in counseling, I presented two completed papers—one on the theory, the other on the research described above, already submitted for publication as one monograph (Piechowski, 1975b). I felt that this was more than enough. I expected the counseling faculty to be duly impressed, since instead of a proposal, I was offering work already completed and with some substance. But because the theory was unfamiliar, they failed to be duly impressed. They asked me to make a comparison of Dabrowski's unknown theory with theories that were known to them, specifically Carl Rogers's client-centered therapy and Maslow's hierarchy of needs and his concept of psychological health. In due course, I carried out the comparison, not only with Rogers and Maslow, but also with 10 other theories of counseling and psychotherapy (Piechowski, 1975a). To do this, I studied the nature of scientific theories and the concepts on which they are founded. I could see that the concepts of Dabrowski's theory had good form. As a biologist, I knew that the concept of levels, with their structure defined by dynamisms, was a good concept. The overexcitabilities were not only good descriptive terms but also had a biological basis as the ways in which a person's nervous system handles experience. What made these terms good was that they described properties that were part of a person's biological makeup. Thus, the theory was constructed with terms that allowed measurement, and the measurement made possible the study of individual differences. It must be noted that the developmental theories of that time—Piaget, Kohlberg, and Loevinger—presented presumed universal patterns with no provisions for individual differences at any level.

As a former molecular biologist, I could see that Dabrowski's theory met the criteria of a scientific theory. The theory of positive disintegration had good formal structure, was empirically verifiable through research, and had provisions for uncovering individual differences (Piechowski, 1975a). This is why it appealed to me from the beginning. Worth pointing out are the 72 hypotheses formulated by Dabrowski and Kawczak that give the theory a well-articulated, formal definition (Dabrowski et al., 1970).

As I was coming into contact with psychology, I could not understand the long-standing divorce from biology, especially the human brain. Seeing the exclusive focus on general laws of learning and general personality, I asked: Where do they address individual differences? I'll give one telling example that is still largely in force today. So much effort has gone into studying and measuring intelligence, and yet little research by mainstream psychologists has been directed to where intelligence is expressed most sharply—in highly gifted children and adults—and with an enormous range of individual differences that are far from being fully investigated.

Limited DP Is Not Necessarily Limiting

Developmental potential is a necessary concept in Dabrowski's theory to explain differences in attained level of development. Barry Grant, whose research on moral development I discuss later, pointed out that spelling out unequal endowment for development creates one of the strong objections to Dabrowski's theory in egalitarian-thinking educators and social scientists (Grant, personal communication, March 24, 2007). My counter to this is that under optimal conditions, even children with limited developmental potential can grow up to be good citizens with a strong sense of fairness.

An illustration to make this point comes from a longitudinal study of adolescent character development by Peck and Havighurst (1960). In that study, one boy, Ralph, was at age 17 self-reliant, responsible, endowed with a sense of fairness, well-liked as a team member and as a leader, unafraid of authority, and virtually free of adolescent conflict and rebellion. The secret? A family climate that fostered trust and autonomy. His developmental potential, seen through the Dabrowskian lens, was quite limited. There was little evidence of intellectual, imaginational, or emotional overexcitabilities, but under optimal family conditions, his development was unhampered. (Growing up on a farm had a lot to do with it, too, through many opportunities to develop a sense of competence.) Peck and Havighurst placed him in their highest category of maturity of character: rational-altruistic. A limited potential does not limit a child from becoming an upright, positive human being, provided the conditions of growing up are close to optimal, as they were in Ralph's case.

Arthur was a different boy. Overweight, aloof from others, bright but often hostile, imaginative but self-centered, impulsive but conflicted and guilt-ridden, he grew up with a mother who openly disliked and ridiculed him. His father, who lived elsewhere, had no interest in his son and only tolerated him. Yet the team of observers, to whom Arthur was the epitome of emotional immaturity and instability, noted that by age 17 he had become more stable and had more self-control. They said—and this is highly significant in light of repeated observations, tests, and interviews over a period of seven years—"Nothing and no one in particular has helped him of late years." In my view, without his intelligence combined with his strong imaginational and emotional overexcitabilities, he would have ended up in an institution—mental or penitentiary. Nevertheless, it is remarkable that he did grow and become more mature, because he had the capacity for intelligent emotional assessment of others and himself, despite the absence of a nurturing and modeling adult. Arthur is a striking example of strong developmental potential overcoming an extremely unfavorable environment.

The Problem of Primary Integration

After getting my degree in counseling from the University of Wisconsin, I took a faculty position at the University of Illinois at Urbana-Champaign. My first graduate student, Margaret Lee Schmidt, chose for her Master's thesis the comparison of Kohlberg's and Dabrowski's theories (Schmidt, 1977). Her analysis led her to several conclusions, three of which are relevant here. One, that the first four stages of Kohlberg's sequence of moral reasoning are encompassed within Dabrowski's Level I (primary integration). Two, that the study of authoritarian personality (Adorno, Fraenkel-Brunswick, Levinson, & Sanford, 1950) was the best description of behavior characterizing Level I. And three, that Level I is not a personality structure, but instead is the result of limited developmental potential of people trying to survive in a ruthlessly competitive and economically uncertain world. While Dabrowski, just like Adorno et al., viewed primary integration as a rigid personality structure, now it makes more sense to see it as the outcome of social conditions. If people are operating at Level I, it is because this is the condition of their world, not because they are constituted that way (Piechowski, 2003).

The growing understanding that depression in men often manifests itself by outbursts of workaholism, anger, irritability, shaming, and blaming (Real, 1997; Scelfo, 2007) should prompt increased caution about assigning Level I to observed behavior. Furthermore, there is nothing primary about primary integration. It is not the starting point of development, and it conflicts with our evolutionary design for primary affectional attachment (Bowlby, 1969). We are born as social beings programmed for social interaction through cooing, smiling, and calming in loving arms. Asocial character develops because of emotional injuries that repeatedly break the bond of attachment. If it looks like an integration, it is due to the defensive armor to protect oneself from emotional hurt.

Levels are not real; they are abstract concepts (Piechowski, 2003). They do not have a beginning or an end in the manner of stages of development. It cannot be said that a newborn has a personality; therefore, primary integration cannot be assigned to a baby. All of these arguments force us to reconsider the concept of primary integration.

Self-Actualizing People and Level IV

For one of the readings in my course on personality, I chose Maslow's *Farther Reaches of Human Nature*, published in 1971 after his death. His frequent reference to self-actualizing people as the measure of psychological health and as a standard of right and wrong persuaded me to read his descriptions of self-actualizing people. Reading it was an *aha!* experience; here were rich descriptions of the thoughts, feelings, and motivations of people who were like Saint-Exupéry.

Using the Saint-Exupéry's material, I set out to identify the characteristics of self-actualization. First, I compiled a list of descriptors of self-actualization from Maslow's chapter in *Motivation and Personality* (Maslow, 1970), in which he delineated 16 characteristics of self-actualizing people. Then I tried to identify these characteristics in each of the 113 units from Saint-Exupéry. The task of working out the intersection of the 16 characteristics of self-actualization with the 30 dynamisms of Dabrowski's theory was extraordinarily tedious, yet deeply satisfying. Of Level III, only two dynamisms, hierarchization and positive maladjustment, were strongly represented in Saint-Exupéry's profile, but of Level IV, all but two were present. There were no traces of Level II. This, to me, convincingly demonstrated that when Maslow described self-actualizing people, he was looking at the same kind of people on whom Dabrowski had been formulating his idea of Level IV (Piechowski, 1978).

As Saint-Exupéry was Dabrowski's choice, I submitted the paper under my name and his. I sent a copy to Dabrowski but got no response. It took almost two years before I got the galleys. They came without Dabrowski's name on them. As it turned out, he wrote to the editor of *Genetic Psychology Monographs* asking that his name be dropped from the paper. To his credit, he did not block the publication, but it was odd that he did not inform me of his decision. So I asked him, and he explained that every paper on his theory should have his name as the first author. However, there was also another reason. He felt strongly that Maslow's belief that satisfaction of lower needs would more or less automatically move people toward self-actualization was fundamentally wrong. He didn't know that Maslow had changed his position and realized that self-actualization does not necessarily follow satisfaction of all of the needs below (Maslow, 1971). I believe he must not have read Maslow's description of self-actualizing people nor gotten through my paper (it is rather dense). His conclusion was that his theory and Maslow's could not be commensurate. He never understood that by providing a theoretical structure for Maslow's concept of self-actualization, his theory was showing its power. Here were two independently developed conceptions that had a perfect correspondence. How often does this happen?

Objections to equating self-actualization with Level IV came not only from Dabrowski but also from people who read Saint-Exupéry's biography and found that his relationship with his wife was less than ideal and that he had a mistress. This violated Dabrowski's saying that people at a high level of development have deep and loyal relationships. However, a person's profile cannot be expected to conform completely to ideal type—Maslow did list imperfections in the characteristics of self-actualizing people—and additionally, the idealism of a person expresses the level toward which they are moving. An analogous case can be seen with Leo Tolstoy who, after 10 years of happy marriage, acted on his ideals of a simple life, renouncing his wealth and, instead of writing, dedicated himself to educating peasant children (Marsh & Colangelo, 1983). With 10 children to raise, his wife objected to this radical curtailing of income, and this caused serious conflict.

The study of Saint-Exupéry paved the way for an analysis of the self-actualization profile of Eleanor Roosevelt, and of her personal growth and inner transformation (Piechowski, 1990; Piechowski & Tyska, 1982). Other case studies of self-actualizing people based on the framework of Dabrowski's theory followed (Brennan & Piechowski, 1991). Any attempt to negate the validity of Saint-Exupéry's self-actualization profile would have to face the similarity of his and Eleanor Roosevelt's profiles, despite their vastly different personalities. There is also the striking similarity in their philosophies of life. They both stressed the necessity to be actively engaged in life, be it socially, politically, or creatively. This is what makes for living fully. They both tended to be concerned with problems that are universal and central to human existence, and to the existence having meaning, and they both wanted to awaken their fellow human beings to the utter urgency of these problems (Piechowski & Tyska, 1982).

The fit between Level IV as the structural skeleton and self-actualization as the flesh of rich description with which to cover the bones is too good not to be true. Rev. Charles Payne produced a case study of the emotional development of Paul Robeson—singer, actor, and a protest leader, a man of high moral stature—showing him to be both self-actualizing and meeting Level IV criteria (Payne, 1987).

Anna Mróz (2002a) studied seven remarkable persons, aged 30 to 63, whose level scores ranged from 3.3 to 3.8. She obtained autobiographical narratives in three sessions in a dialogue format. The first two were devoted to the life story itself and her questions, the third to checking for understanding and accuracy. She used the Miller method to find persons deeply engaged in multilevel growth (Miller, 1985; Miller & Silverman, 1987). Of the 37 initially asked to participate, 19 filled out the questionnaire, and seven stayed with her to the end.

One of her subjects was a painter, 52 years old, married. As a boy, he was very introspective and found that he could not communicate to others his inner world nor obtain from them an idea of their world. "A blocking on both sides, and nothing could be done about it," he said. But he continued to look for means of communication while safeguarding his individuality. In his early twenties, while studying art, he found a friend with whom he could communicate without speaking: "Sometimes we were saying nothing. We could sit for hours and look at each other. At times we had conversations without speaking." Later with his wife, he experienced a relationship that was "something more than a mutual understanding of souls." His personal growth continued through integrating his life as a husband, father, teacher, and artist. His overriding consideration was a growing sense of responsibility in all aspects of his life.

For a 30-year old actor in Mróz's study, his time in nature until the age of six—he referred to himself as a "child raised in the woods"—was a source of such ecstatic experiences that it literally took his breath away. At such moments, he felt he wasn't breathing. Starting school was a shock for this free-roaming, beautiful spirit. In his early teens in order to adapt, he assumed a mask of tough masculinity. But inside himself, he cried in his loneliness and sought to regain his childhood experiences and to find communion with others. In his later teens, he devoted more time to being alone, to getting rid of the mask and facing himself. During his years of studying art, he found that "people can be beautiful" and that "individualism within a group" is preferred. He developed a deep relationship with a woman who soon became ill. The imminent threat of losing her brought pain and anxiety ("I was very much afraid I won't see her the next day"). As a young adult, he rebelled against God's indifference to human pain, but now realized that the experience of oneness with God includes the experience of pain as part of life: "I saw her suffering, but then I saw suffering through her, all of it, how much there is." He began work with youth: "Now is the time when everything that grew in me, and continues to grow, be given to others."

Another of Mróz's subjects, a nun, was very much frightened in her childhood by the war (WWII) and the threat to her father's safety. Yet she remembered herself as a happy child and very religious. Even as a child, she was aware that she had to work on herself—that more was needed than piety. She realized that she could place herself in God's presence and pray without words. In fact, verbal prayers became a hindrance. In religious ceremonies, she liked to stand with the banner, using it to conceal herself from people. The immediacy of God's presence, she said, was a gift of the ease of making contact, given to her freely. She underwent many tests, as every spiritual person must. Her empathy grew deeper and stronger, and her inner life was growing in depth. Her guiding motive was "to not betray the God who dwells in me" and to progressively purify her intent. She experienced God as outside space and outside time. She worked with children and married couples. To her, God was acting like a "marvelous educator." She felt herself to be God's temple. The last phase of her life at age 63 bespeaks the realization of the personality ideal, the principal dynamism of Level V—in sum, a profound inner transformation.

People whose developmental "center of gravity" is at an advanced level can be found; one only needs to know how to look and where to look. I have described Ashley, 44 years old, a university professor from whom I had three consecutive annual responses to measures of developmental level and overexcitability. She devoted her life to teaching—she is perhaps the most hardworking teacher I have met—while her vacations have been spent in highly concentrated study. Ashley's reports were scored at level 4.1, 4.2, and 4.3, respectively, by the Miller method (see Miller's chapter, this volume). Scores for Level IV extend from 3.6 to 4.5; consequently, Ashley's scores reflect a very advanced multilevel growth, approaching Level V. The scores themselves cannot reflect the profound changes that took place. Characteristically, and in agreement with Dabrowski's theory, the first report had a number of responses that were scored at Level III. The last full report had none. Nancy Miller and Frank Falk, who did the scoring, remarked that of the 270 protocols they scored, this is the highest level material they have seen (Piechowski, 1992b).

Tom Brennan found these types of people by strategic nomination (Brennan, 1987). Janneke Frank (2006) identified an inspirational teacher of gifted students and carried out an in-depth case study of his advanced multilevel development. Janice Witzel (1991) found them serendipitously among never-married women who turned out to be gifted, happy, self-actualizing, and invisible. Thanks to the single qualification—"well thought of"—the women nominated for Witzel's study were outstanding in their achievement, often despite lack of support in their environment, making their achievement even more amazing. They had a high level of energy, had drive for autonomy and development of their own powers, responded to opportunities and help offered, had high self-esteem, lived a deeply satisfying way of life, and were able to let go of experiences without devaluing. They were actively altruistic by being engaged in heavy-duty volunteer work. And despite such high qualities, as single women, they were unnoticed. They fit Maslow's criteria of self-actualization, which makes them good candidates for advanced multilevel growth (Witzel, 1991; Piechowski, 1998).

Perhaps the question to decide is this: Do all self-actualizing people meet the criteria of Dabrowski's Level IV? The reverse, all people who meet the criteria of Level IV are self-actualizing, can be safely assumed to be true. If this is to be studied, then the criteria for identifying them should come from Maslow's description of self-actualizing people and not by the means of the Personal Orientation Inventory (Shostrom, 1963). As I have argued elsewhere, that inventory is basically limited to the Rogerian concept of openness to experience and does not include the much more telling characteristics in Maslow's description (Piechowski & Tyska, 1982).

The Problem of Level V

If Level IV is not easy to grasp, particularly if one has an unrealistically idealized notion of it, Level V presents an even greater problem. Who can say they know personally someone so advanced as to qualify for this lofty plane of the most advanced development? How perfect can one expect such a person to be? Is such a person possible at all in our midst who would be like Jesus Christ, Saint Francis of Assisi, Gautama Buddha, Paramahansa Yogananda, or the Dalai Lama? Would Mother Teresa be a good example, her detractors notwithstanding? Shall we look among the saints? Religion, if followed with conviction, imposes a demanding personal discipline. Consequently, one could argue that a person without a religion would have no chance of attaining the most advanced level. However, there are secular people who do attain Level V—some might say without the outside help of a religious discipline. In view of this, I always felt that the most convincing examples of high levels of development are secular.

My first candidate for Level V was Dag Hammarskjöld, the great Secretary General of the United Nations (1953-1961), awarded posthumously the Nobel Peace Prize. My intention was to analyze his *Markings*, but the task seemed daunting, because some of his reflections are cryptic and also not always an immediate record of his own feelings. Dag Hammarskjöld chose to serve all nations, but especially the small emerging nations of the world. It was not an easy choice; he knew the stranglehold of loneliness. Because he made the United Nations operate according to the ideals of its charter, he has been called Servant of Peace. The inner transformation that he forged in his life opened to him transcendental realms:

> *Now you know, when the worries over your work loosen their grip, then this experience of light, warmth, and power. From without—a sustaining element, like air to a glider, or water to a swimmer. . . through me there flashes this vision of a magnetic field in the soul, created in a timeless present by unknown multitudes, living in holy obedience, whose words and actions are a timeless prayer.* (Hammarskjöld, 1964, p. 84)

The metaphor of a magnetic field in the soul offers a glimpse into the inner source of inspiration and energy that is not powered by egoistic desire, but by the willing surrender to an inner ideal, what Dabrowski called personality ideal (Piechowski, 2003).

At some point, I received a copy of *Peace Pilgrim: Her Life and Work in Her Own Words*. Here was an extensive account of an authentic life that convinced me of true representation of Level V (Peace Pilgrim, 1982; Piechowski, 1992b; 2008). She was born Mildred Norman in 1908 on a farm in New Jersey. Her family wasn't churchgoing. Even as a child, she had a bearing that made other children listen to what she had to say. She did not find her mission in life, to work for peace, until after her marriage and divorce and 15 years of work with emotionally disturbed adolescents and adults. She described those 15 years as a struggle between the lower and the higher self—a determined effort to start living what she believed. Then, at a certain point "in the midst of the struggle came a wonderful mountain-top experience, and for the first time I knew what inner peace was like. I felt oneness—oneness with all my fellow human beings, oneness with all of creation. I have never felt really separate since."

The way she described the phases of her inner growth and spiritual maturing reads like a textbook case of multilevel growth. She drew a jagged line of the inevitable ups and downs of the higher self combating the lower self, followed by a high plateau with only occasional dips out of higher consciousness, and finally the steady smooth upward incline after inner peace was hers for good. She stressed that even though the battle had been won and inner peace had been achieved, inner growth continued (Peace Pilgrim, 1982; Piechowski, 1992b).

Dabrowski was well aware that secondary integration was not a final plateau. However we may try to conceive of the highest state, we can be certain that it grows in depth and intensity. This is how Peace Pilgrim described her inner state after having attained inner peace for good; it is her version of Hammarskjöld's "magnetic field in the soul" and Dabrowski's personality ideal:

> *There is a feeling of always being surrounded by all of the good things, like love and peace and joy. It seems like a protective surrounding, and there is an unshakableness within which takes you through any situation you may need to face….* (p. 22)
>
> *What I walk on is not the energy of youth, it is a better energy. I walk on the endless energy of inner peace that never runs out! When you become a channel through which God works there are no more limitations, because God does the work* through you*: you are merely the instrument—and what God can do is unlimited. When you are working for God, you do not find yourself*

> *striving and straining. You find yourself calm, serene, and unhurried.* (p. 26)

Her mission was to work for "peace among nations, peace among groups, peace within our environment, peace among individuals, and the very, very important inner peace...because that is where peace begins" (Peace Pilgrim, 1982, p. 25). Peace Pilgrim started her pilgrimage of 25,000 miles on foot for peace in 1953, the dark period of the Korean War and rampant McCarthyism. Although there were then small peace groups, the peace movement was not yet born (Peace Pilgrim, 1982; Rush & Rush, 1992). Some years into her pilgrimage, she undertook a 45-day fast in order to stay concentrated on her prayer for peace. Her prayer consciousness became an unbroken continuous state of being: "I learned to pray without ceasing. I made the contact so thoroughly that into my prayer consciousness I put any condition or person I am concerned about and the rest takes place automatically" (p. 73).

A great many people got to know her as she walked from coast to coast in the years between 1953 and 1981. A documentary, *The Spirit of Peace*, brings impressive evidence of the impact of her mission on, for instance, prison programs that drastically reduce recidivism, and on arbitration with the same goal as Gandhi's, that both sides be winners in resolving a conflict. Lawyers involved in arbitration using her *Steps Toward Inner Peace* said that, after 20,000 cases, they have had a steady 80% success rate, *independent* of who is the arbitrator. In the compilation of her talks and in the testimony of those who knew her intimately, there is ample material revealing her consistently high level of energy, kindness, unshakable inner peace, and dedication to her mission to raise people's consciousness for peace (Peace Pilgrim, 1982). This material gives insight into the inner and outer life at Level V of one of our contemporaries (Piechowski, 1992b).

Peace Pilgrim's upbringing was not religious; her search for God was prompted entirely from within, and so was Dag Hammarskjöld's. Etty Hillesum was raised conventionally in the Jewish tradition, but she searched for that essential part of herself that she felt was locked away. It brought her to a life of prayer and an intimate communion with God (Piechowski, 1992a; Spaltro, 1991). She reached deep inside herself and conquered hatred. Amid Nazi horror, she achieved inner peace. She spoke from first-hand knowledge when she affirmed that "everything we need is within us"—everything to give our life meaning, to secure inner peace, to solve the problems of our time. Like Peace Pilgrim, she affirmed repeatedly that inner peace is the necessary foundation of world peace (Piechowski, 1992a). Etty Hillesum's (1985) diary is perhaps the most detailed record of multilevel development yet.

Abraham Lincoln, raised in his mother's Baptist creed, as a young man rejected religious dogma (Wilson, 1998). In his personal growth, he experienced periods of inner conflict and depression resulting in profound inner transformation. Elizabeth Robinson (2002) and Andrew Kawczak (2002) offer a brief analysis of the phases of positive disintegration in Lincoln's life and conclude that he reached secondary integration.

The Roominess of Dabrowski's Theory: Levels as Larger Universes

The complexity of Dabrowski's theory should not be underestimated (see Table 3.4). Personal growth is much like scaling a mountain rather than a sequential unfolding of childhood, adolescence, and adulthood. Imagining personal growth as ascent of a mountain, with all of the peril, tests of courage, and perseverance, suggests that not everyone has the strength, endurance, and determination to go far; few manage to reach the summit. Also, not everyone is interested in climbing and may prefer to remain in the valley. Some may not even be aware of the mountain. The endowment for how far in scaling the figurative mountain an individual can go constitutes developmental potential. An endowment for multilevel development signifies that a person starts already a significant distance up the slope. A person with limited potential starts in the valley and does not reach far.

Table 3.4: Levels of Emotional Development According to Dabrowski's Theory of Positive Disintegration (Piechowski, 2003)

Level I: Primary Integration
Dog-eat-dog mentality
Dominant concern with self-protection and survival; self-serving egocentrism; instrumental view of others

Level II: Unilevel Disintegration
A reed shaken in the wind—Matthew, XI, 7
Lack of inner direction; inner fragmentation—many selves; submission to the values of the group; relativism of values and beliefs

	UNILEVEL DYNAMISMS
Ambivalences	Fluctuations between opposite feelings; mood shifts
Ambitendencies	Changeable and conflicting courses of action
Second Factor	Susceptibility to social opinion; feelings of inferiority toward others

Level III: Spontaneous Multilevel Disintegration

*Video meliora proboque deteriora sequor.** —Marcus Tullius Cicero

Sense of the ideal but not reaching it; moral concerns; higher versus lower in oneself

MULTILEVEL DYNAMISMS

Multilevel dynamisms are ways of critically perceiving and evaluating the world, others, and oneself, leading to the work of inner transformation

Hierarchy of Values and Social Conscience

Hierarchization and Empathy	*What is* contrasted with *what ought to be*: Individual values Universal values lead to authenticity
Positive Maladjustment and Empathy	Protest against violation of ethical principles

Emotionally Charged Self-Reactions and Self-Judgments

Dissatisfaction with Oneself	Anger at what is undesirable in oneself; self-loathing
Inferiority toward Oneself	Anger at what is lacking in oneself, of not realizing one's potential
Disquietude with Oneself	Disharmony in one's inner state of being
Astonishment with Oneself	Surprise in regard to what is undesirable in oneself
Shame	Shame over deficiencies and others' view of one's moral standard
Guilt	Guilt over moral failure; a need to repay and expiate

Level IV: Organized Multilevel Disintegration

Behind tranquility lies conquered unhappiness.—Eleanor Roosevelt

Self-actualization; ideals and actions agree; strong sense of responsibility on behalf of others' well-being and inner growth

	DYNAMISMS OF INNER RESTRUCTURING
Subject-Object in Oneself	The process of critical examination of one's motives and aims; an instrument of self-knowledge
Third Factor	The executive power of choice and decision in one's inner life; active will in self-regulation and self-determination

*I regard the better but follow the worse.

Responsibility	Taking on tasks for the sake of one's own and others' development; empathic responsiveness to social needs
Inner Psychic Transformation	Inner restructuring at a deep level, with lasting consequences beyond return to lower-level functioning
Education of Oneself	A program of change
Autopsychotherapy	Self-designed psychotherapy and preventive measures
Self-Control	Regulating development and keeping in check interfering processes; leads to autonomy
Self-Awareness	Knowledge of one's uniqueness, developmental needs, and existential responsibility
Autonomy	Confidence in one's development; freedom from lower-level drives and motivations

Level V: Secondary Integration

A magnetic field in the soul—Dag Hammarskjöld

Life inspired by a powerful ideal, such as equal rights, world peace, universal love and compassion, sovereignty of all nations

Personality Ideal	The ultimate goal of development—the essence of one's being
	DYNAMISMS CONTINUING ACROSS LEVELS
Creative Instinct	Becomes the dynamism of perfecting oneself
Empathy	Connectedness; caring; helpfulness
Inner Conflict	In the beginning, a clash of drives; then inner conflict becomes emotional (unilevel) and conscious (multilevel)
Identification	Identification with higher levels and personality ideal
Dis-Identification	Distancing from lower levels and drives
Disposing and Directing Center	Status of will: I: Identified with the main motive (drive) II: Multiple, fragmented, or shifting in direction III: Ascending and descending as a consequence of which level it is attached to (=identified with) IV: Unified V: Personality ideal

One could say that the theory is spacious; each level is a large universe with much room for many individual developmental paths. Any level can hide widely contrasting types of development, just as under the same IQ there is a wide range of individual intelligence profiles.

Each level has room for many possible patterns and alternative pathways. Barry Grant studied cases of advanced moral development, to which he applied four theories of development: Kohlberg, Gilligan, Dabrowski, and Blasi (Grant, 1988; 1990; 1996). He sought to introduce a dialogue between individual lives and theories, to use the theories to illuminate lives and the lives to check the theories. With four theories in the game, which case was going to have the best fit with any of the four? The development of one of his subjects ("Hendricks") had striking parallels with Kohlberg's own. "Both men were influenced by moral questions raised by *The Brothers Karamazov*; both believed in democratic values." And further, "both men grappled with moral relativism and sought a rational foundation for a universal morality as an alternative to it." Kohlberg found his solution in universal principles in the form of moral reasoning he called "stage 6 justice reasoning" (Grant, 1990, p. 86). Hendricks's solution was to take "rationality as an attitude toward finding and debating truth—tolerance, open-mindedness, awareness of merit in competing views" (p. 87). His rational approach is a morality in the making, rather than a morality that is based on universal principles. Hendricks presents a challenge to Dabrowski's scheme. Grant says Hendricks would be at Level III or IV, because "he has developed a hierarchy of values and, with a strong sense of responsibility, seeks to live out his ideals." However, Grant's exhaustive case study (162 pages) came up with no evidence of inner transformation in the life of this man committed to peace but not to inner growth.

Another of Grant's cases, "Hope Weiss," demonstrates the possibility of multilevel growth being compatible with relativism. Having been raised on Dabrowski's theory, I always believed that relativism of values, and hence moral relativism, belong in the unilevel universe. But Barry Grant explains that there are three kinds of relativism: *descriptive relativism*, which holds that the basic moral tenets of peoples and societies are different and in conflict—this would fit my earlier narrow conception; *normative relativism*, the view that what is right for one society or person is not necessarily right for another in a similar situation; and *meta-ethical relativism*, which says that basic ethical judgments cannot be justified one against another in an objectively valid way. Hope Weiss's morality combines normative and meta-ethical relativism. Her moral stance was rooted in a sense of a changeless self, which she felt she always had: "My essence has always been the same. I don't know if that's true for everybody....As far as I can remember, from before kindergarten days, I'm really the same inside" (Grant, 1996, p. 121). She believed that there is more than one right response to many situations; consequently, she rejected the idea of universal principles of moral judgment. Her morality was grounded, above all, in compassion. Seeing a person in need, she felt compelled to help.

Hope Weiss's behavior is characteristic of a multilevel way of functioning, and yet she does not feel that she arrived there through a process of positive disintegration; rather, she felt that she had always been that kind of a person. This suggests that it should be possible to find more persons who are born with an unusually strong empathy and an unchanging sense of self. Ann Colby and William Damon (1992) interviewed Suzie Valdez who for years has been "feeding, clothing, and providing medical care for thousands of poor Mexicans living in the surrounds of the huge Ciudad Juarez garbage dump." She said that she always had love: "I love everybody; I mean love. The Lord has given me a love for these people that I myself don't understand" (p. 47). Charleszetta Waddles, another deeply committed person in Colby's and Damon's study, recalled her mother saying to her, "I wish I had a heart like you," and about herself, she said, "I had compassion; I was forgiving, but at that time I didn't call it by that name. I said, 'Well, I just can't help it, I'm free-hearted'" (p. 212).

Two British studies reported people who had, since childhood, a life-long continuous awareness of "this never failing flow of Life—Love—Power...the central spark of life in us" (Maxwell & Tschudin, 1990, p. 195) and being always essentially the same: "I don't feel that *essentially* I have changed much.... I think I always had the idea that the essential 'me' was timeless and free and only for the present suffering all the inhibitions of being encased in a body" (Robinson, 1978, p.141).

Perhaps those who are aware of their essence from a very young age do not need to undergo positive disintegration, while others do, because finding their essence is their life's task that impels seeking, questioning, doubting, scrutinizing, evaluating through positive disintegration, and inner transformation.

Grant's study demonstrated that no single theory, not even the four theories together, could account in full for the developmental pathways of each of the four morally advanced cases. Individual lives are incomparably richer than any theory, or even a combination of theories. As Goethe said, "Gray is all theory, green is the tree of life."

The Pearls of Level II

Coming into contact with Dabrowski's theory, one tends to focus on the higher levels, III and IV, and be disdainful of Level II; yet this level deserves understanding and a huge amount of empathy. This did not become clear to me until I read *Women's Ways of Knowing*, by Belenky, Clinchy, Goldberger, and Tarule (1986).

Level II is not easy to grasp in all its multiple possibilities. I remember once saying to Dabrowski that unilevel disintegration was eluding my understanding. He jokingly answered, "I don't understand it either." Level II is not always characterized by disintegration, because it carries the possibility of partial integration, or adaptive integration, that follows the conventions and dictates of society and one's immediate environment. Level II may carry inner instability that we would see in oscillations of mood, inconsistent ways of acting, or shifting from one extreme to the other. But it is also possible to have a fairly integrated worldview of conventional values or a sort of intellectual rationalism. Fulfilling the expectations of others, family, or society ("second factor") in extreme cases may lead to anorexia and bulimia in gifted women (Gatto-Walden, 1999). Inner fragmentation ("I feel split into a thousand pieces") and unpredictable shifts among many "selves" are often experienced. In adolescence, a failed attempt at identity, which Elkind (1984) called "the patchwork self," is another example of the inner disorganization. At this level, personal growth becomes a struggle toward achieving an individual sense of self.

When a sense of self is undeveloped, personal growth moves toward gaining a sense of one's individuality, coming into one's own as a person. When people trust external authority, depend on it for defining who they are, they derive a sense of self from their role: "I've never had a personality. I've always been someone's daughter, someone's wife, someone's mother" (Belenky et al., 1986, p. 82). As long as this does not change, there is no inner development—a Level I (and not yet II) condition remains. A crisis erupts when the authority is exposed as wrong, misleading or exploitative, and abusive. This can happen in a family, in a church, or in the whole nation as it did during the Vietnam War. Feeling betrayed, people reject authority because it failed them. They begin to look for self-knowledge and self-definition in people like themselves, and eventually in themselves.

The first step is liberation from passive acceptance of external authority and replacing it with trust in subjective knowing. The second step is the quest for self. In a radical shift, a person moves away from dependence on external authority to listening to her own inner voice. But the voice is undeveloped, and whatever comes from the "gut" is taken uncritically. The voice does not yet represent the true self. If emotional growth leads no further than the person's "gut feeling," it will be swayed by moods, opinions, and chance experiences—what Dabrowski called "ambivalences" and "ambitendencies." It is then locked in the unilevel range and remains there. But continued growth is definitely possible, moving toward a sense of self.

One of the women in *Women's Ways of Knowing* described how she ceased to obey the whims of external authorities dictating matters of right and wrong. She stopped thinking of herself as dumb and ignorant:

> *I can only know with my gut. I've got it tuned to a point where I think and feel all at the same time and I know what is right. My gut is my best friend, the one thing in the world that won't let me down or lie to me or back away from me.* (Belenky et al. 1986, p. 53)

Other women expressed similar change in themselves, the first stirrings of their own inner knowing: "It's like a certain feeling that you have inside you. It's like someone could say something to you and you have a feeling. I don't know if it's like a jerk or something inside you. It's hard to explain" (p. 69).

It is possible that the feeling of an inside jerk suggests what Gestalt psychologists and Gendlin (1981) have described as the internal shift of things falling into place when a problem is solved.

> *There's a part of me that I didn't even realize I had until recently—instinct, intuition, whatever. It helps me and protects me. It's perceptive and astute. I just listen to the inside of me, and I know what to do.* (p. 69)

Another woman described how she had to leave her past and start anew:

> *Being married to him was like having another kid. I was his emotional support system. After I had my son, my maternal instincts were coming out of my ears. They were filled up to here! I remember the first thing I did was to let all my plants die, I couldn't take*

care of another damned thing. I didn't want to water them; I didn't want to feed anybody. Then I got rid of my dog. (p. 78)

This woman divorced her husband, moved to a different town with her son, and began exploring alternative lifestyles.

Following the rules—isn't that what school and church, the principal agents of socialization and trimming individuality, are about? To break away from the trust in rules is particularly difficult if there is no guidance from anyone. The quest for self is arduous:

> *I always thought there were rules and that if you followed the rules, you'd be happy. And I never understood why I wasn't. I'd get to thinking, gee, I'm good, I follow the rules. I do everything they tell me to, and things don't go right for me. My life was a mess. I wrote to a priest that I was very fond of and I asked him, "What do I do to make things right?" He had no answers. This time it dawned on me that I was not going to get the answers from anybody. I would have to find them myself.* (p. 61)

Fluctuations in the sense of self, but also exhilaration and optimism in the process of change, are expressed by three different women:

> *I'm a different person each day. It's the day, I guess, depending on how it is outside or how my body feels....* (p.83)
>
> *I'm only the person that I am at this moment. Tomorrow I'm somebody different, and the day after that I'm somebody different....I'm always changing. Everything is always changing....* (p.83)
>
> *It's hard to say who I am because I don't really think about more than tomorrow. In the future, I'll probably have a better understanding, because now I simply don't know. I think it will really be a fun thing to find out. Just do everything until I find out.* (p. 83)

Opening to novelty and change, several women expressed in imagery of birth, rebirth, and childhood—a significant step in personal growth, even though it is far from multilevel:

> *Right now I'm so busy being born, discovering who I am, that I don't know who I am. And I don't know where I'm going. And everything is going to be fine....* (p. 82)

> *The person I see myself as now is just like an infant. I see myself as beginning. Whoever I can become, that's a wide-open possibility....* (p.82)
>
> *I actually think that the person I am now is only about three to four years old with all these new experiences. I always was kind of led, told what to do. Never really thought much about myself. Now I feel like I'm learning all over again.* (p. 82)

I feel very strongly that emotional growth within the unilevel universe of Level II should not be underestimated but respected and explored further. This raises the question as to whether it is possible to facilitate a transition to multilevel emotional growth if a person's developmental potential is limited. And is it possible to imagine a harmonious society without a multilevel majority? I feel it is possible—to imagine. Recall the example of Ralph, that showed how optimal families raise children who are responsible, who have a strong sense of fairness and justice, and who care for others even when their DP is short on the critical overexcitabilities, emotional and intellectual. Child development research has indeed established that the optimal conditions for growing up are like those that Ralph's parents created (Bowlby, 1969; Sroufe, 1995).

The above examples show that not all material has to be generated from the framework of Dabrowski's theory. Research literature can be explored to flesh out some of his concepts in living color.

Measurement: There Must Be a Better Way

Research depends on instruments specific to its purpose. Assessing developmental level from autobiographical material is an extremely time-consuming process. Furthermore, Levels I and II are difficult to assess, because most of the dynamisms are at higher levels. In addition, Level I is defined by a total absence of any developmental dynamisms, and the absence of something is difficult to quantify.

David Gage decided to explore new avenues. Multilevel dynamisms, he concluded, could be viewed as themes that are expressed at every level of development: moments of feeling inadequate and unworthy, moments of frustration and anger toward oneself, dealing with questions that cause conflict and doubt within oneself, and so on. Of Gage's three new methods, their validities thoroughly investigated, Definition Response Instrument (DRI) was used in subsequent studies. It consists of six questions corresponding to themes represented by six multilevel dynamisms (Gage, Morse, & Piechowski, 1981).

Katherine Ziegler Lysy was the first to use David Gage's instrument to assess developmental level (Lysy & Piechowski, 1983). She set out to compare measures of personal growth derived from Jung's and Dabrowski's theories. Jung's concept of psychological type identifies three continuous personality dimensions: from extroversion to introversion (E-I), from sensation to intuition (S-N), and from thinking to feeling (T-F). One would expect the last two dimensions to correspond to the overexcitabilities—for instance, thinking to intellectual and feeling to emotional. However, there is very little correlation between overexcitabilities and these dimensions, suggesting that they are different constructs. The Jungian dimensions refer to preferred and *habitual* modes of processing experience; the overexcitabilities refer to the *heightened* capacities for enlarging experience (Lysy & Piechowski, 1983).

Kathy Lysy gave her 42 subjects measures of overexcitability and developmental level. She then correlated the data on overexcitabilities with the data on developmental level. Emotional and intellectual overexcitabilities had a highly significant correlation with developmental level (.57 and .59), while for imaginational, the correlation was .38. (See Miller's chapter in this volume for a discussion of this and more recent findings.)

Dabrowski emphasized that emotional, intellectual, and imaginational overexcitabilities were essential for multilevel growth. He also believed that strong psychomotor and sensual overexcitabilities would hamper development. This is not exactly what was found. Psychomotor and sensual overexcitabilities did not have a lowering effect on developmental level; on the contrary, they were mildly correlated with it. However, the Jungian function of intuition showed a highly significant correlation (.44) with developmental level, suggesting that intuition is an essential component of multilevel potential.

Emotional and intellectual overexcitabilities are the strongest factors in potential for multilevel growth. The strength of these overexcitabilities is critical, because inner psychic transformation cannot be forged without them. While psychomotor and sensual overexcitabilities by themselves cannot enable multilevel growth, they are not an obstacle to it. Clearly, multilevel growth is principally the function of the strength of emotional and intellectual overexcitabilities in concert with intuition. Although Dabrowski discussed intuition as a strong factor in multilevel development, he did not include it among the dynamisms. Lysy's results suggest that it should be included. As intuition operates differently at each level of development, it would be best to place it with the continuing dynamisms, like identification and empathy that extend across levels (see Table 3.4).

A brief word about the continuing dynamisms. They operate at more than one level; some diminish in strength; others grow stronger. Empathy grows stronger and deeper. In the gifted, empathy may operate as a way of knowing—that is, of understanding the world and others through an ability to get out of one's skin to see and feel from the perspective of others (Jackson, Moyle, & Piechowski, in press). Dabrowski stressed the key role of empathy in working out inner transformation toward kindness and taking responsibility for one's own and others' unique development. His conception of empathy resonates well with such traits of self-actualization as acceptance of self and others, democratic character structure, and kinship with others (Gemeinschaftsgefühl).

Conserving versus Transforming Inner Growth

A few of Lysy's subjects showed evidence of inner psychic transformation. Speculating about different strengths and different kinds of developmental potential, we came up with two terms: *conserving* and *transforming*. Potential for conserving growth would allow it to continue through Level II close to Level III, but not any further. Transforming growth, however, would continue. The subjects who were deemed transforming had level scores of 2.3, 2.4, 2.6, 3.0, and 3.1. Of the subjects who were deemed conserving, the highest level scores were 2.4, and 2.6, and 2.8. Recall that Level III scores go from 2.6 to 3.5. A similar, or even identical, score can hide vastly different types of development. Thus, conserving subjects can be found in the lower region of multilevel growth (scores of 2.6 and 2.8), and transforming subjects' scores can be found below the numerical threshold for multilevel growth (scores of 2.3 and 2.4). Yet in their material, there were distinct expressions of a multilevel character. This is probably the closest that we can see in Level II the presence of what Dabrowski called "multilevel nuclei."

Judith Ann Robert (1984; Robert & Piechowski, 1981) took up the task of exploring the distinction between conserving and transforming personal growth. Examining the content of responses to open-ended questionnaires, she found telling differences:

> *The concepts of a hierarchy of values can be found in both subjects, but the conserving subjects lacked inner psychic transformation which enabled them to put their ideals into action.... This concept of inner psychic transformation, which was associated with transforming subjects, is the process by which specific tasks of inner restructuring are carried out. This requires an inward problem solving approach, focusing on one's personal growth and development. And finally, an additional distinction between the subjects was the transforming subjects' sense of responsibility toward others and their own development.* (Robert, 1984, p. 103)

Robert noted that the transforming subjects did not dwell excessively on their inner conflict—the split between higher and lower in themselves—but instead were active in solving the problems presented by their multilevel growth process.

I feel that Dabrowski extolled the virtues of inner conflict perhaps too much, as he believed in the ennobling value of suffering but failed to mention that the ennobling is possible only if one accepts the suffering as something to grow through. Acceptance is essential. It is one of the lessons from the lives of Peace Pilgrim, Etty Hillesum, and Ashley. Rather than condemning, accepting one's inner "what is" as the starting point is a vital step in emotional growth toward realizing "what ought to be" (Piechowski, 2003).

Dabrowski's Theory and Gifted Education

Two persons played a key role in introducing Dabrowski's theory to the field of gifted education: Nick Colangelo and Linda K. Silverman. Nick was my officemate when we were graduate students in counseling at the University of Wisconsin-Madison and graduate assistants at the Research and Guidance Laboratory for Superior Students. I decided to create an overexcitability questionnaire to give to the gifted middle and high school students attending the Laboratory. This was the first OEQ. It had 46 open-ended questions formulated from the 433 expressions of overexcitability that I had collected from autobiographies and Verbal Stimuli I had just finished analyzing. In this way, I obtained the initial material that I put years later in *"Mellow Out," They Say. If I Only Could* (Piechowski, 2006). Nick became interested in the theory and in my project, as did Kay Ogburn (later Colangelo), with whom we shared our office. After we all graduated, Nick and another of our officemates, Ron T. Zaffrann, conceived the idea of putting together a book under the title *New Voices in Counseling the Gifted* (Colangelo & Zaffrann, 1979). It was the first book of its kind and was graced by a general chapter on developmental potential and one on a clinical example of multilevel potential (Ogburn-Colangelo, 1979; Piechowski, 1979a).

Linda Kreger Silverman became an ardent champion of Dabrowsk's theory, organizing training sessions and pulling in R. Frank Falk. Linda spoke about the theory at meetings, workshops, wherever she was invited to speak. The concept of overexcitabilities found ready acceptance, because they are so apparent in gifted children and adults. And then there were those who resonated strongly to the concepts of multilevel growth and inner transformation. Linda Silverman launched *Advanced Development* as a forum to stimulate thinking and research on adult giftedness and Dabrowski's theory. (See the chapters by R. Frank Falk, Nancy B. Miller, and Linda K. Silverman in this book.)

Conclusions and Challenges

1. Dabrowski's theory evolved over many years. The multilevelness research project helped establish the structure of levels, definition of dynamisms, and developmental potential.

2. Dabrowski's theory has good form. Its concepts have been operationalized, which enabled the design of research instruments and methods of measurement.

3. Four empirical tests of the theory became possible: (1) reconstitution of the overall structure of levels from individual profiles, (2) constancy of developmental potential, (3) agreement between clinical and quantitative assessment of level, and (4) three-way agreement in deriving a quantitative index of level between neurological exam, autobiography, and Verbal Stimuli.

4. Intuition makes a significant contribution to an advanced level of development. Although Dabrowski did not include it among multilevel dynamisms, he often spoke of its importance.

5. The concept of primary integration (Level I) needs to be reconsidered, as it is neither primary nor a personality structure but the outcome of the way society is.

6. It is possible to grow into a positive human being, even with limited developmental potential, provided the conditions of growing up are close to optimal.

7. In order to avoid thinking of levels as rigid structures, it is essential to remember that Dabrowski emphasized looking at the person's inner psychic milieu to see whether it was unilevel, unilevel with multilevel nuclei, or essentially multilevel.

8. Unilevel growth process should not be underestimated. The search for one's own voice and sense of self commands respect and empathic understanding.

9. Each level is a large universe with many possible developmental patterns.

10. Conserving and transforming growth overlap at the borderline of Levels II and III. Similar or identical level scores may hide contrasting types of inner growth.

11. Taking Maslow's full description of self-actualizing people, individuals in advanced multilevel growth (Level IV) are self-actualizing. Whether self-actualizing people are also engaged in advanced multilevel process has yet to be examined.

12. Rare persons aware of their own essence, of their self remaining essentially the same throughout their life, do not appear to have gone through positive disintegration. Their lives give evidence of an advanced multilevel functioning. If one views the process of positive disintegration as the search for one's essence—one's true or higher self—then persons who have always had awareness of their timeless essence appear to be exempt from the crushing grind of positive disintegration.

13. Cases of persons approaching Level V, realizing fully their personality ideal, can be found among our contemporaries.

14. Of all psychological theories, Dabrowski's theory offers the most insight into the emotional development of gifted and creative children and adults.

Chapter 4
Dabrowski on Authentic Education

Marlene D. Rankel, Ph.D.[1]

I was fortunate to meet and work with Dr. Dabrowski for the last 12 years of his life. I first encountered his theory in 1968, while a student at the University of Alberta in Edmonton, Alberta, by reading his book *Positive Disintegration* (Dabrowski, 1964a). I remember being intrigued, because Dabrowski took terms usually deemed negative—for example, depression and frustration—and reframed them as positive, thereby turning the world of psychology upside down. He spoke about levels of being in the world and of the need to understand degrees of moral and ethical behavior. In his concept of overexcitabilities and their origin, he emphasized emotion and imagination over intellect. After having read his book, I began to ask others about him, only to find that he was at the same university. I lost little time in seeking him out, and shortly thereafter, I was involved, at his invitation, in discussions of his various published and unpublished books.

Working with Dabrowski was a very intense experience. He had an amazing capacity for work, and I, along with his other students, was challenged to keep up with him. In spite of his intensity, he was very understanding, always considerate, and available if needed. In his office, while pacing back and forth, he dictated his papers and his books to his secretary, who could, if necessary, type faster than anyone I had ever seen. I believe that part of the intensity I felt working with him can be attributed to the various positions he held. For a number of years, Dabrowski had a double appointment, half-time lecturing and doing research in Edmonton,

---

1 Marlene D. Rankel, Ph.D., Psychologist (Retired), Beaumont, Alberta, Canada.

the other half lecturing and counseling—in French, one of his many languages—at the University of Laval in Quebec. He was awarded a Canada Council Research grant, 1969-1972, during this busy period as well. We students and colleagues who worked on his research project were exhausted by his energy level, and when he left for his six-week period in Quebec, we spent the first few days recuperating and sharing our admiration for our mentor's indomitable spirit.

I felt that Dabrowski was a living example of his theory—overexcitable in all domains, but predominantly emotional and intellectual. His authority shone through his every action, and particularly in his smile. Introverted by nature, he disliked talking to large groups, preferring his smaller academic sessions with his students. When he died in 1980, he was sorely missed. Through his theory, his ideas remain alive and inspire students to take responsibility for their own individual growth and to have empathy for the well-being of others. For Dabrowski, I believe, the inauthentic life was not worth living.

Authenticity was an important concept for Dabrowski, as evidenced in his theory and its application to education. In this chapter, I discuss his approach to education as expressed in *Authentic Education* (Dabrowski, n.d. 1), a manuscript with which I was privileged to collaborate. Dabrowski postulated that by using the theory of positive disintegration to reframe mental health and education, public education could be used to facilitate mental health in society.

Mental Health: A Dabrowskian Perspective

Dabrowski, in the early years of his work, emphasized the need to re-evaluate functions other than intellectual ability, expressed as intellectual quotient (IQ), to create a more complex definition of what it is to be human. He clearly stated that if mental health were to be studied in depth, it would require an examination of emotional intelligence, expressed as emotional quotient (EQ) (K. Dabrowski, personal conversation, June 1969), a term unheard of in the early 1960s, but now commonly used. Similar to intellectual ability, Dabrowski believed that there are levels of emotional functioning.

Dabrowski suggested that psychiatrists with sufficient clinical experience would agree with his position that there are levels of emotional as well as intellectual functioning, and the levels of emotional functioning, though more difficult to define and measure, are just as observable as the intellectual levels. His position was that a low level of emotional functioning is associated with biological determinism; our behavior and how we respond are largely the product of our biological instincts. A high level of emotional functioning connotes psychological determinism; we are able to exert self-control and determine ourselves by our psychological perspective and attitude.

Using a sample of 100 individuals of average IQ from his own clinical experience, Dabrowski evaluated 10 emotional and instinctual functions. He used this tentative example, as he called it, to show that in contrast to their average IQ, the emotional and instinctive functions in this group were of a very low level, meaning that their intelligence was used almost solely as an instrument to satisfy their lower-level biological drives. Furthermore, Dabrowski felt that in terms of the emotional sphere and EQ, such individuals are emotionally challenged, if not emotionally retarded. This was extremely radical thinking for his time and, as expected, was either not well received or totally rejected by academics and the medical profession.

In Dabrowski's view, it was clear that psychology cannot derive a statistical norm of mental health in the same manner as was done for intelligence. What then, he asked, is mental health, and he answered using the comparison between R. R. Hetherington's and his own point of view. Hetherington's definition of mental health was "a high degree of personal integrity, being a 'whole', lacking conflicts, being able to realize one's own potential and to be productive" (Hetherington, 1966, cited in Dabrowski, n.d. 2, p. 3). In contrast, Dabrowski, in *Normality, Mental Health and Mental Illness* (Dabrowski, n.d. 2), defined mental health as "an individual and social capacity for development (developmental potential) which is multisided (universal) and which goes in the direction of higher scales of values and of a personality ideal" (p. 3). He stated that mental health is more than realizing one's own potential; one must ask, "Potential for what and in what direction?" Dabrowski's definition also takes into consideration the *role of disintegration* and the *positive role of conflict* in development, and it stresses the need to differentiate developmentally positive and negative potentials. Simply being productive was not a reliable indicator of mental health or of active development.

Dabrowski's conclusions were:

1. The majority of people suffer from an underdevelopment of emotional and instinctive functions.

2. The statistical average is well below the criteria for mental health, and the average human being develops one-sidedly (usually intellectually) and unequally.

Dabrowski believed that the majority of mental disorders have their origins in the predominance of low levels of emotional functioning, to which intelligence is subordinate. With low emotional functioning, individuals use their intelligence to meet their selfish needs. In this context, he defined mental illness as the inability to develop individual and social potentials in the direction of higher scales of values and toward a personal and social ideal.

Thus, he outlined the problem and proposed a solution—not an easy one, since he also was concerned with how we could develop mental health in society. However, Dabrowski reasoned that one could prepare programs for individual and social development that would apply educative methods of loosening, and even disintegrating, various rigid, narrow, and automatic mental attitudes and structures. His theory of positive disintegration, he believed, would not only provide ways of diagnosing and estimating what can be and has to be changed, but also that its application would provide methods for carrying out that task.

And where would this take place? In the home? In the office of psychiatrists, one at a time? Possible, but a slow process at best. Dabrowski was optimistic enough to believe that this change could and should begin in schools, in collaboration with parents. Teachers and counselors, once acquainted with his theory, would apply their understanding of his developmentally positive methods to their students, thereby not only preventing mental illness, but also aiding in the development of mental health. Dabrowski called this application of the theory of positive disintegration *authentic education*, and he regarded this as one of his most valuable contributions to society.

Authentic Education: Facilitating Mental Health in Society

Dabrowski's views on the role of education in facilitating mental health are described in his unpublished manuscript *Authentic Education* (n.d. 1), which forms the basis for this chapter. He hoped that teachers would apply his theory of positive disintegration to the education of children, resulting in a more humane school setting where children who are, what he would term, "psychoneurotic" are appreciated rather than pushed aside as "difficult" or even labeled as mentally ill. (Those familiar with the theory are aware that psychoneuroses are indicators of the potential for advanced development.) His further concern was the lack of such an approach in America and a desire to make educators aware of the nature of the problem and possible solutions.

Introduction to Authentic Education

Dabrowski stated clearly that his manuscript attempts to present a basic concept of humanistic education—true humane education—and not merely training as the methods of an animal trainer would be described. Parents and teachers, he believed, are looking for ways to provide humane education, one that enhances development and respects individual children as unique and unrepeatable, while at the same time awakens children to the knowledge that this is so of others as well as for themselves. Such an education strives for the harmony that respects, not reject, differences, and it is this harmony of true education with higher human values that differentiates the education of human beings from the training of animals.

Idols and Truths in American Education

Dabrowski's assessment of education noted several *idols* in American life and education. The first idol is in the area of psychology, where behaviorism is highly regarded as objective and, therefore, an accurate measure of human beings. Dabrowski's objection is that such measures are suitable only for animals and lower organisms. Observable behavior, in his opinion, can only measure basic primitive dynamisms; the motivations and reasons for behavior remain unanswered by such an approach.

The second idol is the advertising that permeates American culture to the point that time, which could have been spent on thought-provoking inner issues, is sidetracked to the mindlessness of television and radio.

The third idol is the measure of the self based on material goods—the number of cars, homes, television sets, and so forth—determined by comparison with one's neighbor. Material progress becomes the primary goal, and this weakens one's interest in moral and creative progress.

The fourth idol, which emerges from these common traits and from a general attitude of mediocrity, is the attitude of certainty—a sense of self-assuredness. Such persons thoughtlessly impose their values on others, self-assuredly assuming their correctness, which might be represented in the over-simplified and less-than-subtle view of international relations that Americans frequently express.

The fifth and final idol is the American tendency to search for groups that are similar in customs, behavior, and approaches to oneself, which, in Dabrowski's view, is adjustment to mediocrity.

Expressed in terms of Dabrowski's theory, two common characteristics of the American style of life are: (1) unilevelness, and (2) the feebleness of the hierarchization of values. Such attitudes, while expressed by adults, are fostered by the American educational system. The school becomes the center for indoctrination of these attitudes and even attempts to prevent transgression of these attitudes. For Dabrowski, the American hierarchy of economic and financial values, combined with a relatively narrow appreciation for other ways of life, tends to diminish the sympathy of other societies toward America.

For the unilevel American, it is impossible to understand the meaning or value of internal conflicts and, in particular, the problem of tragedy, which Dabrowski found in his practice to be correlated with the real development of man, increasing his subtlety, empathy, and creativity. Issues arising from internal conflicts, such as tragedy, receive little attention in American schools and, in keeping with behavioral psychologists, get "treated" and vanish. What also vanishes is the capacity for future individual development. Sadness, for example, is regarded as negative; yet in their highest forms, both sadness and conflict are recurrent themes in creative and imaginative works of art and poetry. Dabrowski felt that Americans disregard tragedy and drama in the arts and in everyday life, when it is precisely the tragic element of life that makes these things great. This is evidenced in individuals' need to have movies and stories with happy endings.

Problems that could advance the development of multilevelness are overlooked in the American culture in order to return to the more mindless, non-threatening peacefulness of unilevelness and its false security. Dabrowski addressed the problem of adjustment to reality and asked again, "Which reality?"—the false security of unilevelness, with its confidence based in ignorance, or the more alive, often difficult, and often uncertain multilevel reality, which demands that the individual not adjust to that which is not tolerable. From Dabrowski's perspective, this negative adjustment, this mindless conforming to society, is adevelopmental, causing the individual to lose touch with the horizons of creative development. Positive maladjustment through rejection of societal norms when they run counter to higher values—the path of the courageous—becomes a necessity for those who are creative, multidimensional, and multilevel and eager to greet the storm of the higher-level needs. And here, Dabrowski said, we see positive maladjustment expressing the aspiration of "what ought to be" and a slow movement away from that "which is."

In short, Dabrowski viewed American society as immature, and education as based on the common values of the majority of people—values that could be easily measured and statistically analyzed. In this setting, education becomes entirely pragmatic, primarily an ahierarchical (unilevel) education, because it is accomplished under the influence of an external milieu, one which neglects both the child's developmental potential and the inner psychic milieu. Furthermore, since the present system fosters unilevelness, materialistic values, and the dominance of basic needs, it is inevitable that students produced by such a system will not have an appreciation of multilevel experience, creativity, and the developmental potentials often expressed in anxiety and conflict.

Dabrowski further stated that because of the problems outlined in his introductory chapter of *Authentic Education*, he felt it necessary to introduce to America an authentic education based on a multisided, objective, and hierarchical perspective. His manuscript is a gift to unilevel America and, ultimately, to a multilevel world.

On Training and Education

As noted earlier, Dabrowski believed that much of what passes as education was actually training—training intended for, and applied to, animals. On behalf of the well-being of the animals, the emphasis is on fresh air and sunshine. On his own behalf, the owner finds that healthy animals prove to be of more value in the marketplace. In the higher levels of animal training, methods of psychic training are used. These methods have been borrowed from psychology of learning and are based on the methods of reward and punishment used in psychological conditioning. In this approach, rewards are associated with appropriate behavior and punishments with unacceptable behavior.

Parents display a similar awareness of the developmental requirements of their children, including proper food, vitamins, sleep, and fresh air. Dabrowski felt that it was curious that parents do not exhibit a similar interest in or awareness of the normality or abnormality in the different stages of a child's growth. He noted that using a training approach to child-rearing resulted in little or no parental interest in understanding their children's developmental potential, while in an authentic educational approach, such understanding is essential. Training treats children as a herd animals; authentic education treats them as individual human beings.

Dabrowski noted that the differences between children could vary greatly in their developmental potential and its manifestation. Some children display abilities in music, art, drama, or ballet, while others are interested in mathematics or mechanics. Some children present characteristics of emotional awareness of individuals and social interactions, while others do not. Some children express emotional, intellectual, and imaginative overexcitability. These three forms of overexcitability create inner tension, and such children are more difficult to deal with than others. The interaction of the forms of overexcitabilities manifests itself in such behaviors as emotional outbursts and resistance to socialization—for Dabrowski, evidence of psychoneurotic characteristics—positive signs in the theory of positive disintegration. Failure to reframe such behaviors in a Dabrowskian way will probably result in parents' or teachers' retreat to a training approach rather than the true education of these children. Training serves to decrease the frequency of behaviors deemed socially unacceptable. On the other hand, if adults can understand the child's developmental potential, outcomes can be more favorable for both the child and the adult.

To develop the child's potential, which is the basic purpose of education, parents and teachers must understand the difference between education and training. Dabrowski noted that "contrary to the training process, authentic education is designed to encourage a child to transgress [i.e., to pass beyond or over limits] mediocre statistical qualities, and to develop his own hierarchy of values and aims, which he is then taught to realize" (n.d. 1, pp. 32-33). In such an approach, the understanding of adjustment includes taking into account a child's own potential, values, and aims. In contrast, in a training program, differentiation, humanization, and creativity are of little concern.

Intelligence alone is not the sole goal of authentic education, but rather the way an individual uses his or her intelligence. Intelligence in the service of higher human values, such as concern for others as opposed to serving egotistical self-satisfaction, is the measure of the authentic student. When high intelligence is lacking imagination and emotion regarding others and is utterly self-serving, we can have a psychopath, regardless of his or her degrees or prestigious position in life. This, at its extreme, can be the end result of training and, even in a less malignant form, can gel into what Dabrowski referred to as *unilevelness*, which he felt was what the training approach to education exemplifies in America. It is not concerned with the psychological development of the individual child other than, through its efforts by reward and punishment, to eradicate any real evidence of such development in the name of mediocrity. Authentic education, in contrast, concerns itself with the awareness and understanding of developmental potentials and the role that they play in developing a more humane, truly human individual. He called this approach *multilevelness*, for it embraces an awareness of the levels of humanness and the effort required to support its further development in the interest of mankind.

Dabrowski bemoaned the over-emphasis in education on biological, "trainable" children and the need to blind them to their own creative needs in the interest of fostering the authoritarian point of view and approach in American life—one which, once experienced as "that's just how it is," results in teachers who propagate the same method, which closes rather than opens doors to curious, life-loving children.

A second concern of Dabrowski's was the educational system's emphasis on adjustment to the social environment as it is viewed and promoted by contemporary psychology. This approach to adjustment has reinforced values such as empirical verification and objective observation and emphasizes a preoccupation with measurement. Such research does not, and cannot, measure the multilevelness of its subjects. The restrictions required for scientific rigor have also curtailed the number and kind of phenomena that can be investigated, as well as severely limiting the meaningfulness of the questions asked.

Adjustment and Development

Historically, the term "adjustment" has really implied "passivity." Dabrowski stated that in this meaning of *adjustment*, automatic changes in behavior occurred because of changes in the external and internal environments; as the environments change, the individual automatically adjusts to maintain harmony and stability. In the traditional approach, individuals respond—consciously or unconsciously—to adjust to the status quo. In so doing, they exemplify a form of external determinism where their adjustment is expressed by their conscious or intuitive dependence upon the events of the external environment.

Dabrowski's own definition of adjustment was different and much more complex. Dabrowski emphasized the negative and positive aspects of the deterministic attitude toward adjustment as it affects the possibility of the multilevel development of personality and culture. By negative adjustment, he meant unconscious adjustment—non-reflective and without self-control or initiation. It can be seen in the passive acquiescence of persons to higher authorities ("The President must be right"), abdication of personal responsibility for one's own attitudes and actions ("I was just following orders"), and an unconscious comfort in this state. In contrast to positive adjustment, what is missing in negative adjustment is the capacity to appreciate the attitudes and opinions of others and the appreciation of the psychological and cultural differences of others. A social life requires mutual understanding and tolerance, without which further global growth cannot occur.

Dabrowski stated that *maladjustment* can take both negative and positive forms. He described negative maladjustment as "that which is expressed in psychopathic behavior—meaningless anarchy, criminality, and a lack of acceptance of social and moral values" (n.d. 1, p. 42). Negative maladjustment is typified by the most glaring examples of a lack of sensitivity for others. Positive maladjustment, in Dabrowski's opinion, is the basic element of what it is to be human. It is the process that underlies the comprehension and development of a hierarchy of values, and it is manifested in more conscious, reflective types of behavior. Positive maladjustment denotes the progression of an individual from the lower levels of reflexive behavior to the higher levels of conscious reflective action. It is an upward movement from "what is" to "what ought to be"—the foundation upon which the hierarchy of values develops.

The upward movement, tentative at first, is stimulated by the individual as an outgrowth of dissatisfaction and disquietude toward him- or herself, as well as feelings of inferiority. These feelings activate the forces of a personality ideal, and this ability to comprehend what one is and what one could be inspires further struggle leading to the origin of the inner psychic milieu, the internal environment, the center of future growth, and the depository of the developing dynamisms. In this higher level, internal, more conscious "command center," one finds an increase in the creative instinct, a search for the "new" positive adjustments instead of the "old" negative adjustments to the external world. Higher values, not yet realized, exist as seeds of future development—that is, the self-perfection instinct in the dynamisms of autonomy and authenticity. For Dabrowski, positive maladjustment was the developmental enhancement of one individual through his or her own self-education (autoeducation), nervousness, and autopsychotherapy. Dabrowski was writing here about human development over a lifetime, a long and arduous journey from an unconscious adaptation to an external world to a conscious adaptation to an internal world and, thus, the conscious control of one's every action.

Dabrowski (1964a) stated that disintegration can be observed in young children, both at about 18 months and two and a half years, and again in puberty. In the early stage, 18 months to two and a half years, we see capriciousness, dissipated attention, periods of artificiality, animism, and magical thinking, which are closely connected with a wavering nervous system and unstable psychic structure. At the age of opposition, elements of disintegration, such as mood changes and self-contradictory acts, become stronger. Disintegration at the age of puberty is characterized by lack of emotional balance, presence of ambivalence, ambitendencies, attitudes varying between feelings of superiority or inferiority, criticism and self-criticism, self-dislike, maladaptation to the external world, and concern with the past or future rather than with the present. Both of these periods bring about anxiety, stress, and even anger in parents and teachers. It is extremely important that we understand the rich developmental potential in the seeming misbehavior of our most promising children and youth, thus avoiding the part we currently play in destroying it.

Integration and Disintegration

For centuries, Dabrowski said, the term "integration" has been considered to be "healthy." It tends to mean physical and psychological growth—that is, a lack of internal conflict, an ability to overcome external conflict—and it has been seen in general as a healthy tendency toward development. The well-integrated person has been considered capable of quick decision and action and generally acts with "common sense." Because this description has been accepted as "normal," society has come to view disintegration as morbid or pathological. When the term is applied to personality, it strongly suggests that the person in question is unstable, nervous, suffering from psychic illness, or in general maladjusted.

In contrast to the above impressions, Dabrowski offered a different view of the positive and negative aspects of disintegration. He agreed that the self-controlled, unemotional, adaptive individual can appear to be positively adjusted, but he or she is actually adjusted to the environment for personal profit. Many criminals display this attitude of easy adjustment and decision making—for example, the assassins of Lincoln and of the Kennedys. Hitler and Stalin are extreme examples of unfeeling, inhuman dictators, but many more exist in ordinary situations, such as bosses who, in their daily work settings, cause pain, difficulties, and even death to their employees. Thus, from a human perspective, this arrogant, easy confidence is a negative, not positive, integration.

Positive integration, said Dabrowski, is the end point of a series of superficial or severe experiences and "psychic breakdowns," all of which lead to an understanding of the richness of oneself. It is called *secondary integration*, and it is the product of multidimensional, multilevel conflicts. The experience includes psychic overexcitability, states of disharmony, and internal conflict, until it embraces, in its integrative attitude, all of the history of one's previously experienced difficulties, disharmony, and development of one's empathy toward others. In contrast, primitive integration reflects unemotional, underdeveloped inhumanity. Secondary integration is not found in psychopaths.

Dabrowski discussed the problems of disintegration, beginning with the protests in children from the ages of two to four, to the very clear disintegrations common at puberty. In such periods, all forms of loosening and even the breaking of the psychological structure are manifested in, for instance, ambivalent behavior, internal conflicts, feelings of inferiority, inhibitions, and discontent with oneself. With appropriate conditions, such problems can be transformed from opposition to self-expression of creative tendencies. Life itself is for some *the* great experience, being dramatic, tragic, and containing numerous difficulties. Such experiences will increase the attitude of sympathy and empathy toward others, thus containing some elements of positive development.

We also see that the so-called nervous persons with psychoneurotic symptoms present empathy more frequently than normal. They manifest a greater tendency for accelerated development, altrocentric attitudes, and self-sacrifice in their search for perfection. These nervous and psychoneurotic individuals are present in a high percentage of intellectually, emotionally, and imaginatively gifted children and youth, artists, writers, etc. This tendency to reach beyond the norm and mediocrity presents the privilege and drama of psychoneurotic individuals. In this group, we find the sincere, the psychologically fresh, the imaginative, and the impressionable individual. Parents and teachers, said Dabrowski, should be aware that in many children, the deviation from the normal standard is a positive sign and not a negative one.

In the field of disintegration, there are positive and negative forms. Dabrowski claimed that we should be able to distinguish one from the other and, through the use of appropriate educational programs, affect the future of society by reducing the number of psychopaths while increasing the number of genuinely psychologically healthy adults.

Nervousness and Psychoneurosis in Education

What is nervousness? Dabrowski asked, and then offered a general definition describing it as psychic overexcitability. More specifically, he described it as psychic overexcitability in the fields of the senses, imagination, emotionality, psychic motoricity, and intellectual activity. The child who is sensitive to tickling, who likes cuddling, kissing, and hugging, presents sensual overexcitability. The child who likes fantasies or drawing, who lives in a world of meditation and imagination and has very rich dreams, presents imaginative overexcitability. Emotional overexcitability manifests in the child who, upon seeing a crippled dog, a weeping person, or an accident, becomes very emotional and tends to remember or memorize this experience. The child with psychomotor overexcitability is very energetic, restless, and overactive. Such children need to be able to move and are fond of sports. Intellectual overexcitability presents in the child who has a deep, natural interest in cognitive phenomena and asks many questions, along with a demand for reasonable answers. Such children typically enjoy scientific books, and they like to concentrate and be alone. They present a need to solve such problems on their own.

Psychic overexcitability, or nervousness, is regarded by most educators and psychologists as a distracting or disturbing factor, often bordering on neurosis. Parents often share this opinion. An overexcitable child does differ from the ordinary type of child, thus causing difficulties for the school and the family, because he or she evokes the idea of "strangeness." On the other hand, Dabrowski emphasized the fact that these children are also sensitive, empathic, gifted, and creative. They do not easily settle for this reality. Great effort and an understanding attitude are needed to appreciate these children. It is clear that parents and teachers generally have more difficulty with them in periods of negativism. For example, if children are unusually fearful, one must never deride them or make them feel shame.

They should be protected with care and sympathy as they are helped to overcome their fears. Children with psychomotor overexcitability should be given ways to release their energy—opportunities to play, to run freely outdoors, to be active—with empathy for the fact that their energy does not stop with the recess bell recalling class to order. However, they should be encouraged to be quiet in some emotional experiences in order to create a more harmonious personality. Children with intellectual overexcitability should be presented with opportunities to develop their interests, along with encouragement to broaden them. We should stimulate in children an interest in aesthetic, moral, and social problems, as well as psychomotor and sport activities.

A word of caution is added: All methods that try to establish an equilibrium of interests cannot produce too great a transformation, because it is impossible to transform hereditary types of overexcitability. Furthermore, we should not inhibit the development of these traits. We should remember we have the possibility to help the child balance some of his or her basic traits of overexcitability through the development of other forms of overexcitability.

Dabrowski also asked, What is psychoneurosis? Like neurosis, but even less understood by parents and educators, it presents with symptoms such as tension, anxiety, depression, and internal conflict. "It is a hereditary constitutional phenomena with very clear positive potential based on psychological overexcitability, on the nucleus of a mixed psychological types, and with the possibility of the transgression of the individual type" (n.d. 1, p. 57). For Dabrowski, psychoneurotic individuals present a potential for accelerated and deep development, and both external and internal conflicts—that is, difficulties with one's environment and with oneself—are the basis of personality development. Dabrowski offered several examples of psychoneuroses in children.

Anxiety psychoneurosis manifests in the extremely sensitive child from conflicts in everyday life, including concerns with death and injustice, feelings of inferiority, fears of darkness, loneliness, and aggressiveness. The occurrence of anxiety psychoneurosis is predominantly influenced by hereditary potential in the form of emotional overexcitability. Such anxiety symptoms are unpleasant for the child, the parent, and the educator. The sensitive child may hide, inhibit, or push down the symptoms into unconsciousness, which can result in obsessions and gesticulations. The child may become anxious about his or her own anxiety. Through accelerated development and maturation, this appears as existential anxiety—i.e., anxiety about death, lack of personal meaning, vanity or transient values, possible abandonment, and loneliness. Along with such symptoms, there is often deep compassion toward others, sensitivity toward the injury of others, and great empathy.

From anxiety psychoneurosis can emerge multidimensional or many-sided psychic richness, generating literary, artistic, musical, and social abilities. On the other hand, some of these children risk exhaustion through mental disease and breakdown. Support for the child's growth can be given through the opportunity for pursuing creative interests, through security in family and friends, and through the development of independence and self-reliance in thinking and behavior.

Depressive psychoneurosis in a child is connected with anxiety psychoneurosis. It can present in the child who experiences his or her own reality too intensely, who is subtle, emotionally sensitive, and irritable. It is expressed by retreat from reality, psychological rigidity, and feelings of inferiority in relation to the ability to handle everyday affairs. A child such as this feels frightened by reality and cannot bear the injuries and humiliations, some of which exist only in the child's sensitive imagination. He or she shows very strong self-criticism, often experiencing feelings of guilt, with a strong and incorrect evaluation of him- or herself.

> *The child may also manifest many positive experiences and attitudes, such as: ability for inhibition, criticism, weakness of aggressivity, and discontent and disquietude with oneself. Such characteristics contain positive elements for accelerated development, but if left to themselves, without harmonizing and stimulating influences toward the growth of creativity, and without the necessary confidence, security, and persuasion in relation to his abilities, the child could be directed toward negative development.* (Dabrowski, n.d. 1, p. 60)

A balance is required, such that the stimulation of emotional overexcitability and the growth of creative activity, which leads the child out of depression, is still counterbalanced by the capacity for mild self-criticism—one that will not overwhelm the sensitive child as he or she struggles toward maturity.

Obsessive psychoneurosis, compared to anxiety and depressive psychoneurosis, is more severe. In most instances, there is great emotional sensitivity, but in some cases, there seems to be no appropriate psychical discharge or any collaboration with emotional overexcitability—i.e., no perceived discharge of psychological tension in fantasy. These psychoneuroses Dabrowski called obsessions. Obsessions can arise from feelings of inferiority and from feeling "a lack of a place" on this earth. This can be the result of children's perception of injury and humiliation, often with little or no basis in reality.

Obsessions can lead to psychological isolation/autism—that is, to retreat within oneself to a social isolation, which could worsen the obsessive psychoneurotic state. Only a great deal of care and understanding, along with a gradual introduction to the external world and support for one's interests and abilities, can bring about a possibility for improvement and positive development. These children should be convinced, in an authentic manner, that they have values of their own, that their overexcitability is positive, and that their obsessions reveal the deepness of their inner life and their developmental possibility. They should also have the confidence of their parents and teachers, as well as some small confidence in themselves.

The syndrome of psychoneurosis of misfortune or failure is often the expression of the dynamisms of depressive and obsessive psychoneurosis. To protect children from such adverse experiences, Dabrowski suggested that we should examine contexts where severe and/or frequent defeats are likely to occur in the child's world. For example, children are likely to experience psychological breakdowns in contexts such as schools where marks are the sole criterion for success or where extensive criticism of children is linked to enhancing their achievement. Such contexts for children who are psychologically rich and emotionally and imaginatively overexcitable will likely result in the development of the psychoneurosis of misfortune or failure. Unlike other psychoneuroses, Dabrowski postulated that this form does not facilitate further psychological development.

To remedy the effects of the psychoneurosis of misfortune and failure, Dabrowski suggested that adults clearly see these children's independent, differentiated personality, their type, and their sensitivity and irritability, and that they take into account creative potentials so that they can adjust their behavior and the evaluation of the children in relation to these characteristics. The children must not always be failures. Dabrowski suggested that adults, rather than presenting role models, allow the children to follow their own patterns of development and find their own creative elements that will aid them in the attainment of their own unique place in the world:

> *If the children are already presenting symptoms of psychoneurosis of misfortune and failure, it is necessary to elaborate in their education and self-education a gradual method of compensation for previous errors, to excite inhibited creativity, and to create some effects, even if partially artificial, but that always comes from the appreciation of the child's capabilities to equalize the effects of his slow development.* (n.d. 1, p. 63)

Infantile psychoneurosis is the effect of a too-great imaginative potential for fantasy, emotional oversensitivity, and a tendency toward idealization and general accelerated development. Here we encounter the so-called psychological immaturity, which is generally considered a delay in the development of emotional life. Quite often, however, it is not a delay, but an expression of accelerated development. Because of the potential richness of such children, their development takes much longer. These children should have sincerely warm and favorable attitudes for a blossoming of their potential, since they are very sensitive, psychologically fragile, and irritable.

This psychoneurosis expresses itself in the psychological unbalance of the child, laziness, frustration, a tendency toward isolation, withdrawal within him- or herself, and a preoccupation with fantasy. A stress-filled environment can easily be created for such a child if there is a great emphasis on his or her intellectual level and actual age, along with the negative perception of his or her emotional age, and if the child is ill prepared to cope with such an environment.

The education of such children should not be based only on their age and intellect, but it should be related to their emotional and imaginative sensitivity. The positive regression these children experience, of necessity, is not pathological, but is a defensive tendency to return to a less stressful time in their imagination, where they can further develop and strengthen their rich emotional gifts. Supporting children through this process helps them meet the requirements of the external environment.

Dabrowski expressed strong support for the rich, even accelerated developmental potential in a great majority of children with such nervousness and psychoneurosis. These children should be treated individually, and we should be prepared to help them cope with their educational difficulties. Teachers must provide individualized education programs for them. These children should not be regarded as pathological cases, but as valuable individuals of the future. We should, in our vigilance, apply a system of education and self-education, which would weaken the excess of irritability and concomitant danger of falling into the psychoneurosis of failure, in our great effort to create all of the conditions necessary for the positive development of such children.

The Hierarchy of Reality and the Inner Psychic Milieu

Dabrowski stated that the sciences, especially positivistic science, present the attitude that facts and values are completely different from one another—that facts are based on concrete perceptions and logical reasoning, and values are based on subjective attitudes. In contrast, Dabrowski believed that, for individuals with some degree of sensitivity, the reality of a hierarchy of values is generally accepted. He said that we observe that some people are sincere and others false, that one is sly and another direct, and one is domineering and another cooperative, and that one sees dignity in humans while another disdains this dignity.

In his life-long struggle to make clear his view of mankind, Dabrowski moved from a general to a very specific description of a scale of different levels of emotional and instinctive functions, proceeding from the most primitive to the highest level of human functioning, which is characterized by several dynamisms such as self-awareness, self-control, autonomy, authenticity, and great empathy (see Dabrowski, 1996a). Since this chapter is about authentic education, I will elaborate on the dynamism of authentism, as this is the one likely to be of great interest to psychologists and educators.

In the more primitive stage, we deal with pseudo-authentism in group behavior, in which all thoughts and actions lack reflection and are determined by the group. There is little, if any, inhibition seen at this stage. We see natural behavior and activities. The so-called authenticity at this level is nothing other than like-finds-like. All thoughts and actions lack reflection and are defined by the group mentality. Historically, it has appeared in the form of ritualistic dancing and shared ceremonies. It also appears in regional or nationalistic behavior—for example, in patriotism. At its most negative extreme, we see pseudo-authenticity masking what is actually the most masterful criminal or sadist.

At the next level, unilevel disintegration, we become more reflective, exhibiting inhibition in the form of embarrassment. However, we still tend to identify with the attitude of the majority.

The third stage is in clear conflict with the second stage and its so-called authenticity. Gradually, "not what is, but what ought to be" comes into our awareness and our struggle through dynamisms of self-dissatisfaction and feelings of shame and guilt, all of which indicate the arrival of a true sense of authentism.

At the fourth stage, we find the slow organization of authentism and personality. This is due to the collaboration of the dynamisms of the third factor, which transcends the first (biological) and second (social) factors, and manifests in inner psychic transformation, self-awareness, and self-control. Authentism at this stage comes into contact with multilevel dynamisms—that is, social, moral, religious, aesthetic, and intellectual, resulting in the original authentic "I" and authentic "You."

On the highest level, the individual approaches and identifies with one's own personality ideal. Here we find the attitude of authenticity and love, rich in subtlety, no evidence of primitivity, which stabilizes, shapes, and expresses the harmony between the objective and subjective regard for and treatment of others.

The Inner Psychic Milieu

Dabrowski stated that this dynamism of authentism is best described by comparison with the external psychic milieu, which consists of our family, school, professional and scientific groups, friends, and enemies. This external milieu acts on us, and we act on it. We experience frustration, joy, and pain toward it, and we have similar effects on others. We see different levels of attitude and behavior in the various individuals and groups—lower, medium, and higher levels. We have confidence in some and none in others; one gives us a quiet and secure atmosphere, while the opposite is true of the others.

We have an analogous situation in our inner psychic milieu. The persons and groups from the external milieu are replaced by the dynamisms and groups of the inner psychic milieu. Here we find the dynamisms that bring us pain, sorrow, and discontent. We also find our own primitive forces, our competitive forces, timidity, discontent toward oneself, a tendency toward self-improvement—all feelings, attitudes, tendencies, and impulsive and intellectual activities on different levels of collaboration and conflict. Thus, the conflict with the external world becomes internalized, and along with it the possibility that the developmental dynamisms become and remain our friends, the adevelopmental dynamisms our enemies.

In this process of growth and development, we observe the transcendence of the first factor, which is biological and unconscious, through the second factor, which is social and semiconscious, to the third factor, which is emotional-intellectual-imaginative and is increasingly conscious. The third factor selects that in oneself which is higher and disintegrates that which is lower, the end result of which is the fully conscious elaboration of the personality ideal and one's authentic identification with it.

What Directs Our Development—Reason, or Drives and Emotions?

Through the centuries, Dabrowski stated, we have become accustomed to the idea that reason is, and should be, the function that controls our feelings and drives. In other words, emotional and instinctive functions should be subordinated to and controlled by intelligence. This has gone on for so long and is so mindlessly accepted that we are used to treating our reason, common sense, and intellectual activities as high level human activities.

Dabrowski stated that the intellect is an instrumental function, incapable of executing, in many cases, nothing other than the expression of low level emotional and instinctive functions. Even the seemingly most smooth and efficient activities can be the instrument of a socially deceptive psychopath. In contrast, the highest level of human structure and functions, he stated, is one in which the individual's drive is toward a self-conscious, self-chosen, self-affirmed, and self-educated unity of one's basic traits. It follows from this that intelligence will either be in the service of this highest group of functions or in the service of primitive, emotional, and instinctive forces.

Objectivization of the Levels of Instinctive and Emotional Function

Dabrowski elaborated his view of society, everyday life in groups, and he described levels of development within such group settings. We want, and need, the just evaluation of our children in the schools, of ourselves in our work, on the street, and in everyday life. He stated:

> *We require the appropriate treatment of children, of the ill and of the elderly. We require justice in the verdicts of sentencing of the courts and we even want objective justice in international tribunals such as the United Nations, that is, objective justice in international politics.* (n.d. 1, p. 97)

In order to do this, we have, under the influence of scientific objectivity, attempted to measure human behavior with little progress in relation to emotional and instinctive functions. Those functions have been, in general, regarded as ones in which the phenomena can only be evaluated subjectively. Dabrowski noted that psychology, sociology, and law demonstrate that there are no strong objective criteria for our behavior. He believed that objectivity of perception exists and is shared in all cultures, more and more through developmental experience, by the higher and especially the highest levels of development, as described in his theory of positive disintegration. The higher the level of development, the higher will be the multidimensional and multilevel internal psychic milieu, and the more likely the possibility that such persons will hold similar opinions of concrete phenomena. He stated that higher-level persons, regardless of nationality, racial, or cultural backgrounds, are closer to one another than they are to their countrymen in relation to judgments regarding the humane treatment of our fellow man.

We cannot accept that the protection of children, of the elderly, of pregnant women, of the handicapped, and of the poor is a matter of whim, yet we see such matters dismissed worldwide by socially and emotionally primitive individuals and groups. As long as such atrocities exist, autonomous, authentic, responsible persons in a global world will not cease from their demands for tribunal justice, in spite of the weakened state of the United Nations. They are prepared to sacrifice their lives for a hierarchy of elaborated and accepted ideals. Dabrowski gave, as an example:

> *Januaz Korczak, physician, writer, and above all, educator. He was Polish and of Jewish origin. When the decision was made in the Second World War to burn in a crematorium at Treblinka all the children attending his school, he decided to go with them even though he had received an amnesty from the Nazis.* (n.d. 1, p. 93)

His decision was based not on intellectual pondering, but on the highest level of the instinct of self-preservation:

> *The basis on which the decision was taken was the content of his life experience and the need to identify his moral and educative beliefs with his actions. The decision arose from the compassion and love he had for the children and his fidelity for them. For Korczak, it was the only comprehensible act, unique, authentic and essential, beyond all the "for" or "against" of intellectual deliberation.* (n.d. 1, p. 94)

In so doing, he expressed the attitude, "*when the sheep perish, the shepherd should also perish*" (n.d. 1, p. 74).

Conclusion

And so what has changed in the field of education since the time that Dabrowski and I worked on the *Authentic Education* manuscript? Not much. I believe that in North American education today, the major focus is still an "objective" one in which students are assessed exclusively using an IQ scale, without reference to emotional intelligence. The understanding of educational ability appears to be contained within a unilevel framework—one within which neither students nor teachers flourish.

We have much current research on emotion which freely speaks of EQ yet lacks awareness of the multilevelness of emotional functions. A case in point is the application of the term "gifted," which, in education, is typically associated with intelligence. This may not be the case in the literature in gifted education, but it seems true in school programs for gifted students. For Dabrowski, giftedness referred to the *tragic gift* of multilevelness, one which brings both agony and ecstasy, the former of which, in deep disintegration, can last for years. Educational systems that focus only on intelligence and academic achievement are still training, rather than educating, our children.

Chapter 5
Philosophical Aspects of Dabrowski's Theory of Positive Disintegration

William Tillier, M.Sc.[1]

Kazimierz Dabrowski's theory of positive disintegration is built upon four central philosophical ideas: multilevelness, "existentio-essentialism," the incompatibility of socialization in relation to individual development, and finally, the necessity of disintegration in the developmental process. The multilevel approach is reminiscent of Plato's description of reality and forms the cornerstone of Dabrowski's theory. The basic assumption of multilevelness is that mental functions can be differentiated into several levels and that development consists of transitions from lower to higher levels.

Although Dabrowski's hierarchical schema is quite challenging, it provides a more realistic description of the complex nature of mental processes and human experience than the traditional, reductionistic approaches of psychology, especially behaviorism. Two levels represent the lowest and highest forms of human experience and function, with developmental, transitional levels in between. The lower, "horizontal" level is marked by the influence of biological instincts and socialization—rote adherence to external, social mores—while the highest, self-determined levels are characterized by multilevel experience, self-consciousness, and autonomy. Quantitative and qualitative differences between these levels of

1 Bill Tillier, M.Sc., Psychologist (Retired), Department of Solicitor General and Public Security, Government of Alberta, Canada.

experience, reflecting individual differences in sensitivity and developmental potential, can be readily observed and measured.

Dabrowski coined the term "existentio-essentialist" to describe how he uniquely combined two traditionally disparate views of human character: one reflecting the essentialist approach of the Platonic tradition, and the other, a more modern existentio-existential approach found in the works of Kierkegaard and Nietzsche, among others. The inherent essence of a person's character is considered the initial foundation of development. However, Dabrowski observed that in the usual course of development, individual essence often remains submerged, as individuality and autonomy are effectively overpowered by socialization and group conformity. Advanced growth must involve a disintegration of this initial, lower-level integration and break free to create opportunities for the discovery of one's true essence, leading to self-insight and a series of conscious and volitional existential choices that will subsequently shape and refine one's raw essence to create a unique, autonomous personality.

In creating his novel theory of personality and development, Dabrowski incorporated and synthesized several important traditional philosophical concepts, including ideas from Plato, Kierkegaard, and Nietzsche.[2] He also contributed a number of unique concepts, including his approach to advanced development (secondary integration), developmental potential, and the role of positive disintegration in the developmental process.

Multilevelness

When I was a student of Dabrowski's, I asked him what I should read to give me a background to his approach, and he replied, "Plato." He said that traditional psychological approaches cannot account for the wide range of observable human behavior and that no existing theory can simultaneously account for the lowest and highest behaviors that people display. Therefore, Dabrowski (1964a) initiated a paradigm shift in thinking about psychology and psychological development by introducing the multilevel approach. In applying a multilevel, Platonic-type description of reality to psychology, Dabrowski developed a hierarchical model that incorporates two basic levels of sensory perception, imagination, cognitive (intellectual) and emotional function, one representing the lowest level of function, and

2 Among Dabrowski's other major influences were Spanish philosopher Miguel de Unamuno (1864-1936), French philosopher Henri Bergson (1859-1941), and German philosopher Karl Jaspers (1883-1969).

one representing the highest. Dabrowski was confident that levels of both external and internal reality can be differentiated and that major differences between higher and lower levels can readily be observed, described, and used to characterize and distinguish different levels.

This differentiation roughly mirrors Plato's description of the four levels of existence; lower level attempts to describe existence are mere opinions, shadows, or inadequate copies of the higher, more authentic, and truer ideal forms. For example, if I draw a right triangle, regardless of my artistic ability or mathematical precision, it will represent only my flawed opinion or less-than-perfect copy of the more real, ideal *form* of the right triangle as described by Pythagoras' theorem. In a similar way, socialization produces mere mass copies of personalities, personal identities, social roles and expectations, et cetera. On the other hand, as we will see, the higher alternative is for the individual to discover and subsequently shape and create his or her own unique ideal personality and then to live by its values, thus approaching the individual idealized form of one's self to the extent that that is ever possible.

The articulation and description of higher levels allows various dimensions to be compared on higher levels versus lower levels, creating an important vertical contrast. Dabrowski conceptualized psychological development as "the transition from lower, automatic, and rigidly organized mental structures and functions to higher, creative, self-controlled and authentic forms of mental life—developmental psychology is unable to give a satisfactory account of this process without the use of the concept of multilevelness" (1973, p. ix).

In summary, psychological development is a function of the level of organization, and using the multilevel approach, we can differentiate different forms and levels of development among people. Multilevelness differentiates psychological dimensions and functions into several levels and provides a significant new methodology to understand the fundamental differences observed in human development and behavior.

Plato's Cave

Dabrowski's multilevel description of development shares several aspects in common with Plato's approach. As we have seen above, Plato described four levels of existence, each with a characteristic level of consciousness and perception. For Plato (Cavalier, 1990), lower levels were associated with limited consciousness and with crude, simple, or mistaken perceptions. Plato was famous for the mathematical complexity of his description of reality, but he also made his approach readily accessible in his analogy of the cave. The average person is a prisoner, sitting among his or her peers in a large underground cavern. The group passively watches life unfold on the wall of the cave in front of them. Taking all autonomy away, the prisoners are chained to their seats and unable to turn around to comprehend their circumstances; their senses are so dulled that they do not even realize their bonds. Unbeknownst to the group, this perceived life is simply a low-level illusion, a procession of images projected on the wall. This shadow play is contrived by the politic of the day and delivered by puppet masters. Positioned behind the prisoners, these puppeteers (representatives of the state and educational system) use shadow puppets to portray life as they want it to be perceived. To further emphasize the contrived nature of this illusion, Plato describes an artificial source of light—a campfire at the back of the cave provides the light for the puppet show.

At some point, a prisoner begins to question things and makes the decision that he or she wants to discover the truth. Eventually, this somewhat special prisoner (Plato referred to him or her as the philosopher or the intellectual) is able to break free and see the overall situation. The prisoner stumbles toward a dim light seeping in from the entrance to the cave. Guided by this tenuous ray of sunlight, the prisoner must make a long and treacherous journey, eventually leading to the surface. This arduous path demands tremendous strength, determination, and a special inner essence or character. Many try but fail to make it to the surface. For those who do stumble into the sunlight, life now takes on a completely different perspective; there is a qualitative paradigm shift in perception.

Plato recognized that the prisoner's impulse may be to stay in the sun and perhaps even look for more opportunities to ascend, so he clearly described the moral imperative of the prisoner who has "seen the light"—to return to the cave and help enlighten his or her peers. Further individual enlightenment must be curtailed until the last prisoner is free from the cave. Unfortunately, in transitioning from the bright sunlight back into the dimly lit cave, the prisoner is temporarily blinded and flails to discover his or her way. The remaining prisoners hear a wild story that they can barely comprehend, and fearing that this escaped prisoner has gone mad, they react by killing the enlightened messenger.

Individuals at the level of primary integration in Dabrowski's model share much in common with the lot of Plato's prisoners. For Dabrowski, the average person passively accepts socialization, endorsing an externally derived day-to-day reality with very little critical question or review. Dabrowski believed the well-socialized person lives out an imitative, externally prescribed series of roles, with very little consciousness, very little individuality or authenticity, and therefore, he considered the average person to be at a primary, basic level of development.

Jackson's Evolution and Dissolution

In applying multilevelness to psychology, Dabrowski endorsed the multilevel approach of John Hughlings Jackson's work on the nervous system.[3] In his influential 1884 Croonian lectures, titled "On the Evolution and Dissolution of the Nervous System," Jackson outlined an evolutionary, level-based model of the nervous system that described differences between lower and higher levels (Jackson, 1884; also, see Taylor, 1958). Three variables distinguish among levels: lower levels are simpler, more organized, and more automatic or reflexive; higher levels are more complex, less organized, and more deliberate or volitional. In addition, the operation of lower levels tends to be subordinate to the control of higher levels. Jackson described evolution (development) as the movement from lower to higher levels and therefore toward more complexity, less organization, and more deliberate, voluntary actions. Dabrowski included these attributes in his definition of higher levels: "[B]y higher level of psychic development we mean a behavior which is more complex, more conscious and having greater freedom of choice, hence greater opportunity for self-determination" (1972, p. 70).

Dabrowski emphasized that higher levels differ on both quantitative and qualitative dimensions when compared to lower levels. Psychology commonly recognizes quantitative differences—for example, intelligence is commonly differentiated into levels on the basis of differences in test scores. However, Dabrowski perceived that advanced development displays another important aspect: at some point, major qualitative differences appear—for example, basic perception of reality is literally different for individuals at the highest levels compared to persons at lower levels. Qualitative differences become an important descriptive feature; they starkly differentiate advanced development from lower-level function, thus providing an evidentiary basis for the classification of personality and development.

3 One of Dabrowski's professors was the eminent Polish psychiatrist Jan Mazurkiewicz. Mazurkiewicz developed a neo-Jacksonian approach, emphasizing qualitatively and developmentally different kinds of consciousness and mental functions resulting from different levels of brain organization (see Kokoszka, 2007).

Essence and Existentialism

Dabrowski (1972) believed that an individual's genetics are important contributors to his or her eventual development. I recall that he used to say that the best genetics cannot be suppressed by the worst environment, and the worst genetics cannot be assisted by the best environment, while the outcome of so-so genetics *is* determined by the environment. Each individual possesses an inner essence, composed of the central qualities and traits of one's personality. However, this essence is not strictly fixed; rather, it exists as a potential that may or may not be developed. In addition, this essence may be positive and act to enhance development, or it may be negative and act to limit development. It also may include a broad spectrum of features, including influences from our animal ancestry, uniquely authentic human traits, and perhaps a flash or two of genius.

The expression of this individual essence is also not a given. Dabrowski (1973) believed that personality must be achieved—constructed through a series of individual, conscious choices that distinguish between that which is "more myself" versus that which is "less myself." As development progresses, insight and self-awareness emerge. At a certain point, "the individual becomes aware of what is his own 'essence'; that is to say, what are his aims and aspirations, his attitudes, his relations with other people" (Dabrowski, 1973, p. 109; also, see McGraw, 1986). The individual constructs a personality ideal based upon this initial essence, along with his or her imagined possibilities, dreams, and aspirations. As the image of the personality ideal becomes increasingly clear, the individual can compare and contrast this ideal with his or her initial essence, and based upon vertical, multilevel comparisons, he or she can make conscious and volitional choices about what to emphasize and what aspects to inhibit. In this way, the full and final expression of one's character reflects both the essence of who one is, as well as the ongoing choices that one makes.

In addition to "character" essence, Dabrowski also described several other innate factors that play critical roles in determining the developmental trajectory of an individual. These include the creative instinct, the instinct toward self-perfection, dynamisms, the ultimate combination of drives and emotions that provide the energy for development, and finally, a constellation of factors that he referred to as developmental potential. Dabrowski defined developmental potential as "the constitutional endowment which determines the character and the extent of mental growth possible for a given individual" (1972, p. 293). Several key features can be used to assess developmental potential, including overexcitability, special abilities and talents, and autonomous factors (primarily the third factor).

We can summarize Dabrowski's unusual "existentio-essentialist" approach by saying that the individual must become aware of his or her unique traits—i.e., essence—and subsequently make volitional existential choices that shape and express this essence to fully express an individualized personality ideal. Dabrowski makes it clear that "essence is more important than existence for the birth of a truly human being," and he goes on to say, "There is no true human existence without genuine essence" (Cienin, 1972a, p. 11). Recognizing the unique contributions of essence, developmental potentials, and existential choice, and understanding how they interact provides us with a powerful new insight into understanding development.

Socialization Squelches Autonomy

Influenced by Jahoda (1958), Dabrowski used a positive approach in defining mental health. Rejecting definitions based simply upon the absence of mental disease or upon some quantitative measure of social adjustment, Dabrowski defined mental health based upon the presence of various new and qualitatively different characteristics—for example, the presence of an autonomous, consciously derived hierarchy of values reflecting the unique personality of the individual. These qualitative differences among levels reflect the developmental status of an individual.

Following Jackson, Dabrowski (1964a, 1972) hypothesized that lower levels demonstrate simpler, more organized, and more rigid, resilient psychological structures. However, Dabrowski's observation was that these structures are typically subordinate to biological forces (instincts) and the influence of the social environment. Thus, at the primary level, personal ideals, goals, and values are subordinate to externally derived mores and standards and display very limited self-consciousness, individuality, or autonomy. The so-called "average" socialized individual displays a well-unified, organized, and coordinated integration of psychological features that forms the basis of traditional conceptualizations of psychological integration and that usually connote a positive aspect.

However, Dabrowski differentiated two types of integration: the lower, initial primary integration reflecting socialization, which carries an adevelopmental connotation, and a higher, secondary positive integration associated with advanced development, autonomy, and self-determination and thus reflecting mental health. Dabrowski suggested that individuals at the primary level do not exhibit individual personalities, and he went so far as to conclude that the "absence of the development of personality means the absence of mental health" (1964a, p. 122).

In describing primary integration, Dabrowski noted that behavior is commonly organized in the service of self-satisfying instincts and impulses. Social roles are often acted out and manipulated in order to achieve ego-satisfying goals. Many of these individuals are charismatic and strong, often taking on leadership roles in society. Unfortunately, some of these individuals continue to act in egocentric and self-satisfying ways, with little appreciation of the damage they may be doing or for their social responsibilities. The image of the psychopath as a suit-wearing, "win at any cost" businessperson or the self-justifying politician comes to mind (see Babiak & Hare, 2006).

Our educational and political system (Plato's puppet masters) is predicated upon creating and encouraging individuals who can excel in the "dog-eat-dog" business and political world. That society develops and so esteems these "winners," "indicates that the society itself is primitive and confused" (Dabrowski, 1970, p. 118). Dabrowski was further concerned that definitions of mental health based upon an individual's adjustment to prevailing social norms do not represent authentic human development or function. Adjustment to a society that is itself "primitive and confused" is adevelopmental and holds one back from discovering individual essence and from exercising choice in shaping and developing one's self—Dabrowski's very criteria for mental health (Dabrowski, 1970).

Dabrowski was not the first to be concerned with the negative impact of socialization on human authenticity. Kierkegaard (Kaufmann, 1969) clearly spelled out similar concerns, saying that reliance on social roles and church doctrine prevents the individual from "real action." McDonald captures Kierkegaard's position, saying:

> *Kierkegaard's central problematic was how to become a Christian in Christendom. The task was most difficult for the well educated, since prevailing educational and cultural institutions tended to produce stereotyped members of "the crowd" rather than to allow individuals to discover their own unique identities.* (2006, section 2, para. 1)

The crowd robs the person of individual responsibility. Instead of defining one's self based upon external social mores and roles, Kierkegaard

(Kaufmann, 1969; Palmer, 1996) suggested that the only true freedom for an individual is the heavy responsibility of being able to choose one's self—to construct one's self, one's beliefs, and one's values through the successive decisions that one makes in day-to-day life. In a position similar to Dabrowski's, Kierkegaard connected consciousness with the vertical comparison of the lower, actual situation versus the higher alternative of what is possible—Dabrowski's adjustment to what "is" versus adjustment to want "ought to be" (1967, p. 194).

This consciousness creates self-doubt and anxieties; once we become conscious of a door, we wonder what is behind it and whether we should choose to open it or not. While many try to deny the existence of the door and its attendant choices, the only true solution is to become fully conscious of reality and live with the dread and anxiety associated with choosing. Kierkegaard said that these choices are critical in creating a self: "A man possesses his own self as determined by himself, as someone selected by himself" (cited in Dabrowski, 1967 p. 36). To deal with and surmount these anxieties and to follow through in making a choice based upon one's values and faith reaffirms and demonstrates human authenticity.

I can illustrate the point from my own life experience. While learning to fly, during my first solo flight, I looked at the seat beside me and saw that it was empty. I was immediately struck by the awareness that I was alone and that my life was up to me now—I alone had to land this airplane. All of a sudden, I became aware of a choice and felt the uncertainty and angst over the *possibility* that I *could* choose *not* to land, but to crash instead. I did decide to land, and before my next flight, I paused for a moment to bolster my faith that I would make the same decision again. Kierkegaard and Dabrowski would probably say that, in this realization and in making the conscious choice to land, I had taken responsibility over my life as an individual, and in doing so, at least for this moment, I had chosen the authentic path. Of course, my instructor expected me to simply carry out my training to land the plane safely (by rote if necessary), and I also had the conscious thought that I wanted to perform well and not let him down. However, had I simply landed without the internal realization of my existential choice, I would never have had this experience of self-awareness, momentary uncertainty, and dread, or the subsequent feeling of self-determination and self-satisfaction.

Nietzsche was even more critical of the role played by society. Nietzsche suggested that all schemes of morality are simply dogmas of the day representing "herd moralities" that deny individuals from developing their own values by averaging mores "to the middle and the mean"

(Nietzsche, 1968, p. 159). The morality of the herd reflects a homogenization, where the group mean now dictates values and ideals, representing the place where the numerical majority finds itself. Reflecting Kierkegaard and Dabrowski, Nietzsche also felt that adopting mores derived from socialization suspends the individual from the need to review his or her individual value assumptions and the responsibility to develop an individual, autonomous morality. The individual becomes content to simply conform and loses any internal motivation to develop him- or herself. Using the analogy of a camel, an unquestioning beast of burden, Nietzsche suggests that the average person learns to kneel and accept the expectations and duties imposed by society, reacting with fear and guilt if he or she fails to do so. In particular, Nietzsche rejected religion, suggesting that belief in religion absolves the individual of the responsibility of self-development.

Exemplars of Advanced Development

In contrast to primary integration, advanced development is characterized by more complex (but less well organized) structures that now become subordinate to a new master—individual autonomy—characterized by self-control, full self-consciousness, and the creation of an internal value structure that comes to direct behavior. Dabrowski contrasted individuals exemplifying primary integration with persons capable of empathy and self-reflection—for example, individuals like Abraham Lincoln, Socrates, Gandhi, and Mother Theresa. These individuals consciously place the needs of others ahead of their own needs, and they lead by example. This group represents the higher end of the developmental continuum, and their secondary integration reflects an autonomous force that Dabrowski called third factor, reflecting self-definition, self-determination, and the growth and expression of "one's own forces"—the criteria Dabrowski used to define mental health (Dabrowski, 1973, p. 39). To emphasize the critical importance of this autonomous variable, Dabrowski defined personality as the achievement of a "self-aware, self-chosen, self-affirmed, and self-determined unity of essential individual psychic qualities" (Dabrowski, 1972, p. 301).[4]

Contrasting the socialized individual, Plato, Kierkegaard, and Nietzsche also presented conceptualizations of the advanced individual, and each approach emphasized self-control, self-responsibility, and self-

4 To better clarify the unique requirements of the hierarchical approach of psychology in a book-length treatment, Dabrowski (1973) redefined a number of psychological concepts and developed several new concepts, reflecting the multilevel, dynamic, and developmental points of view.

determination. Plato described three levels of individual function corresponding to three levels of the soul: (1) the worker class, corresponding to the "appetite" of the soul (from the waist down); (2) warriors who are strong and brave, corresponding to the "spirit" of the soul (the heart); and (3) the governing class, characterized by intelligence, rational thought, self-control, and love of wisdom. Ultimately, only a few individuals represent the governing class, a class corresponding to the "reason" aspect of the soul (essentially the head). These philosopher kings develop through the discovery of ideal forms, Plato's ultimate level of reality (see *Wikipedia, The Free Encyclopedia*, 2007).

For Kierkegaard, the discovery of one's mortality triggers consciousness and signals the activation of true existence. Although very critical of religious dogma, Kierkegaard emphasized a faith-based approach in which true selfhood requires being willing to take a leap of faith and to choose the self that one truly is, risking despair in not being able to achieve this ideal. "Faith is the most important task to be achieved by a human being, because only on the basis of faith does an individual have a chance to become a true self. This self is the life-work, which God judges for eternity" (McDonald, 2006, section 5, para. 2). Unfortunately, in everyday life, normality hides the true reality of being; however, when pushed to the edge of a cliff, or when realizing that one is alone in an airplane, one tends to see ordinary life from a new, clearer perspective.

Part of our developmental task is to try to see ourselves more objectively. Both Kierkegaard and Dabrowski suggest that most people view themselves too subjectively and relate to others too objectively. One of Dabrowski's key developmental features is subject-object in oneself, "a process of looking at oneself as if from outside (the self as object) and of perceiving the individuality of others (the other as subject, i.e., individual knower)" (Dabrowski, 1972, p. 305). This perceptual shift allows one to develop insight into one's mental life in order to better understand and critically evaluate oneself.

Kierkegaard (Palmer, 1996) described what he called stages in life's way, comprising three spheres of selfhood that the individual may choose from, each characterized by its own unique worldview. The lowest, aesthetical sphere is illustrated by the sensuality and hedonism of Don Juan. This level is subhuman, because one is governed by the same forces that control animals. Today, this level may be illustrated by the selfishness of the "dog-eat-dog" businessperson who values profits and deal-making above all else. As mentioned above, this corresponds to Dabrowski's primary level of integration. In order to break out of this inauthentic existence, the individual must embody Kierkegaard's famous "either/or" (Palmer, 1996). The individual must either accept his or her lower self or consciously decide to will an end to the old self and take a "leap of faith" to build a new, true self.

The next, ethical sphere is characterized by ethical and moral responsibilities as expressed in a commitment to self-perfection, attaining one's ideals, and in commitments to others. Like Dabrowski, Kierkegaard was less concerned with what ideals are chosen than with the process—the autonomy employed in establishing one's ideals.

The final, religious sphere involves another leap of faith—this time, a personal leap into an infinite abyss. One does not come to know God through belief in ideas or through the reasoning of the intellect; one comes to know God through making an eternal leap of faith. In making this final leap, the individual also finally constructs him- or herself. This moment highlights the responsibility of self-construction. One is initially filled with angst, anxiety, and dread. This anxiety reflects the realization of the burden of making eternal choices, but it also reflects the exhilaration and the freedom of being able to choose. Each choice is frozen in time as it carries fourth into eternity. However, each new moment is another opportunity to choose again. As Kierkegaard said, the self is constructed through repeated avowals of faith—that is, the self continually relates to itself and to faith as its creative power through the day-to-day choices one makes and the ongoing leaps of faith that these choices demonstrate. Individuals attaining this high level of development are rare; Kierkegaard called them "Knights of Faith." For Kierkegaard, this process of self-creation produces an authentic individual value structure culminating in authentic human acts; thus, to make this final leap is to be an authentic human. Ultimately, the sum of our choices, values, personality, and acts will stand to be judged by God.

Like Kierkegaard, Nietzsche also began with a severe critique of moral dogma and of the role of religion. His solution was to declare God dead and shock us into facing the here and now of our existence. He asked us to imagine a Godless world where we are free to create, and *must* create, our own moral ideals, thus emphasizing immediate and concrete responsibility for our actions in the day-to-day, here-and-now world. In describing human development, Nietzsche presented a hierarchy of three outcomes. At the lowest level is the "last man," composed of the herd or slave masses reflecting content, comfort-seeking conformers who display no motive to develop. The middle level, the "higher man," is an individual who must be more and who must write his or her own story. Finally, Nietzsche described an ultimate role model for the ideal human, the *übermenschlich*, although he acknowledged that this standard might be unrealistic for most people to be able to achieve. Nietzsche (1961) frequently used the term "übermenschlich," which is commonly translated as "superman," but can also be translated as "overman" or "hyperman."[5]

We have already mentioned the analogy of the camel that Nietzsche used to describe the masses. In a transformation similar to Plato's prisoner discovering the sunlight, a few of Nietzsche's "camels" come to question the status quo and transform themselves into lions seeking to capture freedom and autonomy. Nietzsche used a lion to symbolize the higher man, noting that it takes the might of a beast of prey to steal freedom away from the dogma of socialization—the "thou shalt"—the idea that others tell us what we must believe, what we must accept as truth, and what we must do (and our corresponding love of blind compliance to these external rules). The lion must kill the dragon of the "thou shalt" to create an opportunity—the right to pursue new values and a freedom for new creation.

At the highest level, the lion must transform into a child in order to create new values. Not having been acculturated and with no sense of the "thou shalt," the child is innocent and without guilt. The superhuman/child thus represents a new model of individuality—"the spirit now wills its own will, the spirit sundered from the world now wins its own world" (Nietzsche, 1961, p. 55). Nietzsche described the individual's will to power as the need to become more, the will to act in life and not merely react to life. In a description reminding us of Dabrowski's third factor, the will to power is not power over others, but the feelings of creative energy and control over oneself that are necessary to achieve self-creation, self-direction, and to express individual creativity. The individual uses his or her will to power to reject, reevaluate, and overcome old ideals and moral codes and to create new ones. Nietzsche (1961) said that this is a continual process of self-overcoming by which superhumans take control of their genealogies and write their own stories (members of the herd have their life stories written for them).

5 The word übermenschlich can be broken down as such: über: from the Latin for super; ύπερ: Greek for hyper; menschlich: German for human (being).

Disintegration in the Process of Development

Jackson's (1884) approach to development was influential in the early understanding of mental illness, stating that the highest levels with the most complexity will display the least organization and will therefore be less stable, more fragile, and prone to breakdown. In Jackson's widely accepted view, mental illness involved "dissolution" of higher levels that allowed the expression of lower, simpler, and more automatic ones.

Dabrowski (1964a) rejected this position and presented the idea that in many cases, the breakdown of higher-level integrations (Jackson's dissolutions) plays a key role in evolution; these integrations are required developmental features that are needed to transform and reorganize one's internal psychological makeup. Dabrowski emphasized how difficult it is to break free of peer pressure and overcome the inertia of socialization, and his observations led him to conclude that psychological development requires that these early integrations be broken apart. Autonomous, individual development cannot take place based upon a foundation of biological instincts and socialization. On the contrary, advanced development consists of a conscious and deliberate inhibition of lower instincts, impulses for self-satisfaction, and the inhibition of externally derived, stereotypical, socially based reactions. Development consists of a conscious and deliberate expansion of autonomous features—for example, the creation of an individual hierarchy of values and description of one's personality ideal.

Dabrowski observed that the lives of people who display secondary integration invariably exhibit long periods of disintegration, characterized by strong conflicts, crises, and suffering. "The consequence of these observations was a hypothesis that in normal individuals every manifestation of development is, to a greater or lesser degree, related to disintegration, and that in very creative individuals development is strongly correlated with inner disharmony, nervousness and some forms of neurosis" (Dabrowski, 1970, p. 20). Dabrowski (1964a) also suggested that this reorganization is not primarily cognitive or intellectual. Instead, it involves a basic breakdown and reconstruction of the emotional structures. Dabrowski called this process *positive disintegration* to stress its developmental direction and to differentiate it from negative disintegrations described by Jackson and by traditional conceptualizations of mental illness.

The theory of positive disintegration delineates three phases of disintegration—unilevel disintegration and two types of multilevel disintegration. Unilevel disintegration is characterized by conflicts with a horizontal focus—conflicts between impulses, features, and emotional states on the same level. These conflicts feature strong ambivalence and ambitendency—the individual is equally pulled, first one way and then the other; however, there is little practical difference between the available alternatives. There is very limited consciousness or self-consciousness involved in the decision making. These conflicts are not developmental *per se*, because they do not provide "a way up," and they involve little transformation. Unilevel disintegrations usually end in a reintegration back at the initial level; without reintegration, prolonged periods of unilevel disintegration may create crises "without exit" (Dabrowski, 1970, p. 135), leading to suicidal tendencies or psychosis.

For Dabrowski, the crux of development involved a qualitatively new type of conflict, a vertical or multilevel conflict between higher and lower levels of functions. The discovery of higher levels in the external environment and the subsequent awareness and self-consciousness of multilevelness in one's own psychological structures creates the forces necessary for multilevel positive disintegration. The "vertical solution" to internal conflicts is the hallmark of development. "One also has to keep in mind that a developmental solution to a crisis means not a reintegration [at the same or lower level] but an integration at a higher level of functioning" (Dabrowski, 1972, p. 245). Ultimately, and in the ideal situation, development culminates in the formation of a secondary integration based on self-definition and autonomy.

Nietzsche's description of human development, delivered through a character named Zarathustra, mirrors Dabrowski's. Zarathustra is descending from a mountaintop cave, where he has spent 10 years seeking wisdom. On his descent, he passes a man who had previously known him, and the man comments that it is apparent that Zarathustra is now different; he has become the enlightened one—a child. Coming to the first village he sees, Zarathustra stops to watch a circus tightrope walker. He begins to speak to the assembled crowd, who assume that he is part of the circus act. "And Zarathustra spoke thus to the people: *I teach you the Superman*. Man is something that should be overcome. What have you done to overcome him?" (Nietzsche, 1961, p. 41). Zarathustra continues "[Y]ou have made your way from the worm to man, and much in you is still worm. Once you were apes, and even now man is more of an ape than any ape" (Nietzsche, 1961, pp. 41-42).

Using the analogy of the tightrope walker, Zarathustra says that we are a rope, a bridge connecting animal and superman. To develop, we need to go across this rope, risking the fall into the abyss below while moving away from animal toward superhuman. The crowd rejects Zarathustra's story, and he warns us: "You Higher Men, learn this from me: In the market-place no one believes in Higher Men. And if you want to speak there, very well, do so! But the mob blink and say: 'We are all equal'" (Nietzsche, 1961, p. 297). The people in the mob have accepted their roles and collective definitions from their cultural milieu. For the mob, there are no Higher Men; all stand equal before God.

As we have seen, Nietzsche's solution was to declare God dead, thus resurrecting and freeing the Higher Man by creating the opportunity for the individual to exercise autonomy and to spark the desire to release his or her higher potentialities. "God has died; now *we* desire—that the Superman shall live" (Nietzsche, 1961, p. 297). Unfortunately, the mob reacts to Zarathustra in much the same way that Plato's enlightened prisoner was received; he is considered either insane or simply a fool, and Zarathustra laments his reception: "I want to teach men the meaning of their existence: which is the superman, the lightning from the dark cloud man. But I am still distant from them, and my meaning does not speak to their minds" (Nietzsche, 1961, p. 49).

Just as Plato's prisoners unquestioningly derive their values from their social shadow play, Nietzsche's mob uncritically takes the ideals of "good and evil" from the cultural and religious conventions of the day. Nietzsche called on us to resist the impulse to submit to "slave morality" and to "undertake a critique of the moral evaluations themselves" (Nietzsche, 1968, p. 215). Zarathustra tells us that the superhuman must overcome his or her acculturated self and apply the will to power to a momentous new creativity—to building a truly autonomous self. Thus, superhumans move beyond "good and evil" through a deep reflection on their own basic instincts, emotions, character traits, and senses; they go on to develop their own individual values for living, analogous to the hierarchy of values and personality ideal described in Dabrowski's theory. Emphasizing the need to create one's own values, Nietzsche said, "Fundamental thought: the new values must first be created...we shall not be spared this task!" (1968, p. 12). Nietzsche emphasized that the process of value creation and the new values must not be prescriptive: "'This...is now my way,...where is yours?'

Thus, I answered those who asked me 'the way.' For the way…does not exist!" (Nietzsche, 1961, p. 213).

Again reflecting Dabrowski's approach, the shift to a superhuman perspective involves a qualitative change in the way one views life. The "here and now" takes on a new perspective. Life is not lived for the promise of some better future (for example, in heaven). Rather, every second of life is now seen and valued for its intrinsic worth and contribution to our existence. In eliminating God, Nietzsche also eliminates Kierkegaard's eternal and ultimate judge; therefore, in creating a new value structure and self, Nietzsche's superhuman now must take on the responsibility of becoming judge of his or her self. "Can you furnish yourself your own good and evil and hang up your own will above yourself as a law? Can you be judge of yourself and avenger of your law?" (Nietzsche, 1961, p. 89).

This developmental process represents the rebirth of man and the creation of new, human, life-affirming values in this real and finite (temporal) world. These new beliefs reflect our intrinsic will to be more and our ability to transcend, to constantly overcome our old self and to create a new self and new works.

Nietzsche described the chaos and hardship involved in self-creation, including the need to overcome seven "devils" on the way to personality development (Nietzsche, 1961, p. 90). Reminiscent of Dabrowski's personality ideal, the superhuman develops a clear, internal view of his or her "calling" that now must be followed and applied through self-mastery. The will to power is involved in this development in two stages. First, social morality (analogous to Dabrowski's second factor) is used to gain control over nature and the "wild animal" within us (Dabrowski's first factor). Subsequently, "one can employ this power in the further free development of oneself: will to power as self-elevation and strengthening" (Dabrowski's third factor) (Nietzsche, 1968, p. 218). Emphasizing the idea of overcoming, one overcomes the external, lower elements of oneself to achieve the ideal, representing the higher elements of one's self—to "become the person you are" (Nietzsche, 1974, p. 219).

It is important to emphasize that when Nietzsche and Dabrowski discuss ideals, they are not suggesting a prescriptive approach where exemplars and their ideals should be emulated by all—that is, the individual is not encouraged to emulate or desire to become like an external ideal. As Nietzsche said, "All ideals are dangerous" (1968, p. 130). Rather, the impact of becoming aware of ideals and the lesson of observing exemplars is the realization of the possibility of achieving or emulating advanced development through the creation of an individualized, personal ideal of the self, reflecting one's essential character traits, one's aims, goals, values, etc. The only ideal to emulate is the ideal one creates for one's self.

As mentioned above, Dabrowski reserved the term "personality" for those achieving advanced development. Likewise, Nietzsche (1968) equated personality with the development of the superhuman and said that few people achieve personality, and most individuals are not personalities at all. "[O]nly the few are able and willing to follow their fate, embrace the doctrine of the eternal recurrence and *overcome* themselves and in so doing *become* themselves (McGraw, 2002, pp. 191-192). Nietzsche was adamant that "the '*goal of humanity*' consisted in '*its highest exemplars*,'" the self-ruling, self-creating individuals. They are the all-too-few, fully human, if not superhuman, personalities. Nietzsche contrasted the all-too-few with the much-too-many—that is, the human, slave, and herd-types of individuals (McGraw, 2002, p. 192).

Nietzsche related an individual's potential to develop to the richness and intricacy of his or her emotion, cognition, and volition (the will to power). The more potential a person has, the more internally complex he or she is: "The higher type represents an incomparably greater complexity…so its disintegration is also incomparably more likely" (Nietzsche, 1968, p. 363). Lower forms of life and people of the "herd type" are simpler, and thus, the lowest types are "virtually indestructible," showing few noticeable effects of life (and none of the suffering that characterizes the superhuman) (see Nietzsche, 1968, p. 363).

Nietzsche's view nicely dovetails with Jackson's (1884) and Dabrowski's hierarchical approach to neurophysiology. Nietzsche went on to describe a general, multilevel, developmental disintegration—suffering leads to a vertical separation, allowing the "hero" to rise up from the herd. This uplifting leads to "nobility" and ultimately to individual personality—to attaining one's ideal self. This separation finds one alone, away from the security of the masses and, for Nietzsche, without God for company or comfort. "The higher philosophical man, who has solitude not because he wishes to be alone but because he is something that finds no equals; what dangers and new sufferings have been reserved for him" (Nietzsche, 1968, p. 514). Nietzsche made the need to disintegrate clear, saying, "You must be ready to burn yourself in your own flame; how could you become new, if you had not first become ashes!" (1961, p. 90). A state of extreme vulnerability and over-reactivity (Dabrowski's overexcitability) characterizes this transition: "I love him whose soul is deep even in its ability to be wounded, and whom even a little thing can destroy; thus he is glad to go over the bridge" (Nietzsche, 1961, p. 45). The seed must die for the plant to grow.

The capacity to experience and overcome suffering and endure solitariness are key traits of the superhuman. "Suffering and dissatisfaction of our basic drives are a positive feature as these feelings create an 'agitation of the feeling of life,' and act as a 'great stimulus to life'" (Nietzsche, 1968, p. 370). Nietzsche (1974) attributed all human enhancements to suffering and said that one's path to heaven always leads through one's own hell. Unhappiness, tension, and suffering must be endured, persevered, interpreted, and even exploited by the soul, thus cultivating strength, inventiveness, and courage. Nietzsche foreshadowed Dabrowski's realization that disintegration permeates our existence and leads to new insights, strength, and development. "Thereupon I advanced further down the road of disintegration…where I found new sources of strength for individuals. We have to be destroyers!… I perceived that the state of disintegration, in which individual natures can perfect themselves as never before…is an image and isolated example of existence in general" (Nietzsche, 1968, p. 224). "We, however, want to become those we are…human beings who are new, unique, incomparable, who give themselves laws, who create themselves" (Nietzsche, 1974, p. 266).

These quotations are very reminiscent of Dabrowski's own words—for example: "We are human inasmuch as we experience disharmony and dissatisfaction, inherent in the process of disintegration" (Dabrowski, 1970, p. 122). "Crises are periods of increased insight into oneself, creativity, and personality development" (Dabrowski, 1964a, p. 18). And: "Every authentic creative process consists of 'loosening', 'splitting' or 'smashing' the former reality. Every mental conflict is associated with disruption and pain; every step forward in the direction of authentic existence is combined with shocks, sorrows, suffering, and distress" (Dabrowski, 1973, p. 14).

Physical illness may also play a major role in this transformation; as Nietzsche said, he is "grateful even to need and vacillating sickness because they always rid us from some rule and its 'prejudice'" (Nietzsche, 1989, p. 55). Suffering many serious, life-long health issues himself, Nietzsche defined health not as the absence of illness, but rather by how one faces and overcomes illness—"illness makes men better" (Nietzsche, 1968, p. 212). Nietzsche said he used his "will to health" to transform his illness into autonomy. It gave him the courage to be himself. In a practical sense, it also forced him to change his lifestyle, and these changes facilitated a lifestyle more suited to his personality and to the life of a philosopher.

Conclusion

A consideration of the major philosophical foundations of Dabrowski's theory illustrates four major themes. First, a multilevel approach is vital in understanding the complex and broad variety of phenomena presented by psychology and development. A weakness of traditional approaches has been a reductionistic and simplistic view that cannot account for the wide disparity observed between the lowest and highest behaviors. Although the multilevel approach presents its own challenges, it is a much more realistic reflection of human reality, and Dabrowski refines and applies it as a critical component of his full-fledged theory of personality development.

Second, Dabrowski presents a unique view of the antecedents of development that combines elements of the essential approach to human character with that of existentialism in an approach he called the existentio-essentialist compound. This approach charges the individual with the responsibility of discovering his or her individual essence and subsequently shaping and refining it in a process of literal self-creation.

Third, each author presents an illustration of the socialized person. Plato's prisoners, the crowd of Kierkegaard, Nietzsche's mob, and Dabrowski's primary level all illustrate individuals dominated by and adhering to an external system of social mores and standards. Each clearly shows how adherence to an external standard robs the individual of the opportunity for growth and blocks the development of true individuality and autonomy. Each author also describes a higher form of development that involves overcoming this adherence and achieving autonomy. These authors also describe certain conditions and limitations on this process—for example, Plato makes it clear that not every prisoner can break free and make the journey out of the cave and into the sunlight. Similarly, Kierkegaard makes it clear that not everyone can face the abyss, manage the anxiety and dread, and make the leap of faith necessary to achieve higher individual development—his Knight of Faith. Nietzsche also has reservations about the hardships involved in making the transitions of the self required to first become the Higher Individual and ultimately the Superperson. Dabrowski presents his concept of developmental potential to describe the possibilities of individual growth. Again, for Dabrowski, it appears that not everyone can achieve the ultimate level of secondary integration characterized by a self-created, autonomous personality. All of the authors are clear that exemplars of advanced development exist, and they hold them out to us as role models of development, illustrating for us the *possibility*, as Dabrowski liked to say, and the *process*, but not advocating for the *content* of advanced growth.

Lastly, each author emphasizes the struggle involved in confronting the status quo and the tremendous anxiety, even dread, that results. Nietzsche writes at length about the need for the individual to disintegrate in order to create opportunities for growth. Foreshadowing Dabrowski, Nietzsche places the subsequent task of development squarely on the shoulders on the individual, including the tasks of creating an individualized value structure and a unique idealization of the self that will become the guidepost for individual growth. As we have seen, Dabrowski made disintegration the central element of the developmental process and elaborated its features from a psychological point of view.

While Dabrowski's approach may be radical within contemporary psychology, as this chapter illustrates, it is certainly not radical as an approach to psychological understanding or development. Dabrowski's ideas represent the logical extension and application of several major philosophical approaches, highlighted above. Dabrowski combines these philosophical elements—including multilevelness, the discovery and shaping of essence into personality, and the developmental role of positive disintegration—into a unique systematic approach that is a new paradigm for philosophy, psychiatry, psychology, and related disciplines like education to better understand personality and its development.

Chapter 6

Creativity in Dabrowski and the Theory of Positive Disintegration

Dexter Amend, Ph.D.[1]

> *What, then, is the new mission of Don Quixote, to-day, in this world? To cry aloud, to cry aloud in the wilderness. But though men hear not, the wilderness hears, and one day it will be transformed into a resounding forest, and this solitary voice that goes scattering into the wilderness like seed, will fructify into a gigantic cedar, which with its hundred thousand tongues will sing an eternal hosanna to the lord of life and death.* (Unamuno, 1921, p. 329)

Miguel de Unamuno (1864-1936), the Spanish scholar, novelist, poet, and mystical philosopher, well known for his *Tragic Sense of Life* (1921) was read by Dabrowski probably as an undergraduate in philology. Unamuno was exiled from Spain in 1924, owing to his criticism of the military dictatorship. When he was later granted amnesty, Unamuno refused to return and thereafter lived in France. Dabrowski frequently referred to Unamuno as a heroic figure who made outstanding creative contributions to human culture and who showed in his life authentic human values. Dabrowski was quite familiar with the Don Quixote of Cervantes and Unamuno. He thoroughly identified with this dreamy, impractical, but essentially good man who felt called upon to redress the wrongs of the whole world—an exemplar of creativity in the theory of positive disintegration.

1 Dexter Amend, Ph.D., Psychology Faculty, Division of Social Science and Philosophy, Spokane Falls Community College, Spokane, Washington.

Creativity, the attribute a creator must have to create or be creative, is a new word to psychology and English dictionaries. First appearing in the 1950s and '60s, "creativity," the noun, like "network" and "infrastructure," has been newly invented (created) to meet needs to express recent developments in human experience (Piirto, 2004). My account in this chapter of Kazimierz Dabrowski's creativity resonates well with ancient, original meanings, which connected creativity with agricultural growth processes, newness, intuition, and divinity—as in the case of the Greeks, who called poetry "divine madness" (Piirto, 2004).

Dabrowski: The Divine Madman

Throughout his life, Dabrowski was oriented toward and moved by the highest spiritual realities. At the same time, he experienced extreme personal suffering of depression, anxiety, and "creative striving" to transend his mortal conditions of biological life cycle and psychological type. Dabrowski loved music. He was an accomplished musician and would have pursued music as a career were it not for his thorough preoccupation with human suffering and his concern for the well-being of others, especially sensitive and vulnerable psychoneurotics. Dabrowski's understanding of the positive role of psychoneurotic suffering in human life and personality development was not readily or easily communicated. His sensitivity, vulnerability, and profound response to the scope and detail of his own experience, as well as that of others, enabled him to appreciate and creatively employ many literary forms to communicate his message. Under the pseudonym Pawel Cienin (Little Shadow), Dabrowski published *Existential Thoughts and Aphorisms* (1972a) and *Fragments from the Diary of a Madman* (1972b). These small volumes permitted the author to convey directly in the language of the heart and spirit the basic issues and problems described and explained in the theory of positive disintegration. Dabrowski was painfully aware of the limitations of discursive thinking and writing, as well as the errors that they impose when attempting to represent the full range and exigency of human experience, especially the highest, most refined, and subtle aspects of personality development. This chapter will begin with poetry and end with a mysterium.

Three Philosophical Poems

The philosophical poems that follow were salvaged by Marjorie Kaminski Battaglia (2002) from reams of poetry and other of Dabrowski's writings—unexamined and hidden in the shadows of the National Archives of Canada. Translated from Polish by Elizabeth Mika, the poems appear in Kaminski Battagilia's wonderfully poignant and detailed hermeneutic and historical study of Dabrowski and the theory of positive disintegration (TPD).

More than other literary forms, poetry stimulates, exercises, and expands intuition—the capacity to sympathize and identify with the other, such as the hero in a story. "A Voice from Far Away" (below) echoes Unamuno's "Cries Allowed in the Wilderness"—the new mission of the hero Don Quixote. The poem does not speak to you, the reader. The poem implicates you through your intuition. You become the "you" of the poem, which happens to you. In a "Representive of Positive Disintegration," we—humanity—are engaged in a life-growth process of pain and suffering leading to the highest reality. With "Humility," we consider and contemplate a most basic and sublime human quality involving vulnerability, courage, compassion, responsibility, and the highest authentic human values.

A Voice from Far Away

It's not time yet,
It's not time
Between you, between the continuity of consciousness.
There is a dark forest
It's already thinning out
There's already light coming through
But around you—night.
From far away slowly comes dawn
But around you, but right near you
Creeps the unknown,
The unknown is closing in on you.
Endure, tighten up, there's a far away dawn;
It's knocking on the window.

A Representative of Positive Disintegration

Don't we have to sensitize ourselves to ourselves and others;
Doesn't one wonder about the good and evil in the world;
Doesn't it stir developmental potentials;
Don't fear, sadness, and creative striving lead us toward fear and trembling?
Don't nervousness, psychoneurosis, feeling of inferiority create a hierarchy in us—
a way of growth toward humanity, toward freedom;
Is the fact that we cannot adjust,
That we suffer,
And we strive toward what we ought to be,
But we have obsessions, positive regressions that we cannot
reconcile reality with love;
Doesn't the fact that we despair; that we have thoughts of suicide,
that we are terrified of the world's suffering,
Create in us an inner milieu, hierarchical,
Doesn't it inspire creativity?
I think that all this is a positive loosening,
Is the renewal of life.
It is the main cause of transformational changes;
That's why there are so many of the nervous and neurotic, and great artists;
That's why the way upward goes against oneself.
Against psychic integration.
That's why we're going into the darkness to find light.
That's why we are going into sickness to find health;
That's why we are entering fear and trembling
To find dreams about a different reality;
Because they seem to be not just dreams that we encounter in fear,
stumbling through the fields of sadness;
And through neurotic anguish.
Because who would find, who would learn, who would search,
If he does not suffer, if he's not fearful, if he's not kneeling in dust,
And encompassing his whole soul.
So let's not reject psychoneurosis, nervousness,
Because this may be the royal path,
Long and high to the land of growth and maybe also love,
And maybe also of the highest reality.

Humility

Humility is courage
but not servility;
Courage because it must be so,
Not due to an impulse,
Not due to temperament,
But because of truth;
Humility is the lack of demonstrativeness,
It is love without complications,
It is autonomy not only from others,
But also within oneself and against oneself;
It is identification in understanding, in kindness, but without approving of wrong;
It is modesty not preoccupied with itself
It is the sense of mission without grandiosity,
It is cooperation without domination and without subordination.
It is independence from what people could say,
But at the same time intense attention to what others say and do in truth.
Humility—is a union with truth within oneself and beyond oneself.
A union one can intuitively sense without seeing,
A union one is searching for,
A union one is desiring
It is the silent understanding that we don't know anything,
That we don't understand anything,
Although we have the compulsion to know and understand, the compulsion to see,
That we have the responsibility to remember or forget the hurt;
It is the awareness that nowhere exits perfect greatness, perfect love and perfect certainty and wisdom.

These poems evidence and creatively evoke most of the important concerns and considerations which occupied Dabrowski's life and which find their expression and organization in his theory. In this chapter, creativity is less an object of discourse and more a means to foreground aspects of Dabrowski's thinking, which deserve more attention and further study, such as Henri Bergson's influence on Dabrowski, the primacy of creative instinct and emotional and instinctive functions generally, the prominent role of intuition, and the transcendent and spiritual dimensions of TPD.

Working with Dabrowski

Looking at Don Quixote, his partner, his windmills, and the excellent sun, and reading Michael Piechowski's English rendition of the "Psychoneurotics' Manifesto," represented in Figure 6.1, reminds me of collaborating with Kazimierz Dabrowski on the brochure for the Second International Conference on Positive Disintegration. Dabrowski wanted to keep the Don Quixote and "Greetings to Psychoneurotics" from the previous, first conference brochure, but he wanted me to rewrite the text for the second. I had read and studied Dabrowski's source texts: *Positive Disintegration* (1964a), *Personality-Shaping through Positive Disintegration* (1967), and *Mental Growth through Positive Disintegration* (1970). Preparing the text for the conference brochure forced me to analyze, organize, and summarize my experience and knowledge of TPD. This I did in daily meetings with Dabrowski, examining and discussing meanings and working out precise wordings. I remember, when ending the section in the brochure on Philosophical Perspectives, formulating the following: "...the theory is primarily concerned with a fundamental transformation from inner experience determined by behavior (or external interaction) to behavior determined by inner experience" (*Second International Congress on Positive Disintegration*, 1972).

Figure 6.1. "Psychoneurotics' Manifesto," part of the *Second International Congress on Positive Disintegration* (1972) Brochure

Be greeted, psychoneurotics!

For you see sensitivity in the insensitivity of the world,
uncertainty among the world's certainties.

For you often feel others as you feel yourselves.

For you feel the anxiety of the world and its bottomless narrowness and self-assurance.

For your phobia of washing your hands from the dirt of the world,
for your fear of being locked in the world's limitations,
for your fear of the absurdity of existence.

For your subtlety in not telling others what you see in them.

For your awkwardness in dealing with practical things, and
for your practicalness in dealing with unknown things,
for your transcendental realism and lack of everyday realism,
for your exclusiveness and fear of losing close friends,
for your creativity and ecstasy,
for your maladjustments to "that which is" and adjustment to "that which ought to be,"
for your great but unutilized abilities.

For the belated appreciation of the real value of your greatness which never allows the appreciation of the greatness of those who will come after you.

For your being treated instead of treating others, for your heavenly power being forever pushed down by brutal force,
for that which is prescient, unsaid, infinite in you.

For the loneliness and strangeness of your ways.

Be greeted.

Dabrowski and I collaborated for several months preparing the Neurological Exam, which was presented at the Second International Conference (Dabrowski & Amend, 1972). Our work involved operationalizing various procedures for eliciting and interpreting levels of responses and finding words to describe them. Collaborating on the Neurological Exam gave me special insight into Dabrowski's clinical and therapeutic approach. Dabrowski administered the Neurological Exam on me, as well as on several clients as I observed, and he instructed me in becoming minimally proficient at administering it on others. Observing Dabrowski work closely with clients, I saw how very consciously, sensitively, and respectfully he treated them. I began to appreciate the profound role intuition plays in synthesizing diagnosis and treatment, and why he called interaction with his clients "collaboration."

My colleagues and I were fortunate to be drawn into Dabrowski's intense and creative life work. All his life, including during his '70s, he daily approached his work with unrelenting urgency, a contagious ardor into which we were compassionately implicated. Intimately and immediately, we were engaged and expected to participate individually and in group activities. The great and sometimes unbearable tension of collaboration with Dabrowski, famously called "control through love," was instigated and maintained by unending appointments, meetings, assignments, and deadlines that sensitized us to Dabrowski, each other, and to our own inner workings. Astonishment, dissquietude, dissatisfaction, shame, guilt, and inferiority in relation to oneself—the theory's disintegrating dynamisms—crystallized within us. Other components of the theory—subject-object in oneself, the experience of "higher and lower"—became increasingly obvious in our behaviors, which were reflecting our lived experience of the theory. The daily discussions about ourselves and clients, our analyses of protocols and cases, and our attempts to describe, define, and assess aspects of TPD immersed us in a milieu which catalyzed, amplified, transformed, and facilitated our own growth. While we may have thought we were assisting Dabrowski to "concretize," validate, and publish TPD for posterity, in fact we were primarily and predominantly engaged in our own unique and unrepeatable heroic journey of personality.

Creativity in TPD: Central to Development

In thinking back and remembering our collaboration with Dabrowski, when we would discuss client interviews, analyze autobiographies and Verbal Stimuli responses, and when referring to our own and others' ongoing experience, how frequently Dabrowski would say: "It is something like creative instinct." There seemed to be so many different, quite disparate expressions of creativity. However, as I continued to study and apply the theory to my life, I came to realize and appreciate more and more that all experiences and orientations toward *otherness* were for Dabrowski forms of creativity:

> *CREATIVE DYNAMISMS. Different abilities and talents finding their expression in a search for* "otherness," *for non-stereotyped facets of reality. All developmental dynamisms are creative by their power of transforming the individual and his perception of reality.*
>
> *CREATIVE INSTINCT. An assembly of cohesively organized forces, often of great intensity, oriented toward a search for the new and the different in the external and internal reality. Creative instinct is associated with accelerated development.* (capitalized words in original; emphasis added, Dabrowski, 1972, pp. 292, 293)

What Dabrowski meant by "creativity" has been astutely encapsulated by Sister Lina Gaudet (1981), a long-time collaborator with the author of TPD. Discussing the creative process, when it is evoked, and what conditions attend the development of creativity, Sister Gaudet began by addressing Dabrowski's use of the term "instinct." She explained his distinction between phylogenetic and ontogenetic instincts. For example, self-preservation is a phylogenetic instinct present in all individuals, while developmental and creative instincts are ontogenetic, appearing only in persons undergoing positive disintegration. Dabrowski's distinction between lower- and higher-level instincts, as between self-preservation and self-perfection, is described. And the distinction between lower and higher levels of a given instinct is made—such as creative instinct expressed under the influence of drugs or other means to escape the "present reality" vs. creative instinct expressed through a person's unique talents and special abilities in service of his or her personality ideal.

Sister Gaudet (1981) observes that human development is itself one great creative tension giving rise to specific creative dynamisms. She linked creative dynamisms with the process of positive disintegration, beginning with their incipience in unilevel disintegration through spontaneous multilevel disintegration, where strong creativity is associated with accelerated development, and finally, to directed multilevel disintegration, where creative instinct is coordinated and merged with self-perfection instinct.

Sister Gaudet shows that it is ontogenetic, creative instinct that works with developmental instinct to counter and break down self-preservation and other "primitive," phylogenetic instincts, instigating positive disintegration and thus freeing a person from the constraints of the biological life cycle and psychological type.

Creativity and Mental Health

Sister Gaudet pointed out that the presence of creativity makes disintegration positive—that creativity is absent in pathological disintegration and psychopathy. Creativity is generally associated with mental health and the success of education, and therapy consists in the promotion of the client's forms of creative abilities (Gaudet, 1981).

In *Creativity and Mental Health in the Process of Positive Disintegration*, Tadeusz Kobierzycki (2002), of the Music Academy of Frederic Chopin, analyzed and summarized Dabrowski's life-long studies on gifted Polish children during 1935-1949 and 1958-1965. This long-term study investigated the relationship between mental disorders and creative processes and shows a clear connection between psychoneurosis, creativity, and mental health. Listed below are the dates and English titles of several late Dabrowski Polish publications from Kobierzycki's bibliography suggesting the importance of creativity in TPD: *Creative Dynamisms in Psychoneurosis* (1976), *Personality, Disintegration, Creativity* (1978), *Is a Suffering Creative?* (1979), *On the Problem of Creative Development* (1979), *Mental Health of Creative People* (1979), *Personality, Mental Health, Creativity, Psychotherapy: Attempt to Synthesize* (1979), and *Disintegration, Psychoneurosis and Creative Giftedness* (1983). A long-time collaborator with Dabrowski and founder and director of the Student's School of Mental Hygiene, Warsaw, 1984-1994, Kobierzycki says that creative depression "cleanses the artist and makes way for 'a new creative incentive,' which immunizes against mental illness. Exceptional gifts do not protect from depression. Their presence transforms depression into a 'creative humility'" (Korbierzycki, 2002, p. 403).

Philip Maj's (2002) article elaborated on the relationship of creativity to depression, disintegration, and the dynamisms of the inner psychic milieu:

> *Creativity can be perceived as the inability to reconcile with the world, which causes depression.... [The] creative instinct...loosens and disintegrates the inner milieu. A creative person experiences perplexities as someone who is different from the world, but most*

> *of all as someone who is different from himself, which gives him an inferiority feeling towards himself and sometimes also a strong feeling of guilt.* (p. 377)

Creativity and Intuition: Bergson's Influence on Dabrowski

Though there is no thorough treatment of Bergson and Dabrowski like Tiller's (2006) examination of Nietzsche and Dabrowski (see also Tillier's chapters in this volume), Maj (2002) drew attention to Bergson's influence on TPD. For example, Maj noted that "Bergson reveals eternity in creative evolution. Dabrowski sees in it a chance for personality development, accelerated by creative instincts" (p. 379). Dabrowski saw all life in the context of a cosmic process of Bergson's concept of *creative evolution.* Benet (1948) described Bergson's creative evolution as explaining:

> *...how intuition penetrates to the essence of the soul—the élan vital, vital impulse or energy—where science cannot extend, and how the individual participates in all the actual processes of evolution, which are taking place continually by dissociation, change, and constant movement. By intensity of feeling and knowledge of the self, the individual can direct the continual evolutionary energy of life into channels he chooses and achieve progress.* (p. 253)

Henri Bergson's (1935) philosophical contributions to his culture were of heroic proportions. He enlivened evolution with spirit, the *Elan Vital*; he championed the primacy of inner subjective experience—his *Matiere et Memoire*, later translated as *Matter and Memory*, in which Bergson explicated intuition as the most valid source of knowledge. In simple, paraphrase, for Bergson, the life force (spirit) and inert matter (spirits opposite) meet and conflict in a cyclic life-death process which waxes and wanes endlessly as creative evolution. Humans are conscious of their participation in creative evolution by way of instinct, intellect, and intuition. Instinct is sympathetic with the life force and is pointed thereto. Intellect is oppositely posed toward matter and is patterned thereafter. If intellect can be freed from its attachment to matter, it can be combined with instinct, forming intuition—the highest form of knowledge, giving direct and immediate access to reality (Jones, 1969). For Bergson (1944), intuition "...meant the kind of *intellectual sympathy* by which one places oneself within an object in order to coincide with what is unique in it and consequently inexpressible" (p. 136). He identified one reality that we can access directly: "There is one reality, at least, which we all seize from within, by intuition and not by simple analysis. It is our own personality in its flowing through time—our self which endures" (p. 176).

Bergson's influence on TPD is evident in Dabrowski's discussion of instinct, intellect, and intuition. For example, Bergson's notion of intellect being detached from matter can be seen in the liberation of intellect from primitive drives:

> *In the process of development, which consists in the cooperation of disintegrative and integrative processes, the intellectual function becomes independent of its subservience to primitive drives and associates itself with higher emotions into a unified structure. This process makes it possible to associate thinking and feeling into a co-determinate structure in which there is mutual determination and further developmental transformation.* (Dabrowski, 1973, p. 4)

Bergson's notion of intuition is embedded by Dabrowski in the experiences of conflict, development, and creativity:

> *Such experiences as inner conflicts, sufferings, a rich history of life, meditative attitudes, assist in the formation of intuitive capacities of a wide scope. They contribute to the growth of empathy in relation to lower and higher levels of human activity.... Intuition synthesizes the results of empirical and discursive data and creates a new coordinated unit which may become the subject matter of further discursive examination on a higher level.... In art, literature, and particularly in poetry, intuition consists of the capacity for a global, synthetic, emotional-intellectual-intuitive grasp of reality.... The wider and more multilevel the development of an individual, the stronger and more distinct are his intuitive capacities.... Intuition is an indispensable component of any creative research and any act of discovery in daily life.* (Dabrowski, 1973, pp. 188-191)

Bergson's influence on Dabrowski may have stemmed from another source—Bergson's actions:

> *Henri Bergson was born in France in 1859 and lived and taught there all his life. When, after the fall of France in 1940, the Vichy*

> *government introduced anti-Semitic measures based on the Nazi model, it was proposed, because of Bergson's international reputation, that he be exempted from them. He refused to be treated differently, resigned his various honors, and, although at that time an enfeebled old man who had to be supported while standing in line, registered with the other Jews. He died a few days later, in January, 1941.* (Jones, 1969, p. 264)

Creativity and Self-Perfection: Achievement of Personality

Creative instinct seeks new realities and gives rise to "psychological awakenings," but it must subordinate itself and combine with self-perfection instinct if higher levels of development are to be achieved. When creative instinct merges with self-perfection instinct in service of the personality ideal, it becomes less overt and more "modest," expressed by the great Polish poet and dramatist Mickiewicz like this: "In the words you see the will only—in activity the real power. It is more difficult to be truly good throughout a single day than to build a tower" (Mickiewicz, cited in Dabrowski, 1973, p. 26). Implicit in this passage is what Dabrowski called *the developmental choice*, or *transition to the other side*, the most important developmental milestone, brought on by self-perfection instinct.

Self-perfection instinct synthesizes the work of other dynamisms: third factor, subject-object in oneself, inner psychic transformation, identification, empathy, self-consciousness, and self-control. Through this synthesis, self-perfection enables the individual to transcend the instinct of self-preservation observable in daily life:

> *We have many examples which demonstrate the formation and functioning of the instinct of Self-perfection. Many so-called ordinary people, mothers, fathers, teachers, doctors who systematically express in their everyday work a devotion, a renunciation of egoism, a responsibility and a giving up of their comforts for the realization of moral and social aims and duties, express higher levels of this instinct.*
>
> *The conscious controlled sacrifice of oneself for the salvation of others, and for the building of "values of a higher rank," is an expression of the instinct of Self-perfection.* (Dabrowski, 1973, p. 31)

Self-perfection instinct which introduces the dualism "what is higher" and "what is lower," what is "more myself" and what is "less myself," what is the dependent and inauthentic "I" and what is my autonomous and authentic "I" is the highest, most important contribution to the achievement of personality.

Nothing Can Change Here: A Play

Written by Dabrowski about 1972, translated into English by Elizabeth Mazurkiewicz in 1979, and analyzed and discussed by Peter Roland (1981), *Nothing Can Change Here* is one of Dabrowski's last communications in English on positive disintegration. The play is a "mysterium," or mystery play, a genre originating in ancient Greek tragedies, developed by Christian culture, with eventual influence on Slavic, Polish national drama. Roland ends his enlightening account of Dabrowski's play with a short summary of the work, followed by the last words of the dying hero George:

> *NOTHING CAN BE CHANGED HERE is a mystery play, a work that strives to dramatize spiritual truth, a truth that is not of this world and that even contradicts the logic of this world. George reveals this truth when he says:*
>
> *...that which can be called human in the best sense of the word, is the courage to carry out the tasks in which we believe the true essence of humanity lies, even though they are doomed to failure from the outset. Right to the end we mustn't give way, mustn't back out or accommodate ourselves.... [W]e must continue to be ourselves, to withstand the weight of evil and opposition. We must consciously take the path fate has destined for us.... After all, it isn't so difficult—the greater difficulty lies in existence without that path, trying to find a direction without it.* (capitalized words in original, p. 497)

Conclusion

Creativity was very important to Dabrowski and his theory. Philosophically, Dabrowski's theory and his life were profoundly influenced by Henri Bergson. Like Bergson, Dabrowski emphasized the role of instincts and intuition, beyond intellect, in creative development and in the knowledge process generally. For TPD, creativity is central, pivotal, and essential for advanced development. Central to TPD is creative instinct with creative tension, which dynamizes the disintegrative process from self-preservation instinct to self-perfection instinct. Creativity is pivotal, in that its presence signals mental health. Disintegrations, or growth processes, which are creative, are positive; those which are not, are not creative. Finally, it is unique special talents and creative abilities that define individual essence, achieved in personality.

Positive disintegration is Kazimierz Dabrowski's heroic, creative gift to a suffering humanity. His theory is not a cure or a consolation for suffering, but an explanation of it. TPD is an explanation of Dabrowski's profound and extraordinary subjective experience, of his long and continuous investigation, analysis, treatment, and collaboration with gifted children and adults, and of the age-old connection between madness and genius.

Chapter 7
Dabrowski's Views on Authentic Mental Health

Elizabeth Mika, M.A.[1]

The issue of mental health is a central one in Dabrowski's writings. It underlies his theoretical and clinical insights, permeates his theory, and preoccupies his philosophical and personal inquiry. Many titles of his publications explicitly or implicitly reference mental health, and one of his last books published in Poland, still not translated, is titled, not surprisingly, *W Poszukiwaniu Zdrowia Psychicznego* [*In Search of Mental Health*] (1996b).

Dabrowski's interest in defining mental health reflected to a certain degree the spirit of the time. With the expansion of the humanistic trends of psychology in the 1960s and '70s, theoreticians and practitioners spent a considerable amount of effort trying to establish workable criteria for distinguishing what was and was not mental pathology, and trying to define the concept of mental health. These efforts were all but abandoned in the next decade or so, when biologically-oriented models of mental disorder took reign in psychology and psychiatry. Mental health was understood, almost by default, as the absence of mental disorders. Even a cursory search of the term on the Internet and in library databases yields results confirming this observation; mental health has been most commonly defined, directly or indirectly, as non-illness. The National Institute of Mental Health, for example, states that its mission is "reducing the burden of

1 Elizabeth Mika, M.A., LCPC, Independent practitioner, Chicago, Illinois.

mental illness and behavioral disorders through research on mind, brain, and behavior" (2007).

The advent of positive psychology has shifted discussions on mental health away from mental disorder toward well-being and life satisfaction (Seligman & Csikszentmihalyi, 2000). Even though welcome and needed, this change, from a Dabrowskian perspective, in many instances appears to be unilevel in its character, with its (very American) emphasis on the importance of positive feelings and its pragmatic approach to achieving "abundant gratification and authentic happiness" (Seligman, 2002, p. 293). Dabrowski's unique views, anchored in his concept of multilevelness, are still not widely recognized, much less accepted, in psychology and psychiatry, even though they should be considered a necessary inclusion in any discussion on what constitutes mental health and mental disorder. They are particularly applicable to the gifted and talented population (Mika, 2005), where the most common standards of mental health may not necessarily apply.

In this chapter, I will delineate Dabrowski's views as presented in his book *W Poszukiwaniu Zdrowia Psychicznego* [*In Search of Mental Health*] (1996b). There, Dabrowski reviews nine major concepts of mental health in order to compare and contrast them with his own. Following his lead, I will focus on five of these concepts here—those that I believe are the most prevalent in our current thinking—and show how Dabrowski saw his own definition of mental health as different from the established criteria popular in today's psychology and psychiatry, as well as in society at large.

Mental Health as Absence of Mental Disorders

The first widely accepted concept equates mental health with absence of mental disorders—a view common among lay people as well as mental health professionals. To counteract this position, or more accurately, to modify it, Dabrowski pointed out that many so-called pathological mental states or disorders do not constitute illness but are, in fact, processes necessary for personality development. Such mental states as overexcitability and a majority of neuroses and psychoneuroses are "a necessary condition of clear, multisided development and are one of the basic conditions of mental health, not disorder" (Dabrowski, 1996b, p. 4). The commonly used classifications of mental disorders cannot, in Dabrowski's view, be seen as decisive criteria of mental health and mental disorder. He agreed that there are certain conditions, such as psychopathy and mental retardation, that are clearly pathological, as they preclude possibilities of multilevel development, but he also warned against stereotypical diagnosing of many so-called mental disorders as unhealthy, since associated with many of them there are developmental processes of a creative and positive nature.

Even though our classification of mental disorders has changed since Dabrowski's time and we no longer diagnose people with neuroses and psychoneuroses, at least not according to DSM-IV (American Psychiatric Association, 1994), our understanding of what mental disorder is and what it is not has not progressed much. New and different diagnostic labels do not necessarily enrich our knowledge of the etiology, phenomenology, and teleology of conditions considered as mental disorders specifically, and of human psychological suffering in general (Andreasen, 2007). A clinician following Dabrowski's lead needs to adopt a multilevel approach to diagnosis to be able to assess which symptoms and conditions are unilevel and adevelopmental, and thus indeed pathological, and which ones, even though they may appear disordered, express the processes of growth through positive disintegration.

Mental Health as a State of Psychological Integration

The state of psychological integration, where all mental faculties function smoothly without disharmonies or interruptions, is frequently seen as a necessary condition of mental health. "Keeping it together," in the common vernacular, expresses the desired state and the implied strength and goodness of such integration.

Dabrowski disputed this view, reminding us that disharmony and disintegration are at the core of overexcitabilities, as well as developmentally positive forms of neuroses and psychoneuroses, without which multilevel personality development would be impossible. Overexcitability, which is often associated with developmental asynchrony, as well as giftedness and creativity, introduces disharmony and chaos by its sheer presence. However, it also gives rise to developmental dynamisms, which guide and direct accelerated development. As Dabrowski wrote:

> *[Overexcitability] first provokes conflicts, disappointments, suffering in family life, in school, in professional life—in short, it leads to conflicts with the external environment. Overexcitability also provokes inner conflicts as well as the means by which these conflicts can be overcome. Second, overexcitability precipitates psychoneurotic processes, and, third, conflicts and psychoneurotic*

> *processes become the dominant factor in accelerated development.* (1970, p. 38)

Thus on the one hand, we can observe symptoms suggesting accelerated development in many forms of so-called mental disorders, which are characterized by distinct disintegration. On the other hand, psychopathy, representing integration of mental functions on the lowest level of development—where higher feelings are absent and intelligence is subsumed under low level instincts—precludes development and is contrary to mental health. Yet in many forms of so-called mental disorders, characterized by distinct disintegration, we can observe symptoms suggesting accelerated development.

Being integrated, in the common sense of this term, is also associated with adult psychological maturity, achieved after often tumultuous and disintegrative experiences of adolescence. This maturity is a state desired and promoted by many psychological and psychiatric approaches to mental health and human development, as well as society at large. Psychologically mature, in this understanding, is a person who is capable of adjusting to his or her circumstances, behaves like others, knows what he or she wants, and is independent, reasonable, and understandable to others. However, as Dabrowski pointed out, such a mature person does not reach a higher level of development, only a different developmental phase. This kind of maturity is incompatible with mental health, as it is based on unreflective adherence to low level norms and standards of behavior, which leads to stagnation rather than development.

Many, if not most, highly gifted and creative individuals, especially artists, do not ever achieve maturity as it is understood this way. They remain forever "immature"—naïve; too open; too sensitive; idealistic; romantic; ineffective in their daily functioning; prone to animistic and magical thinking, to extreme expressions of feelings, and to child-like wonder. In short, they are odd and maladjusted by common standards. Dabrowski coined the term "positive infantilism" or "positive immaturity" (1973, p. 153) to describe this kind of immaturity associated with creativity and the capacity for accelerated development, and he listed, among many others, Chopin, Van Gogh, Musset, Slowacki, Kafka, and Shelley as artists who exhibited it in their behavior.

Another argument used by Dabrowski in disputing psychological integration as crucial for mental health has to do with the importance of inner conflicts and frustrations, inherent in positive disintegration, for the development of the multilevel inner milieu and accelerated personality growth. As Dabrowski observed, it is only when we encounter obstacles and frustrations in realization of our goals and desires that we experience internal and external conflicts, ambivalencies, and ambitendencies. Because of these conflicts, an individual endowed with high developmental potential becomes more introspective, more aware of possible choices, and consequently, more conscious of different levels—higher and lower—in his or her feelings, thoughts, and behavior. In these internally and often externally tumultuous conditions, such an individual "introduces into his life a new controlling factor, where higher feelings [begin to control] the lower forms of the instinctual, emotional and cognitive functions" (Dabrowski, 1996b, p. 7).

We can see, then, that the concept of mental health, when based on psychological integration in its common understanding, is contrary to that postulated by Dabrowski. In his approach, authentic mental health is expressed in the dynamic interplay of disintegration and integration of changing localization and scope. A mentally healthy individual has the capacity to undergo positive disintegration and partial secondary integrations on higher levels of development, which lead, eventually, toward a formation of personality on the level of global secondary integration. Lack of this capacity for multilevel development, observed most vividly in mental and emotional retardation characteristic of primary integration, is antithetical to mental health.

Mental Health as Realism in Perceptions and Thoughts, Effectiveness and Productivity, and Ability to Adjust to Reality

The criterion of cognitive realism, with the associated requirement for effective and productive behavior and the ability to adjust to reality, is frequently encountered in approaches to mental health. Realism, both in one's perceptions and life philosophy, is viewed as a necessary requirement of mental health by many psychologists and psychiatrists such as A. Maslow, K. Horney, M. Jahoda, G. Allport, W. Glasser, T. Bilikiewicz, and others (Sowa, 1984, p. 255), and P. Janet (Dabrowski, 1996b, p. 9).

Dabrowski partially agreed with this view, noting, however, that lack of realism in one's cognitive functions may have a developmentally positive value. He stressed the importance of imagination and intuition in accelerated development, saying that many internal processes—which may be only loosely, or not at all, based on reality, such as hunches, dreams, imaginary projects and plans, inner doubts, conflicts, excitations, and inhibitions—awaken our creativity and the need for discovery and innovation. The highest levels of creativity do not depend on accurate perceptions of reality; in fact, excessive cognitive realism can stifle both creativity and personality growth.

The requirement of effective and productive behavior as necessary to mental health is, in Dabrowski's opinion, similarly questionable, since it is difficult to assess effectiveness and productivity involved in many of the most valuable human pursuits. While effectiveness and productivity can be easily observed and measured in the material sphere, there are domains of human activity where such evaluations are very difficult, if at all possible. Emotional development and creative work, for instance, may not always result in tangible products, even though the creative processes involved in both may be of the highest intensity and usefulness to the creator, as well as to society. Dabrowski pointed out that artists are often considered ineffective and unproductive, and the value of work they create is frequently dismissed or underestimated by their contemporaries, who apply pragmatic judgments to both the artists and their art. He observed that it is difficult to talk about effectiveness and productivity of geniuses and eminent individuals, and even more so psychoneurotics, who can be engaged in profound spiritual efforts, although to outside observers they appear inept and inefficient.

Evaluating lives of such artists as Vincent Van Gogh, Miguel de Unamuno, or Juliusz Slowacki through the prism of effectiveness and productivity is impossible, Dabrowski believed, without major modifications to our understanding of both of these terms. While he did not reject this particular criterion as useful in defining mental health, he assigned it secondary importance, noting that it needed to be properly understood within the context of a multilevel approach to reality. He noted that most human traits and behaviors associated with effectiveness and productivity are usually, though not always, indicative of stereotypical and undifferentiated adjustment to social conventions and may signify unilevel integration. As such, they are incompatible with accelerated development, which is the expression of authentic mental health, in Dabrowski's view. As he wrote:

> *Effectiveness and productivity as permanent traits of one's whole character cannot be harmonized with positive and accelerated development, with creativity, with originality. These traits are often*

> *encountered in primitive, stereotypical individuals, exhibiting strong automatic reactions, which are frequently expressive of pathological features.* (1996b, p. 14)

Closely related to cognitive realism and effectiveness and productivity as criteria of mental health is the ability to adjust to reality. Dabrowski questioned the most common understanding of this requirement, pointing out that it usually means giving up, to some degree at least, one's views, standards, and ideals in order to fit in with a group and society. As such, this requirement is incompatible with mental health. To describe different variants of an individual's adaptation to society, Dabrowski introduced the concepts of positive maladjustment (maladjustment to lower-level tendencies in one's own behavior and in influences of one's environment) and negative maladjustment (mental illness and disorder), as well as positive adjustment (dynamic adjustment to ever higher levels in the hierarchy of reality, values, and goals, expressed at the fullest in one's personality ideal; adjustment to "what ought to be") and negative adjustment (adjustment to reality, values, and goals of lower levels to the statistical norm; adjustment to "what is").

The criterion of effective adjustment to reality as a sign of mental health is typically, though not always, used to describe negative adjustment, which is based on either uncritical or opportunistic acceptance of social norms and behaviors and which expresses unilevel pragmatism and moral relativism. It is an attitude of compromise, often adopted unreflectively, with the status quo, where an individual lacks the ability to create his or her own inner truth and convictions and easily submits to various ideologies in order to secure status or material gains. Negative adjustment is often associated with effectiveness—understood as the ability to take advantage of changing environmental conditions to accomplish one's goals, such effectiveness manifests a moral and intellectual indifference, and a lack of interest in one's own development, as well as the development of others.

The extreme end of negative adjustment (and negative integration) is expressed in actions of psychopaths, who use their intelligence in the service of primitive drives. They can be both efficient and productive in accomplishing their goals, since in their pursuits they are not encumbered by such disintegrative experiences as doubts, hesitations, inner conflicts, shame, guilt, and empathy for others. They easily adjust to changing external conditions and are cognizant of reality. Oftentimes, they rise to positions of influence and power, brilliantly (or even not so much) taking advantage of opportunities for personal advancement, which are easily granted in our society to those who impress with their confidence, decisiveness, aggressiveness, effectiveness, and productivity. Dabrowski considered psychopathy to be "the greatest obstacle in development of personality and social groups" (1986, p. 123) and noted that "[our] general inability to recognize the psychological type of [psychopaths] causes immense suffering, mass terror, violent oppression, genocide, and the decay of civilization" (1973, p. 40).

On the other hand, psychoneurotics, who exemplify mental health in Dabrowski's views, are usually impractical and ineffective precisely because of the richness of their inner experiences associated with their accelerated development. Their inner conflicts and doubts, their "overactive conscience," their ideals and visions of a better world, their moral ruminations and questioning make them appear out of touch with reality. They have difficulties adjusting to changing life conditions, since too often the changes disturb deep ties they form with people and places and are incompatible with their highest values. They may not be skilled in influencing reality in tangible, measurable ways, and so their actions may seem odd or purposeless to average individuals. As Dabrowski observed, "Psychopaths have aims but not values. Psychoneurotics have values but not aims. Personalities have both values and aims" (1970, p. 160).

But even individuals with developed or developing personalities, who "have both values and aims," may be perceived, by unilevel standards, as eccentric and impotent. Peace Pilgrim's decision to start walking for peace no doubt struck many of her contemporaries as strange, if not insane (Piechowski, 1992b). Brother Albert's extreme devotion to the poor, which led him to abandon a successful artistic career and live in the slums of Krakow while trying to help the homeless find food, shelter, and jobs, was perceived by many as deranged (Mika, 2004). Some criticized Janusz Korczak's choice to accompany "his" children to the gas chamber in Treblinka as foolish (Lifton, 1997). Many eminent artists, among them Michelangelo, Adam Chmielowski (a.k.a. Brother Albert), Francis Bacon, Fra Bartolommeo, Paul Cezanne, and Willem de Kooning, puzzled and exasperated their contemporaries by their seemingly incomprehensible desire to destroy their art. But as Dabrowski pointed out, this desire, far from being pathological, is usually associated with high developmental potential present in creative individuals. It is an expression of two higher-level instincts that arise at a level of positive disintegration—the instinct of self-perfection, and partial death instinct, which manifest, in individuals striving toward realization of their personality ideal, in a need to destroy or marginalize expressions of their lower-level existence.

These behaviors, though deemed odd or pathological in the eyes of outside observers, represent a strong developmental instinct and oftentimes the highest level of positive adjustment—adjustment to "what ought to be," to the reality of the highest human values and ideals. This kind of adjustment to different, higher levels of reality is characteristic for individuals engaged in accelerated development, who may lack the desire, energy, and skills to adjust to the norms governing the statistical majority. They are, however, very capable of undertaking arduous, long-term efforts toward transcending limitations of their biological cycle and psychological type, and they can progress—through personal crises, depressions, inner conflicts, and states of inner agony—toward realization of their personality ideal. In these endeavors, they are both uniquely effective and even productive, though it is clear that these terms are not quite appropriate to describe these particular efforts.

In Dabrowski's view, the interplay of positive maladjustment, characterized by rejection of what is primitive, automatic, and harmful in the life of one's group and society, and positive adjustment—to one's ideals and the highest human values—expresses an essential characteristic of authentic mental health of individuals and groups.

Mental Health as Psychological Equilibrium

Psychological equilibrium, a concept popular in biological and some psychoanalytic approaches to mental health, is a state of balance between major forces governing our behavior, which makes adjustment to changing conditions and effective psychological functioning possible. The idea of balance as an optimal and desirable state of psychological functioning finds a lot of support in common wisdom, which advocates the "golden mean" approach to life, characterized by harmony and lack of excess.

As Dabrowski pointed out, this approach reflects a unilevel, phase-based view of human life as centered on activities designed to fulfill biological imperatives without major tensions and upheavals. As such, it is incompatible with the multilevel conception of human development presented in TPD, which posits that creative, authentic, accelerated personality development progresses through inner conflicts, grave emotional experiences, depressions, anxieties, obsessions, inhibitions, and intense strivings for transcending one's biological cycle and psychological type—through positive disintegration.

Individuals endowed with high developmental potential—with multiple forms of overexcitability, creative talents, and rich inner milieu—are prone to frustrations, conflicts, and tensions, which, by definition, create imbalance in their lives. This imbalance, however, leads to accelerated emotional growth.

> *Based on everyday observations and clinical studies, we can say that every authentic process of development is based on loosening, or even disintegrating of the primarily integrated attitudes toward our internal and external reality. Inner conflict, which most often is creative in its nature, is coupled with fear and pain; every step toward authenticity is paid for with shocks, sadness, suffering.* (Dabrowski, 1996b, p. 12)

Like integration, psychological balance as a permanent state or disposition is thus contrary to accelerated development through positive disintegration. A prolonged state of psychological balance is symptomatic of either psychopathology, specifically of psychopathy and mental retardation, or, on the highest level of development, of personality. But the latter, secondary balance, is very rarely encountered, in Dabrowski's view. Thus, a state of "moderate imbalance" (Dabrowski, 1996b, p. 13) is a sign of mental health.

Mental Health as Physical, Mental, and Social Well-Being

The criteria of physical, mental, and social well-being are so frequently used in conceptualizations of mental health that they have become an inextricable part of the reigning myth of normalcy, especially popular among mental health professionals in the United States. Sowa, in her discussion on cultural roots and implications of mental health concepts used by psychiatrists, calls this particular myth a "flatly hedonistic superstition" (Sowa, 1984, p. 206).

As Dabrowski observed, definitions of mental health based on an individual's well-being fail to account for the fact that a state of well-being and happiness is often incompatible with the most significant human experiences, such as inner conflicts, hesitations, pain and suffering—both physical and mental—experiences of loss, grief, deepest empathy, or even creativity. In his opinion:

> *...sadness and depression create more of the deepest values than self-satisfaction and psychological contentedness. There cannot be great creativity without tragedy; there would not be any moral reforms and deepest forms of empathy without experiencing sadness, depression, inner conflicts, misunderstandings, and at times even agony.* (1979b, p. 262)

Thus, according to Dabrowski, mental health definitions that emphasize overall well-being promote a constant and negative adjustment to lower levels of reality and do not acknowledge the reality of higher feelings and values, which is always associated with anxieties and worries, depressions, and suffering. Instead, they stress mental and physical balance, hedonism, and conformism, and they fail to include developmental and hierarchical aspects of mental health.

Dabrowski noted that periods of well-being in individuals engaged in accelerated development occur only after conquering multiple difficulties and associated states of positive maladjustment—existential fears and depressions, feelings of guilt, and experiencing a sense of tragedy inherent in human life. In individuals capable of accelerated growth, complete states of well-being occurring on higher levels of development are rare and fleeting. "An individual who is developing must feel badly in different periods of time, must be tormented by sadness, anxiety, depressions, inner and external conflicts. Without these experiences there is no development, there is no growth of self-awareness" (Dabrowski, 1996b, p22). Prolonged periods or more permanent states of well-being are characteristic for people with diminished sensitivity toward themselves and others, and to the existential realities of human life in general.

Prolonged periods of well-being, as Dabrowski wrote, occur rarely and typically are found in individuals with low developmental potential. "An individual who is developing must feel badly in different periods of time, must be tormented by sadness, anxiety, depressions, inner and external conflicts. Without these experiences there is no development, there is no growth of self-awareness" (1996b, p. 22). Dabrowski also pointed out that states of physical, mental, and social well-being do not necessarily coexist in individuals capable of advanced development. He noted that many clearly pathological conditions, such as psychopathy and organic brain damage, are characterized by physical but not mental health. He also listed examples of persons who, even though incapacitated by either a physical defect or grave illness, exhibited a high level of mental health. In his view, the combined state of physical, mental, and social well-being is not encountered in people who exemplify authentic mental health.

The current conceptualizations of mental health maintain the "flatly hedonistic superstition," even though their proponents attempt to distinguish between the hedonic sense of "feeling good" and positive functioning (Keyes, 2002). By doing so, they allow the possibility that positive feelings may not be enough to signal mental health and that positive human functioning may coexist with unhappy feelings and physical problems. However, this is still far from acknowledging that difficult experiences, commonly considered as negative or pathological, are part and parcel of mental health and its necessary component. The prevalent ideas of what constitutes mental health, especially as espoused by the positive psychology, along with the stress on "doing good," strongly emphasize the importance of positive feelings and freedom from symptoms of mental disorders (Seligman, 2002). In this respect, they fall short of the breadth and depth presented in Dabrowski's concept of mental health.

Dabrowski's Concept of Mental Health

Dabrowski's concept of mental health stresses its dynamic, multisided, hierarchical, and teleological aspects. According to his definition, mental health is "the capacity for development toward multidimensional understanding, experiencing, discovering, and creating ever higher hierarchy of reality and values up to the concrete individual and social ideal" (1996b, pp. 22-23). Thus, in Dabrowski's understanding, mental health is not a state but a process; it is more or less continuous psychological growth characterized by attempts at transcending limitations of one's biological cycle and psychological type. This multilevel, multisided development proceeds through positive disintegration and partial secondary integration toward global secondary integration on the personality level, and it encompasses all essential psychological functions—instinctual, emotional, and intellectual, as well as moral, aesthetic, and social values in their multilevel manifestations. Personality is the ultimate goal and result of development through positive disintegration.

Dabrowski described three types of development: (1) average, based on a low development potential; (2) one-sided, based on one strong talent or particular set of skills; and (3) accelerated, which is associated with high developmental potential. Accordingly, he discussed mental health of average people, eminent individuals, and personalities (or individuals engaged in accelerated development), as those three groups represent the three types of developmental potential.

Mental health of average people is characterized by relatively easy adjustment to changing life conditions (i.e., negative adjustment). If occasional periods of maladjustment occur in these individuals' lives, they are not very intense, do not last long, and usually do not leave a lasting mark on their psyche. Average individuals are, in general, efficient, effective, and productive in their activities, are capable of overcoming difficulties, and focus on meeting their basic needs. Among their life goals are usually a successful career, material wealth, high social status, and a degree of influence over others. Their emotional lives are characterized by balance; if they experience sadness or depression, for example, these experiences tend to be moderate and do not lead to self-transformative efforts. Their spiritual lives are consistent with their social norms and are typically defined by stereotypical religiosity.

Eminent individuals exhibit a strong desire for realization of their particular talents and related ambitions. Their psychological growth is limited to one-sided development of the talent and life domains associated with its realization. In their psychological makeup, we can observe sometimes significant developmental discrepancies within and among certain functions. This is especially evident when the leading talent or set of special abilities is related to mathematics, physics, technical abilities, or politics. These individuals, as Dabrowski observed, typically exhibit little or no desire to awaken and develop their inner milieu, and are not interested in self-transformation. They may show lack of empathy in their relationships with others, and sometimes even aggressiveness with tendencies to cruelty. They are at little, if any, risk for mental disorders.

Individuals engaged in accelerated development, or functioning on the level of personality, exemplify hierarchical, multisided, and multilevel mental health, which is an expression of their multidimensional growth. They are focused on development of their own inner psychic milieu and help others in similar efforts. They are devoted to realization of the ever-higher hierarchy of values and show strong strivings toward growing and strengthening of underdeveloped parts in their personality. They exhibit signs of increased psychic excitability—especially emotional, imaginational, and intellectual—in addition to tendencies toward transcending their biological life cycle and psychological type, as well as stereotypical approaches to different areas of life such as education, sociology and psychology, psychopathology, and philosophy. Their life history is full of difficult experiences associated with their need for inner psychic transformation and self-perfection. These experiences most often include neuroses and psychoneuroses, which express their strivings toward ever-fuller understanding, discovering, and creating of a higher reality. Their attitudes toward themselves and others are based on clear perceptions of their concrete personality ideal in its individual and social essence.

From the above descriptions, it is obvious that only the last group—personalities or individuals developing toward personality level through positive disintegration—represent authentic mental health, understood by Dabrowski as multilevel, multidimensional, and accelerated personality growth. Admittedly, by these standards, only a small group of people would qualify as mentally healthy—those few gifted individuals endowed with high developmental potential who function on higher levels of development. The overwhelming majority of society falls short of the standards of authentic mental health. Dabrowski concurred with this observation and noted that society at large would not be able to develop and gain a higher level of mental health if it did not have the clear, concrete hierarchy of values exemplified by lives of the few, who can be seen as models of "what ought to be." These individuals, through their own concrete life examples, show possibilities that awaken and stimulate development—and mental health—of their group and society. The majority of people possess some degree of developmental potential, manifested in their sensitivity, individual talents and special abilities, and more or less developed beginnings of self-awareness and inner milieu. That potential, as Dabrowski wrote, can be developed, and exemplars of advanced development play a crucial role in this process.

Conclusion

Dabrowski's theory of positive disintegration and his unique concept of mental health provide an excellent model of human development in both its disordered, average, and exceptional aspects—a model that is particularly applicable to assessment and therapy of gifted and creative individuals. As Dabrowski argued, the unilevel criteria of mental health and mental disorder prevalent in psychiatry and psychology are insufficient and often inadequate when considered in the context of human strivings for emotional, moral, and spiritual development in the context of multilevel, multidimensional reality of human lives. His ideas on the role of positive disintegration in development and mental health fill this void. He cautioned against using unilevel criteria, such as narrowly understood usefulness and effectiveness, to evaluate multilevel phenomena, particularly creativity, personality growth, and mental health. He reminded us that intense experiences, including states of ecstasy and rapture, depressions and dissatisfaction with oneself, inhibitions, maladjustment to "what is," and strivings to achieve "what ought to be," are characteristic of many artists, scientists, social reformers, and saints, as well as all individuals with any developmental aspirations.

These states—which are clearly far from psychological balance, integration, and well-being and would not be seen as expressive of mental health if judged by the prevalent criteria—stimulate efforts at self-transformation and are essential components of developing individuals' inner lives. They also serve as examples of developmental possibilities and authentic mental health for groups and societies.

We cannot label such experiences as mentally unhealthy without depriving ourselves of what is a uniquely human and perhaps the most valuable aspects of our existence. By pathologizing disintegrative experiences associated with creativity and self-transformation, we stigmatize individuals undergoing accelerated growth and add to their burdens rather than help relieve them. We also reduce the possibility of advancing our society from the flatland of hedonic complacency that it inhabits toward higher levels of development, or at least toward their acknowledgment and appreciation. In addition, by promoting unilevel standards of mental health, we make it possible for psychopathic individuals to achieve power and prominence, which they use destructively in pursuit of their primitive and often inhumane goals.

Dabrowski's theory of positive disintegration offers a promising alternative to today's limited notions of what mental health is. While it may be "positively infantile" to hope that a psychological theory would change the world, one can imagine that adopting Dabrowski's insights would contribute to re-evaluating our notions of mental health and pathology and go a long way toward more authentic assessment of both.

Part II

TPD and Giftedness

Chapter 8
The Theory of Positive Disintegration in the Field of Gifted Education

Linda Kreger Silverman, Ph.D.[1]

Gifted education was introduced to Dabrowski's theory of positive disintegration (TPD) in 1979 through two chapters in the book *New Voices in Counseling the Gifted* (Colangelo & Zaffrann, 1979). Piechowski (1979a) contributed Chapter 2 on "Developmental Potential," in which he made a strong case for the overexcitabilities (OEs) being better indicators of giftedness and creativity than most of the published checklists, IQ tests, and other current methods of identification. In Chapter 11, Ogburn-Colangelo (1979;1989) demonstrated how the theory could be used as a basis for counseling gifted clients. She presented actual transcripts of counseling sessions with a first-year college student who was torn between her desire to have a career in music and her desire to please her parents. The case was beautifully interpreted through the lens of TPD. The combination of these two chapters left an indelible impression on the field. In the ensuing years, Dabrowski's theory gradually has been adopted throughout North America and Australia as fundamental to our understanding of the psychological aspects of giftedness. The aspect of TPD that has most appealed to gifted educators is Dabrowski's overexcitabilities.

1 Linda K. Silverman, Ph.D., Director, Institute for the Study of Advanced Development and the Gifted Development Center, Denver, Colorado.

Dabrowski based his theory on substantial clinical experience with intellectually and creatively gifted children, adolescents, and adults (Piechowski, 1992b; 2006), as well as analysis of the biographies of eminent personalities (Dabrowski, 1970). Until the late 1960s, the research was largely clinical rather than empirical, composed of extensive case studies. Michael Piechowski, then a young professor in molecular biology at the University of Alberta, met Kazimierz Dabrowski in 1967 and became his collaborator and translator. From 1969 to 1972, Dabrowski received a grant from the Canada Council, enabling the first systematic attempts at empirical research on the theory to be undertaken. Piechowski developed content analysis techniques as a means of analyzing massive amounts of narrative data collected on the subjects via open-ended responses to Verbal Stimuli and autobiographical material. A two-volume work, *Theory of Levels of Emotional Development* (Dabrowski & Piechowski, 1977), resulted—the culmination of eight years of close collaboration, during which Piechowski returned to the University of Wisconsin at Madison to obtain a second Ph.D. in counseling psychology. Dabrowski originated the conceptual framework of TPD, and Piechowski contributed the empirical support, the content analysis techniques, application of the theory and the methodology to the study of self-actualizers, and the introduction of the theory into gifted education. As a result, the psychological study of giftedness gained a theoretical foundation, and the theory of positive disintegration gained an empirical basis.

Overexcitabilities

Overexcitability, or psychic overexcitability, is an innate tendency to respond in an intensified manner to various forms of stimuli (Piechowski, 1999). It is a translation of the Polish term, "nadpobudliwosc," which literally means "superstimulatability" in the neurological sense—stronger neurological reactions to stimuli (Falk, Piechowski, & Lind, 1994; Piechowski, 1999). When translated into English, "over" has a negative connotation; however, it would be more accurate to think of OE as an overabundance of energy or the capacity for exuberance and enhanced experience.

Dabrowski's concept of overexcitabilities was first published in his monograph "Psychological Bases of Self-Mutilation" in 1937, and his first paper on types of OEs was published in 1938. The earliest study of OEs in the gifted was conducted by Dabrowski in Warsaw in 1962 (Dabrowski, 1967). Dabrowski (1972) studied 80 gifted and creative youth in Warsaw, including cognitively advanced students and youth involved in the fine arts of ballet, theater, and art. He employed intelligence testing, projective tests, neurological evaluations, questionnaires, interviews, history taking, and case studies. He noted that all of the children he had observed in a school for the arts had characteristic ways of releasing tension and responding to stimulation. Dabrowski categorized these reactions as psychomotor, imaginational, emotional, intellectual, and sensual. The five OEs are innate strengths. They have been considered variables of temperament (Nixon, 1996b) and relate most closely to the temperamental qualities of activity level, intensity of reaction, and threshold of responsiveness (Gottfried, Gottfried, Bathurst, & Guerin, 1994; Silverman, 1998; Thomas, Chess, & Birch, 1968).

> *...Each form of overexcitability points to a higher than average sensitivity of its receptors. As a result, a person endowed with different forms of overexcitability reacts with surprise, puzzlement to many things; he collides with things, persons, and events, which in turn brings him astonishment and disquietude. One could say that a person who manifests a given form of overexcitability, and especially one who manifests several forms of overexcitability, sees reality in a different, stronger, and more multisided manner. Reality for such an individual ceases to be indifferent but affects him deeply and leaves long-lasting impressions. Enhanced excitability is thus a means for more frequent interaction and a wider range of experiencing.* (Dabrowski, 1972, p. 7)

In *Social-Educational Child Psychiatry*, published in Poland in 1959 (revised in 1964), Dabrowski provided his fullest treatment of the five forms of psychic overexcitability, discussing the clinical and educational implications of the OEs, "as well as the challenges they pose in raising a child prone to high levels of stimulation" (Piechowski, 1995, p. 3).

> *Dabrowski emphasized the disequilibrating, disorganizing, and disintegrating action of overexcitability on various areas of psychological functioning.... Overexcitability was defined by the following characteristics: (1) a reaction that exceeds the stimulus, (2) a reaction that lasts much longer than average, (3) the reaction often not being related to the stimulus (e.g., a fantasy image in response to an intellectual stimulus), and (4) a ready relaying of emotional experience to the sympathetic nervous system (fast*

beating of the heart, flushing, perspiring, headaches). (translated and cited in Piechowski, 1995, p. 3)

Only when excitation is beyond the norm does it contribute to developmental potential and qualify as *over*excitability (Piechowski, 1979a). The strength of an overexcitability affects the quality of the person's experience. "The intensity...must be understood as a qualitatively distinct characteristic. It is not a matter of degree but of a different quality of experiencing: vivid, absorbing, penetrating, encompassing, complex, commanding—a way of being quiveringly alive" (Piechowski, 1992b, p. 181).

- *Psychomotor OE* is a surplus of energy or the expression of emotional tension "through general hyperactivity" (Dabrowski, 1970, p. 31). Manifestations include excess physical energy, workaholism, nervous habits (such as tics and nail biting), rapid speech, love of movement, impulsivity, and pressure for action (Piechowski, 1979a; 1999).

- *Sensual OE* includes responsiveness of the senses, aesthetic appreciation, sensuality, and enjoyment of being the center of attention.

- *Imaginational OE* is the capacity to visualize events very well; inventiveness; creativity; fantasy; and poetic, dramatic, or artistic abilities. "Imaginational hyperexcitability can provide a basis for the development of prospection and retrospection, that is to say, the ability to use one's past experience in the planning of the future" (Dabrowski, 1970, p. 31).

- *Intellectual OE* includes probing questions, analytical thinking, reflectiveness, problem solving, and interest in abstraction and theory. This OE appears to be most closely associated with intellectual giftedness, but gifted individuals have repeatedly been found to be high in emotional OE as well (e.g., Bouchet & Falk, 2001; Silverman & Ellsworth, 1981; Tieso, 2007b).

- *Emotional OE* involves intense connectedness with others; the ability to experience things deeply; fears of death, embarrassment, and guilt; and emotional responsiveness.

Piechowski (1979a) suggested that the OEs or "original equipment" are basic components of giftedness shared by many types of gifted and creative individuals. "The overexcitabilities may be regarded as the *actual psychological* potential of the creative person" (p. 49). "The assessment of the strength and richness of these forms should allow a reliable qualitative assessment of creative giftedness" (p. 54). Piechowski's expanded view of giftedness predates Howard Gardner's (1983) attempt to broaden the perception of intelligence in the popular book, *Frames of Mind*. In the *Encyclopedia of Creativity*, Piechowski (1999) asserted that creative individuals must be endowed with certain fundamental attributes: intelligence, talent, and overexcitabilities. The OEs contribute significantly to the creator's drive, vivid sensory experience, relentless searching, power to envision possibilities, and the intensity and complexity of feeling involved in creative expression.

Piechowski and Colangelo (1984) emphasized that the OEs are not specific domains of talent or prodigious achievement. "Rather, they represent the kind of endowment that feeds, nourishes, enriches, empowers, and amplifies talent" (p. 87). Dabrowski's model "promises to uncover for every individual child its principal mode of responding to the world" (Piechowski, 1974, p. 91). The various permutations and strengths of the OEs at least partially account for the wide range of individual differences within the gifted population. Like variables in temperament observed in infants, the overexcitabilities appear to be stable characteristics that differentiate the interests, motivation, and behavior of children with different kinds of gifts.

Research on Overexcitabilities

Michael Piechowski began the systematic consideration of expressions of overexcitability by examining 433 instances of OE found in the autobiographical material of six subjects in Dabrowski's study of levels of development (Piechowski, 1979a). One of the subjects was a historical case study: Antoine de Saint-Exupéry. From this material, he developed an open-ended instrument consisting of 46 items that tapped the different OEs. This was the original *Overexcitability Questionnaire* (OEQ) (Piechowski, 1999), which has been shortened at various times to 41 items (Lysy & Piechowski, 1983), 21 items (Lysy & Piechowski, 1983), and 12 items (Ackerman & Miller, 1997).

Beginning in 1973, Piechowski collected data from gifted junior and senior high school students in a series of studies at the Research and Guidance Laboratory for Superior Students at the University of Wisconsin-Madison (Piechowski, 2006), at the University of Iowa (Piechowski & Colangelo,

1984), and at the University of Denver (Piechowski & Miller, 1995). Two-year follow-up studies were conducted with 27 students, ages 14 to 19, providing an opportunity to observe dimensions of inner growth during adolescence. The results of these studies, involving the analysis of 5,000 responses from 131 students, were recently published in the compelling book *"Mellow Out," They Say. If I Only Could* (Piechowski, 2006). Both the 46-item OEQ and the 21-item OEQ can be found in Appendix 2 of that book.

Identification of the Gifted

Based on Piechowski's hypothesis that the strength of the OEs could be used as a measure of the person's giftedness, several graduate theses and research projects in the United States, Canada, Turkey, and Venezuela have explored the use of overexcitabilities in the identification of gifted and creative individuals from different national, ethnic, and socio-economic backgrounds (e.g., Ackerman, 1993; 1997b; Breard, 1994; Buerschen, 1995; Calic, 1994; Domroese, 1993; Ely, 1995; Gallagher, 1983; Manzanero, 1985; Schiever, 1983; Yakmaci-Guzel & Akarsu, 2006). The instrument employed in these studies was the 21-item *Overexcitability Questionnaire* (OEQ), shortened from the original 46 open-ended questions with the assistance of Katherine Ziegler Lysy (Lysy, 1979; Lysy & Piechowski, 1983). Some sample questions are: "What kinds of things get your mind going?" and "When you ask yourself 'Who am I?' what is the answer?" [The full questionnaire can be found in Falk, Manzanero, and Miller (1997); Lysy and Piechowski, (1983); Piechowski (2006); Piechowski and Cunningham (1985); Piechowski and Miller (1995); and Piirto (1998).]

The narrative responses are coded using content analysis techniques. Two trained raters independently score the OEs on a scale from 0 to 3 according to specific criteria outlined in a coding manual, *Criteria for Rating the Intensity of Overexcitabilities* (Falk et al., 1994). (The criteria are summarized in a chart of "Forms and Expressions of Psychic Overexcitability" in Piechowski, 1997, pp. 368-369.) Ratings are based on richness or intensity of a given response. Raters attempt to reach consensus through discussion of differences. In cases where consensus cannot be reached, the material is often sent to an expert coder for mediation (e.g., Michael Piechowski or Frank Falk). In some cases, the ratings are simply averaged. Interrater reliabilities were calculated for all OEs in 10 studies conducted between 1985 and 1996 (n = 427). Interrater reliability prior to consensus ranged from approximately .66 to .86 (Ackerman, 1996; 1997b). Test-retest reliability for the OEQ completed three to six weeks apart by a group of 60 adults was .65 (Ammirato, 1987). In another study, internal consistency (Cronbach's alpha) for total OE scores averaged .77 for gifted adults (Miller, Silverman, & Falk, 1994).

Validity for the *Overexcitability Questionnaire* is accruing from studies of groups with known characteristics. Falk, Manzanero, and Miller (1997) provided cross-cultural validity for the concept of overexcitability. American artists (Piechowski, Silverman, & Falk, 1985) and Venezuelan artists, employing a Spanish translation of the OEQ (Manzanero, 1985), both evidenced high imaginational OE scores (Falk et al., 1997). Imaginational OE distinguished highly creative junior high students from less creative students (Schiever, 1983; 1985) and differentiated high and low scorers on the *Torrance Tests of Creative Thinking* for sixth graders (Gallagher, 1983; 1985). Imaginational OE was also confirmed in samples of talented high school students studying musical theater, visual arts, and creative writing (Piirto & Cassone, 1994). In addition to scoring higher than their average peers on imaginational OE, gifted preteens and adolescents tend to score higher than gifted adults and graduate students (Piechowski & Colangelo, 1984; Tieso, 2007b). The children in one of Tieso's studies (ages 5 to 15, median age 10) had significantly higher imaginational OE scores than adults on the OEQ-II (Falk, Lind, Miller, Piechowski, & Silverman, 1999b), suggesting to the author that "adults tend to lose their sense of childlike wonder and vivid imaginations as they submit to the realities of adult responsibilities" (Tieso, 2007b, p. 19). The discrepancy between mothers' imaginational OE scores and their daughters' was greater than the discrepancy in imaginational OE between fathers' and sons' scores.

The suppression of imaginational OE in gifted girls may begin as early as middle school. In a second study by Tieso (2007a), a "precipitous decline" in imaginational OE was found in gifted middle school girls compared to gifted elementary-aged girls. Although the gifted group (n = 296) surpassed the typical group (n = 184) in intellectual and imaginational OE, there was a marked decline in both of these OEs for gifted middle school girls. The author commented, "it appears that middle school is an inhospitable place for most gifted females" (p. 237). Middle school may be inhospitable for all gifted students. Tieso reports "an alarming result—all gifted, middle-school students had lower mean OE scores than their elementary peers" (Tieso, 2007a, p. 237).

Emotional, intellectual, and imaginational OEs have distinguished the responses of gifted children and adults from those of unselected samples in the majority of studies (e.g., Piechowski et al., 1985; Silverman & Ellsworth, 1981). Theoretically, these three OEs should be at least as strong as, or stronger than, sensual or psychomotor OE in order to contribute to developmental potential (Dabrowski, 1972; Piechowski, 1975b). However, several studies of OE reveal that psychomotor OE is an important means of differentiating gifted children from other students (Ackerman, 1997a; Bouchard, 2004; Gallagher, 1985; Schiever, 1985; Tieso, 2007b). This robust finding occurred with three different instruments (OEQ, *ElemenOE*, and OEQ-II) and a wide age range in various parts of the United States and Canada. Psychomotor OE differentiated better than the other four OEs between a group of identified gifted high school students and an unselected group in Calgary on the OEQ (Ackerman, 1993; 1997a; 1997b). It was also the strongest OE for a younger group of gifted children (ages 4 to 12) in Texas, using the *ElemenOE* (Bouchard, 2004).

Consistent with the findings of Ackerman and Bouchard, Tieso (2007b), employing the OEQ-II, reported that psychomotor OE was the highest OE score attained by 143 gifted students who participated in a summer program at a university on the east coast. She indicated that "Psychomotor OE may be the best predictor of giftedness among school-age children" (p. 19). By way of contrast, in her second study of 510 children from five school districts, Tieso found that "typical males have higher mean Psychomotor OE scores than gifted males, which contradicts earlier studies…" (2007a, p. 236). Tieso's first sample also demonstrated high emotional OE and intellectual OE scores. She considered the presence of high psychomotor OE and emotional OE to be risk factors for gifted students, which might "lead to diagnoses of ADHD and other behavior disorders" (Tieso, 2007b, p. 20). Apparently, psychomotor OE must be integrated with other overexcitabilities before it contributes significantly to developmental potential (Manzanero, 1985; Falk et al., 1997; Piechowski & Cunningham, 1985).

Research on OEs appears to lend some support to the clinical observation that the gifted have high levels of sensual OE (e.g., Meckstroth, 1991). However, the support is not as sound for sensual OE as for the other overexcitabilities. Comparing OE profiles of gifted adults with a heterogeneous sample of graduate students, Silverman and Ellsworth (1981) found that the gifted group scored significantly higher on four out of the five OEs:

emotional, intellectual, imaginational, and sensual. Sensual OE was stronger in a group of adult artists than in the sample of gifted adults (Piechowski et al., 1985). Artists surpassed the intellectually gifted in imaginational OE and emotional OE, and equaled them in intellectual OE (Piechowski et al., 1985). All gifted samples in the following studies scored high in intellectual OE and exhibited high levels of emotional OE as well: Bouchet and Falk, 2001; Gallagher, 1985; Piechowski and Colangelo, 1984; Piechowski and Cunningham, 1985; Piirto, Cassone, Ackerman, and Fraas, 1996; Schiever, 1985; Silverman, 1983; Silverman and Ellsworth, 1981; and Tieso, 2007b.

Piechowski and Colangelo (1984) compared several groups of gifted and creative individuals from different parts of the country, varying in age from nine through adulthood, and contrary to Tieso (2007a), reported consistency of OE scores across the age span.

> *The youngest gifted groups (age 9 and 11 in the Denver sample) have each the same OE profile of T [Intellectual], M [Imaginational], and E [Emotional] as the gifted adults. This consistency supports the idea of developmental potential as original equipment.* (Piechowski & Colangelo, 1984, p. 87)

Piechowski and Miller (1995) compared data collected on the OEQ with data collected via an interview format (originally developed by Gallagher, 1983) on children 9 through 14. In addition, they investigated the effects of age and gender on OE scores. Prior studies with adult populations had found no correlation between age and OEs (Lysy & Piechowski, 1983; Miller et al., 1994). No gender differences were found in this study, but older children, ages 12 to 14, scored higher than younger ones, ages 9 to 11, primarily due to the difficulty of the younger students in writing their answers. Even so, the two methods were considered nearly equivalent, as the interview format did not generate higher OEs than the questionnaire. Piechowski and Miller recommended that the interview format be used for assessing children below age 12. Further information about reliability and validity of the OEQ is reported in Miller et al. (1994), Piechowski and Miller (1995), and Falk et al. (1997).

Cheryl Ackerman and Nancy Miller (1997) have explored an even shorter version of the OEQ, consisting of 12 of the original items. Their analysis of data from nine studies, conducted from 1985 to 1995, shows that the proposed 12-item version meets acceptable reliability criteria. Further, they argue that the reduced time requirement benefits the respondent, the rater, and, ultimately, the researcher, without appreciable loss of information. To date, this version has not been used in any research studies.

Gender Differences

Piechowski (1986) warned that, in comparing different samples, it was important to be aware of their gender ratio; females tend to produce higher emotional OE scores than males. The significance of gender has been demonstrated repeatedly. Felder (1982), using the OEQ, compared 14 gifted education graduate students, 12 of whom were female, with 16 chemical engineering students, 15 of whom were male. The chemical engineering students were somewhat higher on psychomotor OE, while the gifted education graduate students were considerably higher on sensual OE, imaginational OE, and emotional OE. They were nearly equivalent on intellectual OE. Lysy and Piechowski (1983), studying adults, and Breard (1994), studying children with the OEQ, also found that males scored higher than females on intellectual overexcitability. The primarily female gifted education students scored significantly higher than an unselected group of women at mid-life on intellectual and imaginational OE, but very similarly in emotional OE (Sorell & Silverman, 1983), confirming Piechowski's contention that there is a gender effect for emotional OE. The difference in the performance on emotional OE between the chemical engineering students and the gifted education majors was largely due to the gender ratio of the samples.

Other studies, using both the OEQ and OEQ-II, have also found pronounced gender differences, with females of various ages scoring higher than males on emotional OE (Ackerman, 1997a; Ammirato, 1987; Bouchet, 1998; Bouchet & Falk, 2001; Breard, 1994; Gross, Rinn, & Jamieson, 2007; Miller et al., 1994; Piechowski & Cunningham, 1985; Piechowski & Miller, 1995; Piirto et al., 1996; Tieso, 2007a; 2007b). Males scored significantly higher than females in intellectual, imaginational, and psychomotor OE in Bouchet and Falk's study (2001). Similar to Gross et al.'s (2007) study of gifted adolescents and Tieso's (2007a) study of gifted elementary and middle school students, Bouchet and Falk (2001) found that females scored significantly higher on emotional and sensual OE. As in the study by Miller et al. (1994), the gender differences were attributed to gender-role socialization.

Previous studies show one consistent finding: Emotional OE has been higher for females and intellectual and psychomotor OEs

> *have been higher for males. Sensual OE has been higher for females in many cases. These findings are reflective of traditional gender-role expectations. Our society socializes males to express intellectual and psychomotor abilities, while females generally are socialized to the opposite, by inhibiting such intellectual and psychomotor abilities. Similarly, females are socialized to express sensuality while males are expected to hide sensuality.* (Bouchet & Falk, 2001, p. 261)

While Ackerman (1997a; 1997b) and Gross et al. (2007) found that adolescent girls scored higher than their male counterparts on imaginational OE, Bouchet and Falk (2001) had the opposite finding: "This was the first study to find imaginational OE higher for males than for females" (p. 265).

Newer Methods of Assessing Overexcitability

A new version of the *Overexcitability Questionnaire*, the OEQ-II, was released in 1999—a 50-item self-rating measure employing a Likert scale (Falk et al, 1999b). The OEQ-II was developed over several years, based on the analysis of 300 open-ended responses to OEQ items from several studies. It attained a stable factor structure of five 10-item factors, one factor for each OE. The first sample of 562 college students was obtained from a population of undergraduate students at a large Midwestern university (Bouchet, 1998; Falk & Lind, 1998). The means and standard deviations were as follows: Emotional OE: M = 3.72, SD = .77; Intellectual OE: M = 3.50, SD = .79; Imaginational OE: M = 2.86, SD = .83; Sensual OE: M = 3.28, SD = .87; Psychomotor OE: M = 3.35, SD = .79. Researchers in the United States and Canada provided a sample of 324 subjects (ages 15 to 62) to establish construct validity. Although the mean age of the second sample was five years younger than the original sample, only minor item differences were found (Falk & Lind, 1998; Kort-Butler & Falk, 1999).

Bouchet and Falk (2001) presented research on the OEQ-II involving undergraduate students who had been identified for gifted classes when they were younger (n = 142); who had been in Advanced Placement classes, but not in gifted programs (n = 131); and those who had been only in the standard educational program (n = 288).

> *The items on each factor had loadings of .50 or above. Cronbach's alpha for scale reliability was high: .86 for psychomotor; .86 for*

> *sensual, .85 for imaginational, .89 for intellectual, and .84 for emotional....*
>
> *...[G]ifted and talented students exhibit significantly higher emotional and intellectual OE scores than students in either the Advanced Placement or standard categories. Further, students in the Advanced Placement category scored significantly higher on these OEs than the students in the standard category....*
>
> *...On emotional OE, females scored higher than males in all three schooling categories.* (pp. 263-264)

Since its release, the OEQ-II has been translated into Chinese, Spanish, Turkish, and Polish. Pardo de Santayana Sanz (2006) employed it with 102 gifted and 102 non-gifted children in Spain, ages 8 to 15. Chavez (2004) used the OEQ-II with 90 adults in Mexico—30 creative individuals, 30 controls, and 30 psychiatric outpatients. Chang (2001) had the most ambitious study, involving 2,046 elementary, middle, and high school students in a norm sample and 951 gifted and talented students in fifth, eighth, and eleventh grades in Taiwan. (Results can be found in Chapter 10 in this volume.)

In an investigation of overexcitabilities in families, Tieso (2007b) used the OEQ-II to study the relationship between OEs in gifted children and their parents. She found a high correlation between parents' OE scores and their children's. The vast majority of the variance (78% to 99%) of the OE scores of the children could be explained by mothers' or fathers' OE scores. Similar to the results of Miller et al. (1994), who used the narrative OEQ, males had higher mean scores on intellectual OE, and females had higher mean scores on emotional OE. In Tieso's study, the highest intellectual OE scores were earned by the fathers, and the highest emotional OE scores were earned by the mothers. Females also had higher sensual OE scores than males, supporting the results of Felder (1982) and Bouchet and Falk (2001).

Gross et al. (2007) used the OEQ-II with 248 gifted adolescents participating in summer programs at a university in the south. They compared overexcitabilities with a self-concept measure—The Self-Description Questionnaire II (Marsh, 1990)—and found that while "psychomotor overexcitability boosts self-concept in gifted adolescents," "imaginational overexcitability is clearly the most negatively correlated with self-concept" Gross et al., p. 247). Verbal self-concept scores correlated positively with every OE except psychomotor, and emotional stability self-concept was negatively correlated with intellectual, imaginational, and emotional OE.

A children's version of the OEQ-II has been developed by Susan Daniels, Frank Falk, and Michael Piechowski (in preparation). In 2003, Supporting Emotional Needs of the Gifted (SENG) awarded the researchers a two-year grant (with an extension) to design and test the OEQ2-c, a version of the OEQ-II with readability scaled for 9- to 12-year-olds. Extensive qualitative interviews with parents of highly and profoundly gifted children are currently in progress at the Rocky Mountain School for the Gifted and Creative in Boulder, Colorado. *Living with Intensity: Understanding Sensitivity, Excitability, and Emotional Development in Gifted Children, Adolescents, and Adults* (soon to be published by Great Potential Press) describes the development and reliability of this new scale in differentiating between patterns of overexcitability in typical, gifted, and highly gifted children. The interviews consistently document the challenges and advantages that OEs bring to the lives of the gifted.

Other methods have been developed to assess overexcitabilities in preschool and elementary-aged children. For several years, psychologists in Sydney, Australia, have been analyzing the parent questionnaires of gifted children to determine the presence of OEs (H. Dudeney, personal communication, June 1, 2002). Helen Dudeney, an educational consultant in Australia, has adapted the OEQ-II for parents, changing "I…" to "My child…" (Falk, Lind, Miller, Piechowski, & Silverman, 1999a). This *Overexcitability Inventory for Parents* is now being explored with clients at the Gifted Development Center in Denver. A version of the OEQ-II for teachers is in the planning stages (M. Kane, personal communication, August 28, 2007).

Qualitative case study methods, involving the analysis of school records, observations of children, and interviews with teachers, were employed by Tucker and Hafenstein (1997) to determine OEs in gifted preschoolers. Bouchard (2004) developed the *ElemenOE*, a 30-item Likert scale for teachers to rate the frequency and intensity of children's OEs; the process takes 5 to 10 minutes. The *ElemenOE* was based on an initial compilation of 100 items from Dabrowski's writings, existing overexcitability questionnaires, and checklists for identifying the gifted. These items were evaluated by a content jury of five scholars with expertise in Dabrowski's work. "While the *ElemenOE* has proven reliable for measuring Intellectual and Psychomotor OEs, its reliability on Emotional OE is weak and the reliability of the Sensual and Imaginational scales are unsatisfactory" (Bouchard, 2004, p. 347).

A mixture of qualitative and quantitative methods was used to study the presence and impact of overexcitabilities in high achieving adults. Lewis, Kitano, and Lynch (1992) designed a questionnaire measuring "intensities" (OEs) and characteristics of the gifted and administered it to 31 doctoral students in education, 17 of whom were female. A subset of 11 students, predominantly female, participated in focus groups in which their perceptions could be investigated qualitatively. The researchers found strong evidence of intellectual and emotional intensity, as well as some evidence of imaginational and sensual intensity.

Developmental Potential

A discussion of overexcitabilities would not be complete without reference to *developmental potential.* For Dabrowski, OEs were among the fundamental ingredients for determining an individual's potential for the development of higher order values. Dabrowski (1972) defined developmental potential as the endowment that governs the character and extent of inner psychic growth possible for an individual. Psychic overexcitabilities, intelligence, special abilities and talents, and autonomous factors comprise the individual's developmental potential (Mendaglio & Tillier, 2006). Piechowski (1986) offered a perspective on giftedness based on developmental potential:

> *Giftedness is a multifaceted phenomenon involving the interplay of specific talents, favorable environmental events, and unique personality characteristics.... The concept of developmental potential...broadens the conception of giftedness by addressing the personality correlates of high ability. This model...binds the goals of education to self-actualization and advanced moral development, rather than merely to productivity in adult life....*
>
> *It is often recognized that gifted and talented people are energetic, enthusiastic, intensely absorbed in their pursuits, endowed with vivid imagination, sensuality, moral sensitivity, and emotional vulnerability....*
>
> *These characteristics are found across different talents, in writers, composers, dancers, actors, scientists, inventors, civic and spiritual leaders. Often they are as strong in adulthood as in childhood....*

> *This amplified range of different experiential channels found in creative people as well as those who seek spiritual perfection was correlated by Dabrowski [1964c] with intensified personal growth. People with less fire in their veins look upon those who have it as different, abnormal, neurotic.... To Dabrowski, however, the label was hiding something highly significant—signs of a richer psychological endowment. He found that in youth with superior intellectual and artistic abilities a greater number of so-called neurotic symptoms (anxiety, compulsions, psychosomatic ailments) correlated with a greater number of indices of enhanced modes of experiencing. He concluded that "nervousness and psychoneuroses are phenomena normal in the course of development"* (Dabrowski, 1972). *He saw these as signs of developmental potential....*
>
> *When gifted people, or their parents, are introduced to these concepts, there is often an instant recognition and a reaction of relief.... It helps for once to feel legitimate in one's extraordinary reactions.* (pp. 190-191)

Piechowski (1986) maintained that studying the strength and expressions of OE in gifted and talented individuals had important implications: (1) for understanding the nature of giftedness, (2) as a basis for methods of identifying a broad range of giftedness, and (3) for investigating individuals who were functioning, or had functioned, at higher levels of development. Psychobiographical case studies of individuals who have attained higher-level development reveal that all were gifted individuals and all manifested overexcitabilities (Brennan, 1987; Brennan & Piechowski, 1991; Grant, 1990; Piechowski, 1978; 1990; 1992a; 1992b; Spaltro, 1991).

Dabrowski (1972) posited that at lower levels of development, individuals are at the mercy of their heredity (the first factor) and environment (the second factor). However, those who have crossed the threshold into multilevel development show signs of a third factor—a more autonomous, self-directing dynamism. "Increased consciousness, self-determination, authenticity, and autonomy are the hallmarks of the third factor" (Mendaglio & Tillier, 2006, p. 81). The dynamisms indicate the richness of the person's inner milieu and capacity for transformation. "The aim of this transformation is to make one's ideals and actions one and the same, to live according to the precepts of love, compassion, helpfulness and effective action" (Piechowski, 1986, p. 193). (See the chapters in this book by

Michael Piechowski and Nancy Miller for additional information on developmental potential.)

Gifted children and adults demonstrate the requisite overexcitabilities and intelligence to attain higher-level development, but actualization of that potential is rare. Failure to actualize potential in the emotional, moral, spiritual, and personality spheres may be partially attributed to the devaluing of these spheres in our societies. Perhaps the disparity can be traced to too much emphasis on one's career as a basis for self-definition and neglect of the developing person. In studies conducted to date, women tended to achieve higher levels of development than men (Felder, 1982; Miller et al., 1994). These findings have been explained in terms of gender-role socialization, since women are allowed more freedom to develop their emotions. A shift in focus away from productivity as the *sine qua non* of giftedness might facilitate more balanced development (Grant & Piechowski, 1999; Piechowski, 1986).

Piechowski (1992b) addressed the need to "find and nurture human potential for altruism, self-actualization, and high levels of moral development" (p. 181):

> *We need tools for identification and cultivation of such potentials. Dabrowski's theory of emotional development is such a tool; it is a theory of human transcendence toward a life inspired by universal ideals of human brotherhood, peace, service, and self-realization. The theory arose from his extensive clinical experience with gifted and talented children, adolescents, and adults.* (p. 181)

Conclusion

Gifted Child Quarterly publishes a section before each research article called "Putting the Research to Use." The section before Tieso's (2007b) article was particularly revealing:

> *Dabrowski's overexcitabilities represent a multifaceted lens through which to view the intensities of gifted children. The challenge for researchers and practitioners is to examine these intensities and promote intervention strategies that will enhance students' positive characteristics while teaching them to compensate for the negative. To address this challenge, researchers should explore and explain these sensitivities to gifted students, their parents, and their teachers. Those in charge of identifying gifted, talented, and*

> *creative students should use the overexcitabilities as an additional tool in the multifaceted and inclusive model of identification. Furthermore, teachers must be aware that characteristics indicating a learning disability or behavioral disorders may be characteristics of giftedness manifested through these overexcitabilities. Finally, students and their parents should be assisted in understanding and celebrating students' unique sensitivities and intensities.* (p. 11)

This recent endorsement of TPD in the oldest and most established journal in gifted education is a testament to the acceptance of the theory in the field. Dabrowski's theory has become the key to the psychology of giftedness. The instruments designed by Michael Piechowski, Frank Falk, and their colleagues have facilitated empirical research in support of the theory, as well as increased awareness of TPD internationally. The research base on overexcitabilities of the gifted continues to expand throughout the globe.

Chapter 9

The Dabrowskian Lens: Implications for Understanding Gifted Individuals

Michael C. Pyryt, Ph.D.[1]

This chapter examines research with gifted individuals in the context of Dabrowski's theory of positive disintegration (TPD) and discusses how the theory provides a unique lens for understanding key phenomena in gifted education. Since the theory proposes that one's developmental potential is the result of the combination of overexcitabilities and dynamisms activated (Piechowski, 1975b), this chapter will highlight what is known about overexcitabilities and dynamisms in gifted education. It will also explore how the Dabrowskian lens challenges our traditional notions of gifted education.

Overexcitabilities

The major focus of discussion and research related to gifted education has been on the psychic overexcitabilities (Dabrowski, 1972). The theory of positive disintegration proposes that there are five channels of perception—psychomotor, sensual, intellectual, imaginational, and emotional—that people use to experience the world. The theory suggests that individual differences exist in the amount and mixture of these

1 Michael C. Pyryt, Ph.D., Director, Centre for Gifted Education and Associate Professor, Division of Applied Psychology, Faculty of Education, University of Calgary, Calgary, Alberta, Canada

overexcitabilities, which affect developmental potential. Unless individuals have emotional overexcitability marked by intense concern about relationships with others and the universe, their developmental potential is limited to unilevel developmental stages.

The most extensive study of overexcitabilities in gifted and average-ability individuals is Ackerman's (1997b) secondary analysis of studies using the *Overexcitability Questionnaire* (OEQ) (Lysy & Piechowski, 1983). Ackerman was able to obtain data from 13 North American studies that used the OEQ. Some of the studies explicitly compared gifted and average-ability samples (Ackerman, 1993; Breard, 1994; Domroese, 1993; Ely, 1995). Others simply reported overexcitability scores for gifted (Jackson, 1995; Miller et al., 1994; Piechowski & Miller, 1995; Schiever, 1985) or average-ability students (Felder, 1982; Hazell, 1984; Lysy & Piechowski, 1983; Sorell & Silverman, 1983). The summary information provided by Ackerman (1997b) for 253 gifted individuals and 318 average-ability individuals, ranging in age from 9 to 54, makes it possible to determine the extent to which gifted individuals differed from those not identified as gifted on the five overexcitabilities. Cohen's (1988) *d*, the most popular indicator of effect size, was calculated by dividing the difference between the means of the gifted and average-ability groups by the pooled standard deviations for each overexcitability. It can be expressed as follows:

$$\text{Cohen's } d = (\text{Mean}_{\text{Gifted}} - \text{Mean}_{\text{Average-ability}}) \;/\; \text{Standard Deviation}_{\text{Pooled.}}$$

The obtained values of Cohen's *d* were .29, -.10, .42, .48, and .11 for the psychomotor, sensual, imaginational, intellectual, and emotional overexcitabilities, respectively. Based on Cohen's (1988) recommendations, effect sizes below .20 are considered trivial, effect sizes between .20 and .50 are considered small, effect sizes between .50 and .80 are considered medium, and effect sizes greater than .80 are considered large. This analysis suggests that there are small differences favoring gifted students on the intellectual, imaginational, and psychomotor overexcitabilities as measured by the OEQ. There are trivial differences favoring gifted individuals on emotional overexcitability, and average-ability individuals on the sensual overexcitability as measured by the OEQ.

The original OEQ has 21 free response items, and this instrument requires the use of trained raters to evaluated responses on the OEQ. The publication of the OEQ-II (Falk et al., 1999b) increases our capacity to conduct research related to overexcitabilities. This self-report instrument asks respondents to rate the accuracy of 50 statements (10 for each of the five overexcitabilities). Internal consistency estimates for each of the five subscales exceed .80. Although factor analytic results support the construct validity of the instrument, correlations between the OEQ and OEQ-II were not reported in the technical manual.

Of the total OEQ-II normative sample (n = 887), ages 10 to 76, a subsample of 324 was investigated, and 65% of them had participated in gifted, talented, or honors classes. Bouchet and Falk (2001) provide data for 561 undergraduate students from a large Midwestern university. Students who reported participating in gifted programs or Advanced Placement classes scored higher on the intellectual and emotional overexcitabilities than did students without special placements. The effect sizes were .41 for intellectual overexcitability and .22 for emotional overexcitability. These would be interpreted as small effects. Means and standard deviations were not reported for the psychomotor, sensual, or imaginational overexcitabilities.

Bouchard (2004) developed an observational checklist to measure overexcitabilities in elementary school children (*ElemenOE*). Teachers in Houston, Texas, and vicinity completed the *ElemenOE* for samples of 96 gifted and 75 non-gifted students. Teachers rated identified gifted students as more likely to show intellectual overexcitability (ES = .74) and less likely to show psychomotor overexcitability (ES = -.39). A small difference favoring gifted was found on imaginational overexcitability (.21). Trivial differences were found on sensual (ES = -.18) and emotional overexcitability (ES = .09).

This examination of studies of overexcitabilities in gifted and average-ability samples suggests that, regardless of method used, gifted individuals demonstrate a greater degree of intellectual overexcitability. It's somewhat surprising how few studies have actually been conducted comparing gifted and average-ability individuals. With the exception of the Bouchet and Falk (2001) report, it appears that gifted and average-ability individuals have similar amounts of emotional overexcitability. This finding would suggest that many gifted individuals have limited developmental potential in the Dabrowskian sense and are more likely to behave egocentrically rather than altruistically. Overexcitabilities are only one-half of the developmental potential equation, however. What do the dynamisms tell us?

Dynamisms

The theory of positive disintegration hypothesizes that the interaction between heredity and environment activates certain autonomous inner forces called dynamisms. Piechowski (1975b) provides a description of the dynamisms that are proposed to indicate each of the levels in the theory of positive disintegration. The presence of dynamisms is seen as reflective of disintegration. There are no unique dynamisms that are activated at Level I. Relevant dynamisms activated at Level II include "ambivalence" and "ambitendencies," which reflect initial conflict between "what is" and "what ought to be." Dynamisms activated at Level III include "dissatisfaction with oneself," "feelings of shame," and "feelings of guilt" due to the individual's perceived discrepancy between external reality and the ideal. As one proceeds to Level IV, the dynamisms such as "self-awareness" and "autonomy" provide an individual with a sense of self-efficacy regarding the capability to resolve the inner conflict between the actual self and the ideal self. At Level V, a dynamism called the "personality ideal" is activated. As a result, one achieves the ideal self, and thereby a state of harmony termed "secondary integration."

Mendaglio and Tillier (2006) note that the dynamisms have been largely neglected in the gifted education literature. Probably, this is for conceptual and methodological reasons. Dynamisms add a complexity to the theory that requires persistent reading and re-reading of original sources that were not widely available until recently. It is difficult to convey in a journal article how dynamisms interact with overexcitabilities at various levels of development. Additionally, we are handicapped methodologically by the lack of assessment instruments that directly provide indications of dynamisms present across the lifespan. Typically, case studies, fragments of autobiographical writings, and counseling transcripts are used to provide evidence of the existence of a particular dynamism exhibited by a particular exemplar. There are no comparison studies of dynamisms exhibited by large samples of gifted and average-ability individuals.

In one of the few reports, Mendaglio and Pyryt (2004) analyzed the intellectual requirements needed to activate higher-level dynamisms and proposed that intelligence was required for the dynamisms of "self-awareness" and "empathy." Given this analysis, Mendaglio and Pyryt concluded that intelligence was a necessary, but insufficient, condition for high developmental potential. Nixon (2005) noted that their view of the role of intelligence in the theory of positive disintegration was congruent with Dabrowski's original writings.

The Dabrowskian Lens and Giftedness

The theory of positive disintegration has unique implications for anyone interested in the psychology and education of gifted individuals. First, the model proposes that emotional overexcitability is of primary importance for reaching the highest level of development. The current emphasis on the cognitive domain in gifted education, in conjunction with neglect of the emotional domain, is viewed as misguided. If the goal of gifted education is to foster the highest levels of development, it is essential to identify individuals with emotional overexcitability in addition to intellectual and/or imaginational overexcitability. This would require identification procedures to go beyond individual intelligence measures such as the WISC-IV (Wechsler, 2003) or Stanford-Binet V (Roid, 2003) to clinically determine through interviews, journals, and open-ended responses an individual's concern with relationships and compassion.

The second implication of the theory is that many gifted individuals, because of their emotional sensitivity (Piechowski, 1991a), are likely to suffer internal conflicts when they experience the discrepancy between "what is" and "what ought to be." Rather than viewing such conflicts as negative, the theory clearly views such existential struggles as positive indicators of developmental potential.

Third, the model is consistent with the view that giftedness can be manifested in many ways: intellectually, creatively, emotionally, sensually, and physically. It should be noted, however, that it is the combination of the overexcitabilities that leads to the manifestation of one's gifts. A person who only has the intellectual overexcitability present may be a successful lesson learner. A person who has both intellectual and emotional overexcitabilities is more likely to use that intelligence in humanitarian efforts.

Self-concept development has been conceptualized in terms of three theoretical perspectives: reflected appraisals, social comparison, and attribution (Mendaglio & Pyryt, 1995; 2003; Pyryt & Mendaglio, 1994; 1996/1997). Depending on the theoretical model used, one would expect unique answers to questions surrounding similarities and differences of self-concept processes among gifted and average-ability students. A reflective appraisals approach to self-concept, when applied to gifted persons, would highlight how a person cognitively handles self-referent feedback from significant others. Having greater intelligence would result in more complex interaction with incoming feedback from the social environment.

From a social comparison perspective, one would expect variability in what constitutes a reference group. Presumably, gifted persons select eminent models with which they compare themselves.

From an attribution perspective, gifted individuals will experience competing pressures to attribute success to ability as a natural attribution process and to attribute success to other factors for fear of appearing arrogant.

How giftedness is conceptualized is the other important factor. When giftedness is viewed as high intelligence, particularly when coupled with high achievement, one finds that academic self-concept scores tend to be higher for gifted persons. However, when viewed from a Dabrowskian perspective, expectations regarding self-concept change dramatically. Dabrowski's theory suggests that persons with advanced developmental potential will experience a variety of negative feelings, which are normally associated with low self-esteem. Giftedness from that perspective gives greater importance to self-acceptance rather than the traditional view of self-concept, which can be positive or negative in nature.

Among educators of the gifted, the link between giftedness and perfectionism is clearly established. The tendency toward perfectionism is an item on the most widely-used teacher rating scale for the identification of superior students (Renzulli, Smith, White, Callahan, & Hartman, 1976). Dealing with perfectionism is often cited as one of the counseling needs of the gifted (Kerr, 1991; Silverman, 1993). Typically, educators concerned with gifted children are concerned about two negative impacts of perfectionism: underachievement, and emotional turmoil. In terms of underachievement, Whitmore (1980) reported that perfectionistic tendencies make some gifted students vulnerable for underachievement, because they do not submit work unless it is perfect. In terms of emotional stress, perfectionism is seen to cause feelings of worthlessness and depression when gifted individuals fail to live up to unrealistic expectations. Delisle (1986; 1990) has provided anecdotal evidence that perfectionism places some gifted students at risk for suicide.

One of the difficulties in describing the construct of perfectionism is recognizing the multiple uses that occur in the literature. There is a fine line between striving to reach high standards of excellence and feeling self-defeated through the inability to reach unreasonable expectations. Some writers deal with this dichotomy by contrasting two types of perfectionism.

Bransky, Jenkins-Friedman, and Murphy (1987) distinguish between enabling perfectionism that empowers individuals and disabling perfectionism that cripples individuals. Hamachek (1978) distinguishes between normal and neurotic perfectionism. Other writers (Barrow & Moore, 1983; Burns, 1980; Pacht, 1984) use perfectionism to refer to the negative aspects of the syndrome. Recent research on academic Talent Search participants (Parker, 2000; Parker & Mills, 1996) suggests that achieving gifted students demonstrate signs of healthy perfectionism. Thus, the link between giftedness and perfectionism is not as strong as once thought. Dabrowski's theory of positive disintegration would suggest that perceived positive or negative aspects of perfectionism would be intricately linked with levels of development.

There is a long history in the gifted education literature (Hollingworth, 1942; Terman, 1925) equating giftedness with advanced moral development. Clark (1988) had advanced moral judgment as one of the unique affective characteristics of the gifted. Kohlberg (1969) suggested that there is a curvilinear relationship between IQ and moral judgment. Persons below average in IQ showed scores on moral reasoning tasks that were also below average. For those who were above average in IQ, scores were unrelated to intelligence.

Pyryt and Mendaglio (2001) used meta-analytic techniques to determine the nature of the relationship between intelligence and moral development and to possibly identify correlates of this relationship. Moral development was conceptualized from the cognitive developmental perspective identified with Piaget (1948), Kohlberg (1969), and Rest (1979). This view proposes stages or levels of moral development that evolve as the individual's cognitive structures evolve. Since the assessment of an individual's stage of moral development is typically based on an individual's responsiveness to a moral judgment interview, this construct of moral development is also referred to as "moral judgment" or "moral reasoning."

The results of the meta-analytic study support Kohlberg's original hypothesis of a curvilinear relationship between intelligence and measures of moral development. Apparently, a certain level of cognitive development is necessary for moral reasoning. Once this threshold is obtained, additional increments in IQ do not result in additional increments in moral development. When gifted populations are studied, the low correlation between intelligence and stage of moral development can be accounted for by restriction of range. Still, the tendency to equate levels of giftedness with levels of moral reasoning ability appears premature. It should also be noted that moral development as used in the current study only focuses on moral reasoning. The relationship between scores on moral reasoning tasks and indices of moral behavior remains to be determined. Gifted individuals can clearly exhibit morally reprehensible behavior (Tannenbaum, 2000). Dabrowski's theory of personality places greater emphasis on moral development in the sense of attitudes and behaviors. Inner conflicts result from a clash of values—those represented in the world as it is compared to the way things ought to be. Transition from relativistic values to acceptance of universal moral principles is another attribute of advanced levels of development. Altruistic behavior is a key element of the personality ideal.

Conclusion

Gifted individuals are more likely than average-ability individuals to show signs of intellectual overexcitability. This will be predictive of higher-level potential when combined with emotional overexcitability and higher-level dynamisms. There is limited evidence to suggest that gifted individuals possess these components to a greater degree than average-ability individuals.

Dabrowski's theory of positive disintegration provides a unique perspective on traditional notions of giftedness. It challenges us to prefer compassion to logical reasoning, self-acceptance to self-concept, the personality ideal to the status quo, and living altruism to moral judgments.

Chapter 10
Measuring Overexcitability: Replication across Five Countries

R. Frank Falk, Ph.D.[1]
Buket Yakmaci-Guzel, Ph.D.
Alice (Hsin-Jen) Chang, M.A.
Raquel Pardo de Santayana Sanz, Ph.D.
Rosa Aurora Chavez-Eakle, M.D., Ph.D.[2]

The authors acknowledge the helpful comments and suggestions of Drs. S. Daniels, N. B. Miller, and M. M. Piechowski

Dabrowski's theory of positive disintegration (TPD) was influenced by the highly charged emotional and personal experiences of his youth—particularly the death of his younger sister at age six and the atrocities of World War I (Battaglia, 2002; Hague, 1986). These events, occurring in his early years, profoundly influenced his perception of personality development. His insights are evident in the three fundamental concepts that make up his theory

1 R. Frank Falk, Ph.D., Professor of Sociology (Emeritus), University of Akron, Akron, Ohio, & Director of Research, Institute for the Study of Advanced Development, Denver, Colorado, U.S.

Buket Yakmaci-Guzel, Ph.D., Bogazici University, Istanbul, Turkey.

Hsin-Jen Chang, M.A., Taipei Municipal Zhongshan Girls High School, Taipei, Taiwan.

Raquel Pardo de Santayana Sanz, Ph.D., Francisco de Quevedo School Villasevil, Cantabria, Spain.

Rosa Aurora Chavez-Eakle, M.D., Ph.D., Johns Hopkins University, Baltimore, Maryland, U.S.

2 Co-authors' names were arranged randomly to indicate their equal cooperation. Send all inquires to R. Frank Falk, Ph.D., Institute for the Study of Advanced Development, 1452 Marion St., Denver, CO 80228.

of emotional and moral development: multilevelness, developmental potential, and positive disintegration (Dabrowski et al., 1970). *Multilevelness* refers to a hierarchy of values that are part of "the structure underlying the organization of behavior" (Dabrowski & Piechowski, 1977, p. 12). An individual's level of development is determined by this fundamental structure. *Developmental potential* concerns the strength or weakness of the inner psychic milieu as opposed to the external forces in life. *Positive disintegration* describes the process by which an individual can move up in the levels of development. This occurs when the psychic structure of the existing level gives way to a more self-controlled structure that involves a higher-order organization of behavior.

Together, these concepts create a vast, complex theory, which stresses "the developmental role of inner conflicts and crises, emotional and imaginational hyperexcitability, disruption of primitive functions and structures, generally speaking, the positive nature of the processes of mental disintegrations emphasized and explained in the framework of a developmental perspective" (Dabrowski et al., 1970, p. 116). In this chapter, we discuss the importance of Dabrowski's theory for the field of gifted education and demonstrate how overexcitability can be measured in different languages and cultures. Research findings from four different countries provide support for the validity of the concept of overexcitability.

Giftedness

For many in education, the concept of developmental potential is important to our enterprise. We educate to endow individuals with the skills and knowledge that will allow them to succeed within society. Individuals' potential and various abilities create different opportunities for teachers to assist in development.

For educators and counselors of the gifted, the need to understand the developmental potential of students and to guide them in their life course is of primary concern (Colangelo & Zaffrann, 1979; Jacobsen, 1999; Piirto, 2004; Silverman, 1993; VanTassel-Baska, 1998). In their review of overexcitability research, Sal Mendaglio and William Tillier (2006) note that Dabrowski's theory, and the concept of developmental potential in particular, have played a significant role in research attempting to understand giftedness. They point out that Dabrowski's concept of developmental potential refers to:

> *...the constellation of psychological features that he believed were associated with advanced personality development. These characteristics include three main features: (1) special abilities and talents (like athletic or unique musical ability), (2) the five forms of overexcitability, and (3) a strong autonomous drive to achieve individuality.* (pp. 69-70)

While all three of these characteristics are included within the theoretical definition of development potential, what caught the eye of educators was the concept of overexcitabilities (OEs). In his early work, Kazimierz Dabrowski described five dimensions of heightened excitability: psychomotor, sensual, imaginational, intellectual, and emotional; however, Michael Piechowski is the one who clarified and expanded the definitions based on the investigations that he and Dabrowski conducted of autobiographical and clinical material (Piechowski, 1975b). Piechowski also was able to describe OE in terms that teachers and counselors understood.

A pivotal event for educators was the publication of Piechowski's article "Developmental Potential" in *New Voices in Counseling the Gifted* (Piechowski, 1979a). Piechowski's explanation of the concept of developmental potential intrigued readers, but his description of children's OEs is what those in the field of gifted education identified with most strongly. To quote Piechowski:

> *Nervousness is tension in the nervous system and Dabrowski got the idea from observation of children under conditions provoking tension—in school, naturally. In the old days children had to stand up in silence when the teacher entered the classroom. They sat down in silence. But in that imposed restraint, some squirmed restlessly in their seats, some were relaxed but daydreaming (their gaze vacant or wandering); some sat upright and a little tensed with their eyes closed and the eyelids trembling; a few looked alert and expectant. Dabrowski interpreted this in the following way. The imposition of restraint provokes emotional tension. This tension finds expression in several different modalities. Children that squirm in their seats release their tension psychomotorically; the daydreamers escape the tension into the world of fantasy or spontaneously create pictures and scenes as images of the sources of tension; the upright, tensed children feel the tension emotionally; the alert ones get their mind going and are ready to put their wits to*

> *use. There are five modalities of expressing tension: psychomotor, sensual, imaginational, intellectual, and emotional. They are called forms of psychic overexcitability.* (p. 28)

Overexcitabilities

Teachers and counselors of the gifted now had a conceptualization and description of the behaviors of gifted children that cast them in a positive light. Further, OEs were seen as a possible means of identifying giftedness. Now, instead of relying on intelligence tests or tests of abilities alone, a method emerged which could tap into emotional intelligence (Goleman, 1995), or intensities (Piechowski, 2006). A new way of understanding giftedness appeared on the horizon.

> *The five OEs came to be understood in the following manner: Emotional OE is recognized as intense feelings: positive feelings, negative feelings, complex feelings, and identification with other's feelings. Those with emotional OE have the capacity for strong emotional ties and attachments to others. Imaginational OE is expressed through rich and unusual associations, a creative imagination, and a penchant for inventiveness. Use of metaphors, animistic and magical thinking, and dramatization are also expressions. Intellectual OE involves an insatiable quest for knowledge and is exemplified by endless curiosity. The capacity for sustained concentration and a preoccupation with complex ideas and issues are indicative. Sensual OE is expressed through enhanced sensory gratification—for example, the pleasure of taste or touch or the excess of overeating. Psychomotor OE is characterized by high levels of physical activity and surplus of energy. It is demonstrated through rapid movement that is sometimes compulsive, such as excessive talking, nail biting, or workaholism.* (Falk et al., 1997, pp. 201-202)

Empirical work based on the analysis of autobiographical material began to appear in the mid 1970s (Piechowski, 1975b). Research based on the *Overexcitability Questionnaire* (OEQ) was conducted in the late 1970s (Lysy, 1979) and was published several years later (Lysy & Piechowski, 1983). The OEQ is a 21-item, open-ended questionnaire for ages 13 and above. One of the earliest investigations using the OEQ was reported by Linda Silverman and Bernita Ellsworth at the Third International Conference on Dabrowski's Theory in 1981. They analyzed 31 questionnaires completed by adults identified as gifted and found, to their surprise, that subjects' emotional OE scores were equally as high as their intellectual OE scores. Since then, many studies have been published using the OEQ (see Mendaglio & Tillier, 2006, and Tieso, 2007b, for comprehensive reviews).

To date, two studies using the OEQ have focused on populations outside of North America: a study of Venezuelan artists (Falk et al., 1997) and a study of Turkish high school students (Yakmaci-Guzel & Akarsu, 2006). In each of these studies, the questionnaire was translated into the language common to their subjects, Spanish and Turkish, respectively. Researchers themselves were involved in the original translations, and then several bilingual professionals were used to finalize the translation. In the Venezuelan study, back translations were also completed. Open-ended questionnaire responses were rated in these studies using a coding manual and criteria established by the first author with the help of collaborators Michael Piechowski and Sharon Lind (Falk et al., 1994).

The Venezuelan study demonstrated that artists in both Venezuela and the United States exhibit high levels of imaginational, intellectual, and emotional OE. This study provided "further support for the hypothesis that animistic, intuitive, and emotional thinking are strong characteristics of artists" (Falk et al., 1997, p. 204). Results from the Turkish study show that students with high intellectual abilities score higher on imaginational and intellectual OE as compared to students with low intellectual abilities. Intellectual ability was measured with the Raven Advanced Progressive Matrices Test (Yakmaci-Guzel & Akarsu, 2006). Both studies contribute to the cross-cultural validity of the concept of OE.

The Overexcitability Questionnaire – Two

Conducting studies with the OEQ is labor intensive. In most cases, rating requires two trained coders each spending one or two hours per questionnaire. In addition, some form of consensus is needed when coders disagree. Inter-rater reliabilities in most studies have exceeded 60% prior to consensus; however, because only one score can be used, a means of decision-making must be invoked. Sometimes the two coders discuss disagreements until arriving at consensus. Occasionally, when disagreements persist, responses and scores are sent to an acknowledged expert coder for resolution. In some cases, the two scores are numerically averaged. In a few studies, only one coder has been used. Such scoring methods are extremely difficult when larger sample sizes were desired.

As researchers began to see the need for large-scale studies to explore relationships between groups of individuals—to determine the distribution of OEs and to explore the connection between OE and other variables—they began to look for a more objective test format. My colleagues and I, along with countless students and other dedicated persons, struggled for several years to complete a fixed-choice questionnaire to measure OE. We worked with actual responses from the OEQ along with items constructed by the research team to create the questionnaire. This instrument became known as the *Overexcitability Questionnaire – Two* (OEQ-II). Details of the validation and reliability studies are reported in *The Overexcitability Questionnaire – Two (OEQ-II): Manual, Scoring System, and Questionnaire* (Falk et al., 1999b).

The OEQ-II is composed of 50 items distributed equally on five factors. The factor structure was established by principal components analysis with varimax rotation. There are 10 items for each factor or scale representing each of the OEs. Reliability of the items varies from .84 to .89. Thus, we conclude that an empirically valid and reliable questionnaire is confirmed to measure OE (Bouchet & Falk, 2001; Falk et al., 1999b).

Cross-Cultural Studies

Since its publication, the OEQ-II has been translated into at least three languages that we report here: Chinese, Spanish, and Turkish. The Chinese version is the language as spoken in Taiwan. Two Spanish versions represent the cultures of Mexico and Spain. In this section, we present a discussion of the translation process and the findings from four studies of gifted and talented individuals in Spain, Mexico, Taiwan, and Turkey. Finally, we compare findings from these cross-cultural studies of OE to OE data in a United States college student sample (Bouchet & Falk, 2001).

Study Characteristics

In the study by Pardo de Santayana Sanz (2006) in Spain, there were 204 students; 102 were in gifted programs, selected using high IQ scores, and 102 were non-gifted. The ages of students ranged from 8 to 15. The mean age for the gifted group was 11.05, and the mean for the non-gifted was 11.70. The gifted group was composed of 72% males and 28% females, while the non-gifted group had 49% males and 51% females. Combined, 60% were male and 40% female.

The Mexico study conducted by Rosa Aurora Chavez-Eakle (Chavez, 2004) included 90 subjects. Thirty were individuals who dedicated themselves to full-time artistic and/or scientific creativity, had received national and international awards in their fields, and developed successful careers; 30 were control individuals who were not devoted to activities in these fields. The remaining 30 were psychiatric outpatients without pharmacological treatment at the time of the study. All of the subjects were adults: 46% male and 54% female.

In Taiwan, Hsin-Jen Chang (2001) sampled elementary, middle, and high school students. Her study was composed of two separate samples totaling 2,997 students. Chang included a "norm sample" (n = 2,046) and a gifted and talented sample (n = 951). Students from fifth, eighth, and eleventh grades formed the norm sample, and these students were selected from across Taiwan. Students in the gifted and talented sample came from the same grades, but they were in gifted programs from the Taipei area. The norm sample had a mean age of 12.8 years, with 51% males and 49% females. In the gifted and talented sample, there were 35% males and 65% females. Combined, 45% were male and 55% female.

In Turkey, 500 tenth-grade students formed the sample of the study by Buket Yakmaci-Guzel (2002; 2003). These students were selected from 15 schools and 27 classes in Istanbul. Seven different school types were represented in the sample, including public, private, vocational, science, minority, and foreign private high schools. The number of students chosen from each school type is proportional to the distribution of students in Istanbul. Ages of students ranged between 15 and 20, with a mean of 16.8 years. Males represented 39% of the sample and females 61%.

There are interesting differences among these studies. There are three different languages, four cultures, the age of subjects range from eight to adult, and there are four individual investigators. In addition, it is important to recognize that two of the languages are not part of the Indo-European family: Turkish is among the Altaic family, and Chinese is one of the Mandarin languages. Despite these differences, remarkably similar results were found, as will be shown below.

Table 10.1: Study Characteristics: Comparisons of OEs across Four Cultures

Study	N	Mean Age	% Males	% Females
Spain	204	11.37	60	40
Mexico	90	Adults	46	54
Taiwan	2997	12.80	45	55
Turkey	500	16.80	39	61

Reliability of OE Factors

The four cross-cultural studies reported an acceptable level of internal consistency for items within each factor of OE items. The Cronbach alpha reliability coefficients were consistently high, ranging from .70 to .83 for Spain, .80 to .91 for Mexico, .71 to .81 for Taiwan, and .73 to .77 for Turkey. The overall reliability across studies is .80, a more-than-adequate level for scale items of this type.

Table 10.2: Reliability of OE Factors across Four Cultures

Study	Psychomotor	Sensual	Imaginational	Intellectual	Emotional
Spain	.83	.82	.82	.81	.70
Mexico	.81	.89	.87	.91	.80
Taiwan	.75	.71	.81	.81	.77
Turkey	.77	.74	.73	.74	.73

Translation of the OEQ-II

In Spain, translation was carried out by consulting the original version of the OEQ-II and the version developed for use in Mexico. The Spanish translation had been designed to reflect the cultural and linguistic differences between Spain and Mexico. After creating the Spanish version, a pilot study was carried out with children from 6 to 9 years old to determine the minimal age necessary to understand OEQ-II items. Some changes were made to adapt the language to these ages, and a new form of presentation was proposed because it was easier for young children. The final version was back-translated into English in order to assure equivalence to the original U. S. version.

In Mexico, the OEQ-II was converted from the English version by literal translation. To assess clarity of items, the resulting Spanish version was tested on 10 subjects. Subjects testing the new version were encouraged to comment if they found any phrases confusing or unclear, and they were asked for further clarification when they felt there was ambiguity. After this process, it was decided to use synonyms that were easy to understand in Mexican culture, while avoiding the use of slang words or phrases. Subjects were then asked to compare the meaning of the literal version with the cultural adaptation. The purpose was to determine whether the second version was clearer than the first, while maintaining the original meaning. After this process was completed, the OEQ-II items were deemed instantly recognizable and ready for use with the subjects in this study.

The direct translation in Taiwan was deemed inappropriate for Eastern culture students. Therefore, instead of using the OEQ-II translation, a new scale ("The Me Scale") was developed according to Dabrowski's theory. This study, therefore, is somewhat different from the others, because a different questionnaire was created. The original version of the new questionnaire contained 91 items; five items in each OE factor were reverse scored. For the first pilot study, the new questionnaire was administered to 120 fifth, eighth, and eleventh graders in regular classes. After that, 75 items were reserved, in which five items were reverse scored in each OE factor. This questionnaire was translated into English and sent by e-mail to nine experts who were familiar with Dabrowski's theory, gifted education, statistics, or methodology. After these experts evaluated the 75 items, 66 items were reserved, with only one item reverse scored per OE. Following this procedure, the second pilot test was administered to 220 fifth, eighth, and eleventh graders in other regular classes. After this second pilot study, six items were deleted. The final version of "The Me Scale" contained 60 items, in which 12 items were included for each OE subscale, there were no reverse scored items, and each item was scored from 1 to 7.

Translation of the OEQ-II into Turkish was made first by the researcher and then by five more bilingual individuals independently. Two of these five translators were familiar with Dabrowski's theory and the concept of OEs. Then these translations were put together, examined, and discussed by the researcher and the two translators who were familiar with the theory. Using Turkish language, grammar, and sentence structure, some changes were made, and the final *OEQ-II Turkish Form* was ready to use.

In summary, the Mexican and Turkish versions were both direct adaptations of the original English version for use with adults. The Spanish version was created by altering the Mexican translation for cultural and linguistic variation and then was further refined for younger subjects. In

Taiwan, the attempt at direct translation of the English version into Chinese was deemed ineffective. A new version called "The Me Scale" was developed in Chinese and then translated into English for evaluation. The items were scored for theoretical relevance by a panel of experts familiar with Dabrowski's theory or gifted education. With the exception of the Taiwan study, all versions had 50 items, and each item was scored on a scale of 1 to 5.

Descriptive Statistics

Table 10.3 presents the means and standard deviations for OEs in the studies in Spain, Mexico, Taiwan, and Turkey. The original means from Taiwan were reported in units summed across 12 items, with a range of 1 to 7 for each item. In an attempt to create scores comparable to those in the other studies, means were divided by 12 and multiplied by 5/7 or .71. However, this is an adjustment only, and scores should not be considered totally equivalent.

Table 10.3: Descriptive Statistics: Comparisons of OEs across Four Cultures

OEs	Means		Standard Deviations
Spain			
P-OE	3.41		0.82
S-OE	3.42		0.71
M-OE	3.10		0.81
T-OE	3.61		0.67
E-OE	3.45		0.60
Mexico			
P-OE	3.25		0.75
S-OE	3.71		0.85
M-OE	2.52		0.89
T-OE	3.48		0.80
E-OE	2.87		0.73
Turkey			
P-OE	3.57		0.67
S-OE	3.52		0.65
M-OE	2.90		0.70
T-OE	3.53		0.61
E-OE	3.62		0.66

OEs Taiwan	Adjusted Means	Means	Standard Deviations
P-OE	2.76	46.44	11.46
S-OE	2.83	47.55	11.45
M-OE	2.78	46.77	13.73
T-OE	2.83	47.59	12.29
E-OE	2.97	49.96	11.95

In Figure 10.1, the OE means for studies conducted in Spain, Mexico, Turkey, and the United States (Bouchet & Falk, 2001, described below) are shown. Since these studies used the same metric, it is easier to make comparisons. In general, imaginational OE appears to be the lowest of the five. Sensual and intellectual OE are approximately equal in the four studies. Psychomotor OE and emotional OE are higher than sensual and intellectual OE in the Turkish and United States studies, but both are lower in the Mexico study. The Spanish study is lower on emotional OE and higher on psychomotor OE than sensual and intellectual OE. As a caution, do not be misled by the scale of the figure that only shows units ranging from 2.5 to 3.75; differences in the means in these studies are small. All mean differences are less than 1 point.

Figure 10.1. OE Means for Spain, Mexico, Turkey, and the U.S.

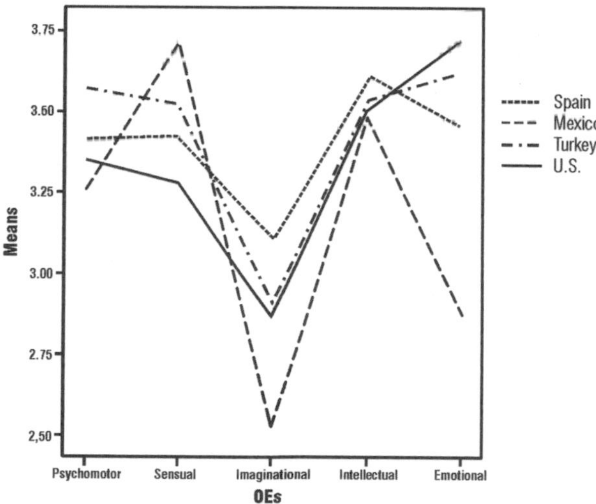

In Figure 10.2, we add the adjusted means for the Taiwan study. The most obvious observation is the small amount of variation among the Taiwan OE means. By contrast, the means from the Mexico study have a large amount of variation. Although the variance is smaller among the Taiwan means, imaginational OE is one of the two lowest means, while sensual and intellectual OE means are approximately equal.

Figure 10.2. OE Means for Spain, Mexico, Turkey, and the U.S. with Adjusted Taiwan Means

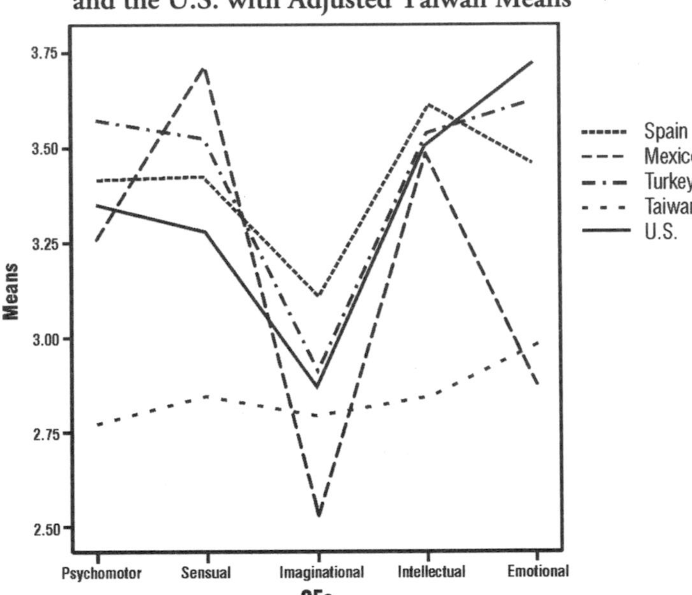

In summary, the emotional OE mean, relative to other means within a study, is highest in Taiwan, Turkey, and the United States. By comparison, intellectual OE is highest in the Spanish study, and sensual OE is highest in the Mexico study. To understand why these differences occur, other sample characteristics must be considered. For example, in the study from Spain, half (102) of the subjects were gifted children, and giftedness in Spain is defined solely by high IQ scores, whereas in other countries, additional information is frequently considered. The Mexican sample included psychiatric outpatients, and we do not know what influence that might have. The Turkish sample included seven different types of high school students.

In Figure 10.3, we calculate a harmonic mean, an average that proportionally weights by sample size, for the four non-United States studies. Because the Taiwan study represents 79% of all of the cases, its influence is substantial. The pattern between these two OE mean graph lines in Figure 10.3 is remarkably similar. The only exception is for psychomotor OE, which has a declining slope for the combined sample and an increasing slope for the United States sample. Again, because of the narrow scale (2.8-3.8), differences are negligible. An earlier study comparing Venezuelan and American artists had similar findings—Venezuelans scored lower on psychomotor OE than Americans (Falk et al., 1997). These findings with regard to higher psychomotor scores for United States subjects may say more about the atypical American culture with its penchant for fast-paced activity than about other cultures.

Figure 10.3. Harmonic Mean for Combined Cross-Cultural Studies and the U.S. Study

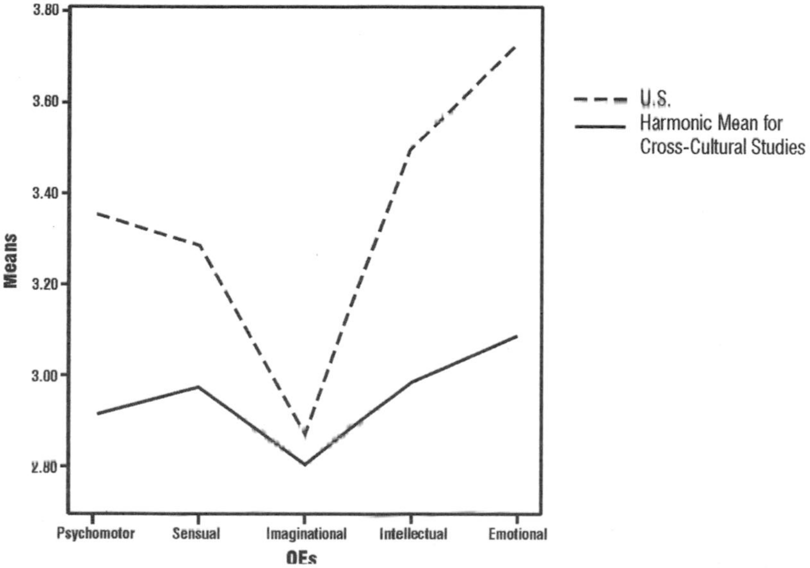

Empirical Findings

Gender Comparisons

In Spain, girls scored significantly higher in emotional OE [$t\ (202) = -3.516$, $p < .001$] and sensual OE [$t\ (202) = -4.824$, $p < .001$] than boys in the total sample. The same held true for the gifted group, with girls higher in emotional OE [$t\ (100) = -3.87$, $p < .005$] and sensual OE [$t\ (100) = -3.628$, $p < .001$]. However, in the non-gifted group, girls were higher only in sensual OE [$t\ (100) = -3.28$, $p < .05$], while boys were higher in psychomotor OE [$t\ (100) = 2.92$, $p < .05$].

In Mexico, the single significant finding with regard to gender differences was that males were significantly higher in psychomotor OE

($z = 2.82$, $p = .004$ Wilcoxon test) than females. The same result was true in Taiwan in the gifted and talented sample; males were found to have significantly higher psychomotor OE ($F = 22.06$, $p < .05$) than females. Gifted and talented females in Taiwan exhibited higher emotional OE ($F = 18.31$, $p < .05$) and higher sensual OE ($F = 3.52$, $p < 0.05$) than males. In Turkey, gender comparisons were not reported.

Intellectual Ability Comparisons

In Spain, the gifted group was significantly higher on intellectual OE [$t(202) = 4.533$, $p < .001$] and imaginational OE [$t(202) = 2.188$, $p < .05$] scores than the non-gifted group. In one area, the non-gifted group was superior: psychomotor OE for the non-gifted group exceeded that of the gifted group [$t(202) = -3.182$, $p < .005$].

Significant differences were found in the Mexico study between three groups for sensual OE ($F = 1\ 1.52$, $p = .0001$), intellectual OE ($F = 16.60$, $p = .0001$), and imaginational OE ($F = 5.56$, $p = .005$). When post-hoc tests were done, it was found that the artistic and scientifically creative group was higher than the other two groups in these areas of OE.

Gifted and talented students in Taiwan were separated for intellectual ability analysis, resulting in three groups: gifted, talented, and a norm sample. Findings indicated that gifted students had higher intellectual OE ($F = 14.44$, $p < .05$) than talented or non-gifted students. Both gifted and talented students displayed higher sensual OE ($F = 63.91$, $p < .001$), intellectual OE ($F = 208.90$, $p < .001$), imaginational OE ($F = 117.34$, $p < .01$), and emotional OE ($F = 18.74$, $p < .001$) than the norm sample.

In the Turkey study, the Raven Advanced Progressive Matrices Test was administered to 500 students. According to the Turkish norms for grade level, students were classified as "above average," "average," and "below average" according to their scores on this test. Findings show that intellectual OE scores of the "above average" group were significantly higher ($F = 9.699$, $p < 0.001$) than the other two groups.

Cross-Cultural Summary

In the three studies reporting gender comparisons (Spain, Mexico, and Taiwan), males scored higher on psychomotor OE than females in at least one group—i.e., gifted, non-gifted, or total sample. Females scored higher on emotional OE in two studies: Spain and Taiwan. In Spain, girls also exhibited higher emotional OE scores in the gifted group, as well as in the total sample; in Taiwan, girls in the gifted and talented groups scored higher on emotional OE than boys. Again, in Spain and Taiwan, girls showed higher sensual OE scores when compared to boys. This finding applied to gifted girls in Spain and in Taiwan to girls in the non-gifted group.

In the cross-cultural studies, gifted groups, including artistic and/or creative persons and above-average students, scored higher on intellectual OE than talented or non-gifted populations. In addition, gifted, talented, and creative persons scored higher than non-gifted populations on imaginational OE. In Mexico, creative subjects had higher sensual OE scores than their non-creative comparison groups; in Taiwan, the gifted and talented groups scored higher on sensual and emotional OE. In only one study (Taiwan) did non-gifted subjects exhibit higher OE scores than their comparison groups; non-gifted students outscored gifted and talented students in psychomotor OE.

Comparisons to the United States Sample

In the United States, a sample of 562 college students was analyzed for gender and intellectual ability differences in OE. Multivariate analysis of variance (MANOVA) [overall $F (5, 540) = 35.74$, $p < .001$] found that males scored higher on psychomotor OE ($p = .01$), intellectual OE ($p = .00$), and imaginational OE ($p = .00$), while females scored higher on emotional OE ($p = .00$) and sensual OE ($p = .05$). These findings were similar to those of the cross-cultural studies, with males scoring higher on psychomotor OE and females scoring higher on emotional and sensual OE. Unlike the other studies, males' intellectual and imaginational OE scores were also higher than those for females.

In a three group comparison of gifted and talented students, Advanced Placement students, and non-gifted students [overall $F [10, 1080) = 3.95$, $p < .001$], college students who had been identified as gifted or talented scored higher on intellectual OE ($p = .00$) and emotional OE ($p = .00$) than those in the Advanced Placement or non-gifted groups (Bouchet & Falk, 2001). This is consistent with findings from the cross-cultural studies in which gifted, creative, and above-average students had high intellectual OE in comparison to talented and non-gifted groups. However, findings regarding imaginational, sensual, and psychomotor OE in some cross-cultural study comparisons were not present in the United States study.

Future Research and Conclusion

Studies such as these raise questions for future researchers. Currently, we do not know the exact score on the OEQ-II (or its translations) that establishes an individual's score as OE. Establishing baseline norms, and perhaps baseline norms for different age groups, is an important next step. The Taiwan norm sample of fifth, eighth, and eleventh graders may provide such a beginning. However, this report does not separate the norm group from the gifted and talented group. Nonetheless, it appears that scores above 2.75 may represent such a baseline. Future research that makes the baseline norms more exact is needed.

Studies such as the ones reported here give us confidence that OE is associated with giftedness. However, measurement continues to require improvement. One recent development in measurement is the English version of the OEQ-II for younger age children. Testing of this inventory, the OEQ2-c, is currently in progress (Daniels et al., in preparation). Early results indicate a reliable instrument that can identify all five OEs in children ages 9 to 13.

Future research should explore variables associated with OE. Currently, two co-authors are pursuing research that examines relationships between neuropsychological variables and OE. Hsin-Jen Chang and her colleagues in Taipei are studying the brain structure along with the neuropsychological and OE measurement of talented students (H. Chang, personal communication, January 8, 2007). Chavez-Eakle is in the final stage of a research project at the National Institute of Psychiatry in Mexico City evaluating the association between molecular variations in the genes coding for the neurotransmitters serotonin and dopamine and the OEs in highly creative individuals (R. A. Chavez-Eakle, personal communication, March 20, 2007). Bold and creative investigations such as these that go beyond current conceptions hold the promise of new insights into OE and its consequence for gifted and talented individuals.

Despite the differences in language, culture, age of subjects, and individual investigator in the studies presented here, the existence of OE is evident in the data. Further, stereotypic socialization to gender roles is present in the expression of OE in questionnaire responses. Gender stereotypes were found to be indeed cross-cultural, extending across diverse populations and resulting in universal gendered responses. Perhaps the understanding of OE responses will shed light on how individuals react to the external environment.

More important for the field of education, we find that OE is able to differentiate gifted from non-gifted populations. One implication of this finding is that in the future, educators may include the OEQ-II as a significant piece of information in their battery of signs of giftedness.

Whether these findings inform us with regard to the theoretical construct of developmental potential is still in question and awaits further research. There is little evidence to date that OE leads to multilevel development through positive disintegration; however, OE has been shown to predict developmental level (Lysy & Piechowski, 1983; Miller et al., 1994). The important news from this replication study is that Dabrowski's theory exhibits cross-cultural relevance and therefore appears to have cross-cultural validity for the concept of OE. This finding holds true irrespective of both culture and language. The fruitful concepts within the complex theory of positive disintegration continue to draw our attention to the intensities of the emotional world and emotional intelligence. This is a crucial area in understanding social and moral development that is only now receiving the attention it deserves.

Part III

TPD in Perspective

Chapter 11

Personality Disintegration and Reintegration in Mystical Lives

Laurence F. Nixon, Ph.D.[1]

When I first encountered the theory of positive disintegration, I was struck by the fact that the stages articulated closely fit the process of mystical development as described by scholars of mysticism, the authors of mystical manuals, and the autobiographical writings of mystics themselves. My interest was further aroused by the fact that the author of the theory provided not only a systematic description of the underlying personality structures at each stage of development, including the connections between the structures at different levels, but also further identified a set of causes for the growth process—developmental potential and external frustration combined with some measure of environmental support. Subsequently, I applied the theory to a review of empirical studies of meditation in an M.A. thesis (Nixon, 1983) and then in a doctoral dissertation (Nixon, 1990). I made use of the theory in an analysis of the beginning stage of mystical development, which I referred to as the mystical struggle. Along the way, I was greatly helped and encouraged by participation in a graduate seminar on the theory of positive disintegration conducted by Andrew Kawczak, as well as by my study of the prodigious body of research undertaken by Michael Piechowski.

---

1 Laurence F. Nixon, Ph.D., Chair, Religion Department, Dawson College, Montreal, Quebec, Canada.

In this chapter, I want to demonstrate the value of the theory of positive disintegration for the study of the lives of religious mystics as given in their autobiographical writings. Elsewhere (Nixon, 1989; 1990; 1994a; 1994b; 1995a; 2000), I have argued that the stages of personality as described in the theory of positive disintegration are found in the lives of mystics, but here I particularly want to focus on some of the factors, temperamental and environmental, that orient an individual toward a mystical vocation—predisposing factors in the form of developmental potential (specifically the overexcitabilities), external frustration, and a supportive environment. And finally, I want to refer to some of the means (e.g., mystical reading, journal keeping, meditation, and asceticism) identified by Dabrowski and reported in mystical autobiographies that are used in the process of organized multilevel disintegration. What follows from these correspondences is a better understanding of mystical lives, and at same time, a better understanding of the theory of positive disintegration itself. I will begin by providing examples of psychic overexcitability in selected mystical autobiographies.

Emotional Overexcitability

Of the five forms of overexcitability, the most important, in terms of developmental potential, are emotional, imaginational, and intellectual. I will restrict my examples of overexcitability in mystical lives to these three forms, and I will begin with some examples of emotional overexcitability, along with a few words of caution about naively taking the descriptions found in autobiographies at face value. For example, evidence of emotional hypersensitivity can be found in *The Revelations* of a 14th-century German nun and mystic Margaret Ebner (1291-1351). She says of herself:

> *I withdrew from all people. I did not want to endure conversation or visits from anyone, except my sisters [i.e., fellow nuns]. I did not like to hear any speech, except about God. It was so totally unbearable to me when gossip or even harsh words were uttered in my presence that I often began to cry.* (Ebner, 1993, p. 86)

Of course, one has to take great care in assessing such passages. Autobiographies are to some considerable extent autohagiographies, and one frequently finds within them statements meant to establish the sanctity, or potential sanctity, of the author. The above passage certainly does that. Furthermore, the report that the subject found ordinary worldly conversation distasteful is one of the many standard tropes found in hagiographical writing. This does not, of course, mean that Ebner did not in fact dislike such conversation, but simply that additional confirmatory evidence is desirable. If the aversion to gossip and the attraction to conversation about God is a standard trope, the emotional reaction of crying that Ebner describes is not. Further support for the presence of emotional overexcitability in Ebner's life is provided by the fact that she is consistent in her descriptions of her responses to behavior she finds not to her liking.

> *When I heard someone was angry with our serving girls and had said to them, "You are not worthy to serve us," heartfelt sorrow overcame me so that I cried and thought, "God has never said that I was unworthy to serve Him." I could not bear the slaughtering of the cattle and when I saw that they were being slaughtered I began to cry and thought that God had never slaughtered me because of my misdeeds. I had compassion for all things and true compassion for everyone whom I saw suffering, no matter what kind of suffering it was.* (p. 90)

Here, Ebner describes the same reaction of crying, and in addition, in this passage, we get to see something of her unique inner life and just how emotionally sensitive she was.

A second example of a mystic who showed signs of emotional overexcitability is the Hindu Swami Paramahansa Yogananda (1893-1952). There are many passages that speak of a turbulent emotional life, such as the following:

> *I still remember the helpless humiliation of infancy. I was resentfully conscious of being unable to walk and to express myself freely. Prayerful urges arose within me as I realized my bodily impotence. My strong emotional life was mentally expressed in words of many languages.* (Yogananda, 1973, p. 3)

Perhaps Yogananda was able to accurately remember the nature and intensity of his emotional life as a pre-verbal infant (who could nevertheless think in "many languages"), but the critical reader has to be excused for entertaining a certain measure of doubt. On the other hand, there are other passages in which Yogananda recalls his adult emotional reactions, which are less suspicious.

> *My own temperament is principally devotional. It was disconcerting at first to find that my* guru, *saturated with* jnana *[spiritual philosophy] but seemingly dry of* bhakti *[devotion], expressed himself chiefly in terms of cold spiritual mathematics.* (p. 145)

When it comes to commenting on his spiritual teachers, one would expect Yogananda to have a predisposition toward seeing their good side, so when he reveals that he is of an emotional temperament in the context of an unflattering remark about his guru, his revelation about his emotional temperament carries more weight.

In the case of a 20th-century mystic like Yogananda, we have sources other than the autobiography. One of these is an account of his life written by Sananda Lal Ghosh, a brother who was particularly close to Yogananda. In his biography, Ghosh (1980, pp. 27-29) describes an incident in which Yogananda as a small child had an extraordinarily strong emotional reaction to the death of a pet goldfish; he sobbed inconsolably for an entire day. While the incident tells us about Yoganada's emotional sensitivity, it does not serve any hagiographical purpose. In fact, if anything, it does the opposite, since Ghosh also includes in his account the fact that the child Yogananda grabbed the family servant, who had accidentally killed the fish, and shook him, crying, "Why have you killed my goldfish? Why?" Then, in order to comfort his son, Yogananda's father fired the servant! There is in such a story no intimation of future sanctity, and tellingly, the story is not related in Yoganada's own account of his life. Hence, it is a relatively credible bit of evidence for the presence of emotional overexcitability.

Space does not permit a detailed and comprehensive articulation of a set of criteria for critical assessment of mystical autobiographies. Therefore, the few examples cited above will have to suffice as illustrations of the kind of caution required.

Imaginational Overexcitability

A number of passages indicating imaginational overexcitability can be found in the spiritual autobiography of the 19th-century French nun Thérèse of Lisieux (1873-1897). She explains that she has a good visual memory: "God granted me the favor…at an early age…of imprinting childhood recollections so deeply on my memory that it seems the things I'm about to recount happened only yesterday" (Lisieux, 1976, pp. 16-17). Another way in which imaginational overexcitability manifested itself was the penchant Thérèse had for making up fanciful stories.

> *[As a child] I loved, too, to tell stories I made up as they came into my mind, and my companions gathered around me eagerly.... The same story lasted for days, for I liked to make it more and more interesting when I saw the impressions it produced and which were evident on my companions' faces.* (p. 81)

Thérèse further reports a tendency as a child to become engrossed in reading material, which led to a state of absorption.

> *...I haven't spoken about my love of pictures and reading.... I owe to the beautiful pictures you* [Thérèse's autobiography is addressed to her sister, Pauline, who was at the time also the mother superior at her convent] *gave me as rewards, one of the sweetest joys and strongest impressions which aided me in the practice of virtue. I was forgetting to say anything about the hours I spent looking at them. The* little flower *of the Divine Prisoner, for example, said so many things to me that I became deeply recollected.* (p. 71)

From this quotation, we see that a capacity for imaginational overexcitability predisposed Thérèse toward an involvement in spiritual reading and meditation—both of which are means used by mystics in their psycho-spiritual development.

A 20th-century Zen Buddhist nun, Satomi Myodo (1896-1978), provides evidence of both visual and aural imaginational overexcitability in her description of her reaction to the separation from her husband.

> *My first hallucination occurred right after the children's father left me.... I had finished a section of the work [in the fields] and was rather tired, so I sat down on a pile of chaff between the fields. In an instant, before I knew what hit me, I fell into a trance.... [S]uddenly, from out of nowhere, I heard a grave voice calling out my name, "Matsuno! Matsuno!" I blinked my eyes open and again heard the voice, saying, "Look over there!" I peered over suspiciously, and...how strange! A moment a field of plain dirt had been there, but now the field was bursting with peas in full bloom. I looked more closely and...what?! The pea field was crawling with green caterpillars.... "The human world is decimated like this too!" This was simultaneously the message of the voice and my own intuition. Then pop! In an instant, the pea field vanished and the place became a dense forest.* (Myodo, 1987, pp. 13-14)

The loss of her husband and subsequently her children eventually resulted in a period of mental illness for Satomi, and we can see an indication of this in the passage below. At the same time, however, she also had an intimation of a transcendental ideal that later took the shape of her personality ideal.

> *...starting from the time my husband left and lasting for about two years, my mental condition was in a very strange spiritual stage. Was it some kind of bizarre mysticism? Was it lunacy? Often, while remaining in this same body, I leaped over the world of humanity and ascended to the distant world of beginningless eternity. There I was completely enfolded in the heart of God. I lost my form and became one with God, the solitary light, which peacefully, truly peacefully, shone out all around. It was indescribable, blissful fulfilment. This condition progressed until I stumbled into the world of absolute nothingness and lapsed into unconsciousness. From this state, I again advanced until hallucinations began to appear.* (pp. 11-12)

The examples of imaginational overexcitability cited above are ones which either developed into dynamisms or practices characteristic of organized multilevel disintegration. But both emotional and imaginational overexcitability play a role in the emergence of the dynamisms of spontaneous multilevel disintegration, as can be seen in the following account of the imaginational (and emotional) overexcitability of the famous Rinzai Zen master Hakuin Ekaku (1686-1769). As a child, Hakuin reacted to a sermon he heard in a way that reveals the presence of imaginational overexcitability.

> *When I was seven or eight years old, my mother took me to a temple for the first time and we listened to a sermon on the hells.... Returning home, I took stock of the deeds of my short life and felt that there was but little hope for me. I did not know which way to turn and I was gooseflesh all over. In secret, I took up a chapter on Kannon from the* Lotus Sutra *and the* dharani *on Great Compassion and recited them day and night.*
>
> *One day when I was taking a bath with my mother, she asked that the water be made hotter and had the maid add wood to the fire. Gradually my skin began to prickle with the heat and the iron caldron began to rumble. Suddenly I recalled the descriptions of the hells that I had heard, and I let out a cry of terror that resounded through the neighborhood.*

> *From this time on, I determined to myself that I would leave home to become a monk....* (Hakuin, 1971, pp. 115-116)

As a result of hearing the sermon on the hells, the dynamism of disquietude with oneself emerged ("I took stock of the deeds of my short life and felt that there was but little hope for me"). The dynamism was further intensified in his bathtub experience, leading to a resolve to become a Buddhist monk. At age 15, Hakuin did leave home to become a monk, eventually passing beyond the stage of spontaneous multilevel disintegration to a more advanced level of personality.

Intellectual Overexcitability

In the autobiographies of mystics, intellectual overexcitability expresses itself in various ways (see Nixon, 1999), but a frequent form is a quest for meaning, the attempt to satisfy which takes the form of spiritual or philosophical reading, seeking out a spiritual guide, and/or meditation. A 20th-century non-denominational Christian mystic, Irina Starr, reports reading about philosophy and religion from an early age to satisfy her intellectual curiosity.

> *It seemed that there was never a time when I was not reading, and for quite some time before this (perhaps a couple of years) I had been reading whatever came to hand, but I was most interested in the books on philosophy, religion and various esoteric subjects which I found on my mother's bookshelves.* (Starr, 1991, pp. 5-6)

A Hindu yogi, Ram Chandra (1899-1983), similarly relates that:

> *From the age of nine, I felt a kind of thirst for Reality and I remained confused and perplexed just like a man drowned in water. I then started reading the* Bhagavad Gita, *but it did not bring to my view the condition I was craving for.... Sometime later, I became interested in philosophy and began to think out the problems in my own way. It was at the age of 15 or 16 that I wanted to read philosophical books.* (Ram Chandra, 1980/1974, pp. 3-4)

At an early age, intellectual overexcitability manifested itself as a metaphysical search for understanding "Reality," as Ram Chandra puts it, and he attempted to satisfy this cognitive need by reading one of the great classics of Hindu spirituality, the *Bhagavad Gita*. As an adolescent, he read philosophical texts, and then as an adult, he found a guru whose teaching and practical instructions guided him into a process of spiritual development.

In the case of D. T. Suzuki (1870-1966), the well-known scholar and practitioner of Zen Buddhism, a search for meaning was prompted by a combination of both intellectual overexcitability and the loss of his father when he was six years old. Suzuki began to question why such a fate should befall him.

> *To lose one's father in those days was perhaps an even greater loss than it is now, for so much depended on him...such as education and finding a position in life afterwards. All this I lost, and by the time I was seventeen or eighteen those misfortunes made me start thinking about my karma. Why should I have these disadvantages at the very start of life?My thoughts then started to turn to philosophy and religion, and as my family belonged to the Rinzai sect of Zen it was natural that I should look to Zen for some of the answers to my problems. I remember going to the Rinzai temple where my family was registered—it was the smallest Rinzai temple in Kanazawa—and asking the priest there about Zen. Like many Zen priests in country temples in those days, he did not know very much....*
>
> *I often used to discuss questions of philosophy and religion with the other students of my own age, and I remember that something which always puzzled me was what makes it rain?...*
>
> *About that time, a new teacher came to my school. He taught mathematics....But he was also interested in Zen....He did his best to make his students interested in Zen, too, and distributed printed copies of Hakuin Zenshi's work* Orategama *[letters written by the Zen master Hakuin to his disciples]....I could not understand much of it, but somehow it interested me so much that in order to find out more about it I decided to visit a Zen master....* (Suzuki, 1986, pp. 3-5*)*

Suzuki's response, a manifestation of intellectual overexcitability, to the loss of his father was to search for answers from what he felt should be an authority (a temple priest), and to engage in discussions with his peers. Eventually, he met a mystical mentor in the form of his mathematics teacher, who introduced him to the autobiographical writings of an exemplar, Hakuin. This, in turn, led to a further search and Suzuki's engaging in the practice of meditation.

Suzuki's intellectual curiosity resulted in his preoccupation with an unanswered question following his father's untimely death. Another example of intellectual overexcitability manifesting in an attempt to solve a spiritual enigma can be found in the autobiography of a 20th-century peace activist and mystic known throughout most of her adult life simply as Peace Pilgrim.

> *When I was a senior in high school, I began to make my search for God, but all my efforts were in an outward direction. I went about inquiring, "What is God? What is God?" I was most inquisitive and I asked many questions of many people, but I never received any answers! However, I was not about to give up. Intellectually I could not find God on the outside, so I tried another approach. I took a long walk with my dog and pondered deeply upon the question. Then I went to bed and slept over it. And in the morning, I had my answer from the inside, through a still small voice.* (Peace Pilgrim, 1991, pp. 1-2)

Peace Pilgrim's way of solving her enigma was to engage in a process of reflective meditation in a nature setting. The result was series of insights that led her to surrender her life to a higher purpose, which surrender went hand in hand with the development of her own personality.

The Role of Negative Environmental Conditions, Especially Loss

While developmental potential, including and especially psychic overexcitability, is necessary for positive inner psychic transformation, Dabrowski held that in most cases, certain environmental factors also need to be present. Most people will accept intuitively that some sort of environmental support would be an asset, but most would not necessarily see a role for negative environmental circumstances. However, the theory of positive disintegration, as its name implies, is a theory characterized by paradox. Personality disintegration can be positive, social maladjustment can be positive, and psychoneurosis can be seen as not an illness. In the same way, negative environmental conditions can also be seen as growth-promoting occasions. Dabrowski's way of putting it is as follows:

> *The author wishes to emphasize that, in his opinion, such [psychic] transformations cannot take place when there is complete*

> *security, and when all basic needs have been satisfied. For the development of higher needs and higher emotions, it is necessary to have partial frustrations, some inner conflicts, some deficits in basic needs, some difficulties....*
>
> *It is also a necessity to have some sadness and grief, depressions, hesitations, loneliness, awareness of death and various other painful experiences which lead us to replace our bonds to what is common, sensual, easy [with]...that which is individual, exclusive, lasting, etc....*
>
> *This means that in the process of fulfilling basic needs, there should remain some dissatisfaction to make room for introducing conditions that would permit the realization of human authenticity, and under which appears and matures awareness of and sensitivity to the meaning of life, to existential, and even transcendental concerns, hierarchies of values, intuition, even contemplation.*
>
> *Unpleasant experiences, and particularly existential shock and anxiety assist the growth of sensitivity to other people and to one's own development. This does not mean that we can discount the possibility of a positive developmental impact of joyful moments, intense experiences of happiness, either past, present or anticipated.*
>
> *We lay special stress upon the creative role of "negative" experiences, because their developmental role is often overlooked and misunderstood.* (Dabrowski, 1970, pp. 35-36)

Dabrowski's statement that personality development cannot take place "when all basic needs have been satisfied," is a reference to Abraham Maslow (1971), who took exactly the opposite position. For Dabrowski, negative life events and frustrations were occasions for growth, and persons who possess psychic overexcitability are the ones who can best take advantage of negative environmental conditions in general and the experience of loss in particular.

> *A normal person on the death of even an intimate friend or relative usually suffers a slight shock, which does not leave deeper impressions. Not so with psychasthenics or neurasthenics, who are inclined to exaggerated self-analysis, phobias, and depression, "striving for ideals and homesick for eternity."* (Dabrowski, 1937, pp. 29-30)

Notice here that Dabrowski suggests that experiences of loss, in combination with psychic overexcitability, can give rise to both the self-critical dynamisms and ideals found in spontaneous multilevel disintegration.

Dabrowski's own studies of autobiographies and his clinical work led him to the view that wherever is found personality growth, so also is found sadness resulting from misfortunes and loss. In Dabrowski's view, "It is characteristic that states of sadness, and frequently states of depression, are encountered whenever we find psychological transformations, misfortune, failure, loss, and breakdown taking place..." (Dabrowski, Kawczak, & Sochanska, 1973, pp. 156-157). This is what one finds over and over again in the lives of mystics (Nixon, 1995b; 1998).

Reference to loss was made above in passages cited from the autobiographies of Satomi Myodo and Daisetz Suzuki. Another example of the type of reaction described by Dabrowski can be seen in the account of Tibetan Buddhist monk Chagdud Tulku Rinpoche (1930-2002). His mother had arranged for him to go on a long and intense meditation retreat when he was 11 years old. While on that retreat, his mother died. After attending the funeral, he returned to the retreat (and subsequently became a monk), in spite of the fact that his maternal uncle wanted to bring him into his home. Here is Chagdud's description of the effect on him of his mother's death:

> *About four months after I began retreat, a messenger arrived with news that altered my childhood completely. My mother's death stunned me. She was young, still in her early forties, and I had not even known she was ill....*
>
> *My mother's death powerfully reinforced for me how hopeless it is to grasp at what is impermanent. I had loved my mother and relied on her, as had my stepfather, my sister and many others, and her love and compassion for all of us were measureless. Yet these strong bonds had not prevented her from slipping from our grasp and dying. Even her wisdom realization, which transcended death, had not averted the loss of her body.*
>
> *My retreat had gotten off to an uncertain start in the first months, as I cheated on my prostrations, but when I returned to retreat after my mother's death, my practice became much more purposeful.* (Chagdud, 1992, pp. 49-54)

As a result of his mother's unanticipated death, Chagdud transferred his attention to higher-level values and found within himself the determination to follow them. Psychic overexcitability, in combination with various frustrations, disappointments, and traumatic events, gives rise to a spiritual crisis, or spiritual emergency, in a spiritual virtuoso. This crisis can easily be seen as a catalyst for the emergence of the dynamisms of spontaneous multilevel disintegration.

Mystical Crisis as an Expression of Spontaneous Multilevel Disintegration

At some point in the career of almost all mystics, there comes a global and sustained crisis of conscience, sometimes lasting for years. What characterizes the condition is a hierarchy of values and self-reproach for failing to live up to the highest value or values. It may be useful at this point to consider some examples. The first is that of the Ming dynasty sage-mystic Lin Zhaoen (1517-1598), whose spirituality is a combination of Taoism, Buddhism, and Neo-Confucianism. Lin was in the process of undertaking studies that were to lead him to a high-status government career, which he abandoned because of his multilevel crisis.

> *When I was studying for the examinations, I wrote two essays: "On Holding to the Mean," and "On the One Thread." At the time, everyone said that my writing captured the principles handed down from Yao, Shun, and Confucius. Delighted, I, too, thought I had grasped them. A year or two later, I suddenly realized that when I tried to embody what I had written in my actions, I did not understand what the words meant. They merely reflected the dregs of the ancients. It was not only that I was deceiving others with them; I was also deceiving myself. Bitterly reproaching myself, I abandoned examination studies and took up the Way of the sages and worthies, determined to seek the means to realize it in myself, obtain it in my mind, and manifest it in my actions. How could I dare to devote myself once more to reiterating mere words?* (Berling, 1980, pp. 63-64)

The second example of a multilevel crisis is that of a 14th-century Islamic mystic Sayyid Haydar Amuli (1319-1385), who gave up a prestigious and lucrative career in the service of the Iranian ruler Fakhr al-Dawlah in order to pursue a process of personal transformation as a Sufi.

> *I...came to take up duties in service [in the Iranian ruler's court]. It was not long before...I acquired such great position and wealth that it is impossible to imagine. In this way, I came to live a life of luxury, prosperity and honour amongst the people, my friends and my fellow townsfolk.*
>
> *I passed some time in this state until a desire for the truth, a desire both instinctive and natural, began to flare up within me and Allah made me aware of the evil and corruption growing in me as a result of my ignorance and forgetfulness of Him. It became clear to me that I was following a way of perversity far from the straight path; it became manifest to me that I was treading the path of misguidance, close to the precipice of sin and crime. It was at this moment that I prayed to the Lord from deep within myself; I implored him to free me from these actions of mine—all my passion and desire was to leave this world and its pleasures. I found within myself that I was ready to turn in the direction of the Real and to set out on the path of* tawhid *(divine unity).* (Amuli, 1989, pp. xviii-xix)

In the case of both men, we find a hierarchy of values (expressed in terms of their respective religious cultures) and, correspondingly, an overwhelming sense of dissatisfaction and self-criticism for not being faithful to what they believed to be the higher value.

Mystical Reading

The response of the potential mystic to a global and sustained multilevel crisis is to seek out an environment that will both stimulate and support the process of spiritual growth that he or she wishes to undertake. Among other things, such an environment exposes the aspirant to mystical writings, orally transmitted teaching, chastisement, encouragement, and counseling regarding various mystical practices. Practices undertaken by future mystics include spiritual reading, asceticism, and meditation. An example of spiritual reading is provided by the 20th-century Hindu Swami Ramdas (1884-1963), who states simply that, "Off and on, he was prompted by [the deity] Ram to read the teachings of Sri Krishna—the *Bhagavad Gita*; Buddha—*Light of Asia*; Jesus Christ—'New Testament;' Mahatma Gandhi—*Young India and Ethical Religion*" (Ramdas, 1994, p. 4). Out of modesty, in his autobiography, Swami Ramdas refers to himself in the third person. His selection of texts is clearly a modern eclectic one, but the point is that he found in these works inspiration for his project of spiritual development.

Most mystics mention spiritual texts that provided them with information, insight, motivation, and encouragement. Another example is Swami Purohit, who describes the positive effect of spiritual reading on him.

> *Thus, I became acquainted with the various schools of yoga. I read the* Geeta *regularly and began to understand it more and more. I read the Gur[u]-Charita, and it instilled into my heart the great principles of devotion. I read the lives of the saints, and these gave me an incentive to practical life [of spirituality].* (Purohit, 1992/1932, p. 31)

Purohit's contention that reading the lives of saints was a source of inspiration for him is consistent with Dabrowski's comment on lives of heroes in his discussion of aids to development in *Personality-Shaping through Positive Disintegration*: "At times a book presenting a story of a hero which, in its psychological and ideological aspects, makes the nuclear dynamism sensitive to the development of personality may be an important factor in stimulating this development" (1967, p. 150).

On the other hand, spiritual reading had its limits for Swami Purohit. At a certain point in his development, he felt that he had to abandon spiritual reading in order to engage in more transformative practices, such as meditation.

> *I wandered from place to place in search of light. I read many books on religion and yoga. At last one day a crisis came. I was reading the* Geeta, *the gospel of Lord Shrikrishna. "Passion, anger, and avarice are the three great enemies. Therefore kill them." Such precepts, though read every day, seemed useless. They must be realised. Study only made me more intellectual. My need was not for knowledge, but for wisdom. Learning could not give me control.... I threw away all the sacred books, including the* Geeta, *and sat down to contemplate and meditate on [the deity] Lord Dattatreya, with all the forces of my mind that I could command.* (Purohit, 1992/1932, pp. 46-47)

Note that in various other mystical traditions (e.g., Zen Buddhism) there are also references to mystical study having a limited role beyond a certain point.

Asceticism

Whatever might be the attitude toward study—whether it is seen as a temporary or a long-term aid to development—all mystical traditions encourage, and all mystics embrace, various forms of asceticism and meditation. One of the unique features of Dabrowski's approach to personality development is that he recognizes the therapeutic value of practices that were not fashionable in his time—such as meditation and, especially, asceticism. Everyone admires the ascetic rigor required to become a good musician, ballet dancer, figure skater, or baseball player. However, the idea that personality development might also require various forms of sacrifice or self-denial is not part of most theories of personality development. For Dabrowski, just as frustrations, insecurities, and losses can provoke a condition of spontaneous multilevel disintegration, self-initiated and self-controlled frustrations and deprivations are necessary in the process of organized multilevel disintegration and secondary integration.

> *In the world of cultural values, sacrifice plays a momentous role.... Suffering and even death may, as it were, give birth to higher values.... Hard experiences do not always dissolve psychic life, they often strengthen and improve it. Fasting, exercise in controlling oneself, and asceticism create resistance, strengthen one's moral vigilance, and increase one's readiness to enter a conscious struggle for the sake of principles one holds. Suffering, if we experience it correctly, makes us sensitive to the sufferings of others, awakens in us a new awareness, and creates a breach in our excessively egocentric attitude toward the surrounding world.* (Dabrowski, 1967, p. 30)

Elsewhere Dabrowski refers to asceticism as an instinct of partial death, and he explains that it plays a role in eliminating lower-level personality structures.

> *As a factor in development, we observe the activity of an instinct of* partial death. *It is a conscious and deliberate program of eradication of the lower personality structures. In order to accomplish this, the disintegrative activity of some dynamisms (for example, the rejection aspect of the third factor, the critical aspect of subject-object in oneself, or the containing aspect of self-control) may be increased in order to destroy the residual structures of primitive levels of the inner psychic milieu. This can take the form of*

asceticism, of resignation from personal ambitions for the sake of serving others, or deliberate and voluntary frustration of one's basic needs. (Dabrowski & Piechowski, 1977, pp. 172-173)

Of course, it should be mentioned that Dabrowski was well familiar with mystical lives, and he even included in *Personality-Shaping thorough Positive Disintegration* an analysis of at least one such life—that of St. Augustine of Hippo; and so it is no surprise that there are a number of correspondences between his theory and models of mystical development, including the place that both have for asceticism. What Dabrowski adds to the discussion of asceticism is an explanation in terms of developmental dynamisms, and he identifies specific developmental functions of asceticism. Mystical autobiographies frequently refer to very rigorous ascetical practices, but perhaps here it is enough to cite an example of somewhat moderate asceticism in a mystical life. It is taken from the autobiography of 20th-century lay Hindu Gopi Krishna (1903-1984).

...I made it a point to assert my will in all things, beginning with smaller ones and gradually extending its application to bigger and more difficult issues, forcing myself as a penance to do irksome and rigorous tasks, against which my ease-loving nature recoiled in dismay, until I began to feel a sense of mastery over myself, a growing conviction that I would not again fall an easy prey to ordinary temptations. (Krishna, 1993, p. 82)

This passage provides a good illustration of the beginning of the dynamism of self-control. Gopi Krishna here provides an explicit description of the mystical practice of the internalization of frustration and painful experiences that, as Dabrowski indicated, are necessary for development. By internalization, Gopi Krishna gained control over his temptations and thereby took control of his personality development.

Meditation

Although he never wrote about meditation in a sustained and comprehensive way, Dabrowski made numerous references to the practice, and when these are systematically organized, what emerges is a model of the functions that meditation can serve at the different levels of personality (see Nixon, 1996a). Here I will briefly mention the role of meditation at the level of spontaneous multilevel disintegration and organized multilevel disintegration. In his discussion of solitude at Level III, Dabrowski says that, "increasing need for reflection, meditation and contemplation augments the need for solitude as a necessary condition of developing the dynamisms of multilevel disintegration" (1996a, p. 116). And in his comments on success, he says that at Level III, there is a:

> *...gradual turning away from external forms of success. [There is a t]ransfer of weight toward moral, altruistic, and creative success. "Lower" forms of success are renounced for the sake of "higher" ones. Sometimes there is a spasmodic elimination of lower kind of success as in trying to achieve the ideal by force. This can be seen in dramatic initial forms of generosity and self-sacrifice. At times, this takes the greater form of asceticism and renunciation of worldly life. The meaning of success is developed in meditation and contemplation.* (1996a, p. 93)

These remarks describe very well the experience that the Hindu Swami Purohit recorded in his autobiography.

> *I practiced the yogic postures, and took a few lessons in meditation. I always slept on a grass mat without a pillow, had my two or three baths regularly, went into the temple, repeated the name of God even when in society, trying to keep my mind occupied with the one thought of God. My conscience became very sensitive, and made me aware of my defects. I knew I had to climb the heights of the Himalayas and tried to equip myself with my whole strength in order to qualify myself for the heavy task that lay before me.* (Purohit, 1992/1932, pp. 31-32)

As a result of his reflection on what was required to achieve spiritual success (here referred to by the metaphor of climbing the Himalayan mountains), the swami undertook a regimen of ascetic practices and meditation. Subsequently, his "conscience became very sensitive," and he was made "aware of his defects." In other words, as a result of his meditation practice, he experienced the dynamisms of spontaneous multilevel disintegration.

At the level of organized multilevel disintegration, meditation can provide an occasion to "reach very high levels of reality"—to achieve some insight into, or foretaste of, secondary integration.

> *It is well known that the state of meditation brings about inner quietude, calm awareness of one's weaknesses, calm equilibration of what has been achieved in the struggles of everyday life. This*

> *inner calm can be considered a meditative inhibition, which strengthens our achievements. In rare moments, one may be given the chance to reach to very high levels of reality. In such moments appear new insights, which in some way stimulate us "upwards." This stimulation as an immediate result of the experience is full of positive and serene tension. It is a calm excitation coming "from above." We could call it a contemplative excitation.* (Dabrowski, 1996a, p. 80)

Elsewhere, Dabrowski elaborates a little more on what he means by reality at a higher level.

> *Reality of a higher level is expressed in philosophical conceptions of development, in existential experiences, in true mysticism, contemplation, and ecstasy. On the highest level, it is not a reality of objects and psychosocial relations but a reality of the ideal. It is the threshold of transcendental reality discovered through first-hand experience.* (Dabrowski, 1996a, p. 93)

This glimpse of a higher reality, achieved by combining asceticism and meditation, is reported in the autobiography of the Ming dynasty Neo-Confucian Gao Panlong (1562-1626).

> *The next day in the boat, I earnestly arranged the mat and seriously set up rules and regulations. For one-half of the day I practised quiet-sitting* [i.e., meditation], *while for the other half I studied. In the quiet-sitting, I did not settle on any one specific way, but just followed the methods Ch'eng and Chu [have] spoken of generally, practising one by one: with integrity and reverence consider quietude as fundamental, observe joy, anger, sorrow and happiness before they arise, sit in silence and purify the mind, realize for oneself the Principle of Heaven. Whether I was standing, sitting, eating, or resting, these thoughts were continuously present. At night, I did not undress, and only when I was weary to the bone did I fall asleep. Upon waking, I returned to sitting, repeating and alternating these various methods of practice. When the substance of the mind was clear and peaceful there was a sense of filling all Heaven and earth, but it did not last.* (Taylor, 1978, pp. 126-127)

Gao chose as his place of retreat a boat moored to a dock in a river. There he established a regimen of study, asceticism, and meditation. From his meditation, he obtained a glimpse of what he understood to be a higher reality, but it was only a glimpse ("it did not last"). Gao's experience of a transcendent reality was what is referred to generically as a mystical experience, and this will be considered below. First, I want to discuss another important aid to mystical or personality development—the mystical mentor.

Mystical Mentors

In almost every mystical autobiography, an important role is indicated for a spiritual advisor, guru, master, or sheikh—someone who instructs and guides the developing mystic on his or her way to further growth. A passage from the autobiography of Moroccan Sufi Ibn Ajiba (1747-1809) will illustrate this point.

> *Our shaykh* [i.e., spiritual guide] *Sidi Muhammad al-Buzidi al-Hasani began to correspond with me. He encouraged me to seek out the companionship and union with God. He wrote to me: "If you want [mystical] knowledge, if you want the treasures of understanding, come!"...*
>
> *When he initiated me (*laqqanani*), I said, "I am in your hand! Do with me what you wish; command what you wish of me!"...From that time on, I made frequent visits to the shaykh... up to the time that God gave me the great illumination....* (Ibn Ajiba, 1999, pp. 78-79)

Ibn Ajiba went so far as to say that, in his view, a sheikh is essential.

> *Know...that there is no way to travel the Sufi path, especially if one is aspiring toward unveiling (*kashf*) and realization (*tahqiq*), without constant and complete obedience and submission to a "realized" (*muhaqqiq*) shaykh, a spiritual guide (*murshid*) joining together esoteric truth (*haqiqa*) and exoteric law (*sharia*). For the spiritual path is perilous and the slightest deviation from the road that is laid out results in missing the goal by a great distance.* (p. 101)

Dabrowski has allowed an important role to be played by an advisor in assisting the development of personality.

> *We must lay stress on the fact that in every phase, and particularly in the initial and following phases—that is, in the period of great conflictive and creative tensions, the period of a very real possibility of a breakdown—the adviser plays a fundamental role in the development of personality.*
>
> *Whereas in the first phase the main role rests with the adviser—that is, with the tutor, teacher, parent, or physician—in the second phase of development the main role passes to the developing individual himself. Nevertheless, this does not mean that help…[is] superfluous in the second phase. On the contrary, the passage from a rather passive sensitization to the phase of the mobilization of one's own forces, to the phase of a strong actuation of one's internal milieu, to the period of disintegration, requires greater responsibility and vigilance on the part of the adviser. The help of an adviser must be increasingly more imperceptible, ever more subtle, ever more "helpful," so as not to interfere finally, injudiciously, and too distinctly in the developmental process of an individual.* (Dabrowski, 1967, p. 151)

Dabrowski's distinction between two overall phases is illustrated by Paramahansa Yogananda in his description of the role played by his guru.

> *[M]y guru was hypercritical of his disciples.…He showed no leniency to anyone who, like myself, had willingly offered to be a disciple.…[H]e always spoke plainly and upbraided sharply… but my unchangeable resolve was to allow Sri Yukteswar to iron our all my psychological kinks.…I am immeasurably grateful for the humbling blows he dealt my vanity.… The hard core of egoism is difficult to dislodge except rudely. With its departure, the Divine finds at last an unobstructed channel.…It was Master's practice to point out the simple, negligible shortcomings of his disciples with an air of portentous gravity.…Master relentlessly continued to dissect me whenever and wherever he chose.…After I had abandoned underlying resentment, I found a marked decrease in my chastisement. In a very subtle way, Master melted into comparative clemency. In time, I demolished every wall of rationalization and subconscious reservation behind which the human personality generally shields itself.* (Yogananda, 1973, pp. 140-145)

It seems that Sri Yukteswar's mentoring approach followed the two-stage model recommended by Dabrowski. In the beginning of his relationship with his guru, Yogananda was unable to be in control of his own development, for as he puts it, "the hard core of ego is difficult to dislodge." At this point, he needed to be constantly challenged. As Yogananda was able to take charge of his own development—for example, in abandoning his resentment—Sri Yukteswar withdrew from taking an active role. As the phrase, "I demolished" in the last sentence of the quotation illustrates, Yogananda was now able to assume responsibility for his own development; he became an active agent.

The precise treatment that Yogananda received from his guru in the first phase of mentoring is not likely that to which Dabrowski is referring in the passage cited above. Dabrowski, given his clinical experience, seems to be referring to vulnerable patients, possibly at risk for suicide. Sri Yukteswar clearly saw his role as one of breaking down a rigid personality structure. Nevertheless, both Dabrowski and Sri Yukteswar understood that mentoring has two phases, and in the second, the mentee has to be allowed space to take responsibility for his or her own development.

There are many other aids to personality development mentioned by Dabrowski, such as keeping a diary "with stress laid on the realization of one's decisions and noting one's achievements within a given sphere [of personality development]" (Dabrowski, 1967, p. 179), and "discharging tension in the world of nature" (Dabrowski, 1967, p. 182), examples of which can be found in mystical autobiographies. In the passage from the autobiography of Peace Pilgrim quoted above, we find an example of the latter. An example of the former comes from the autobiography of 20th-century Zen master Tsuji Somei (b. 1904).

> *During these times of spiritual struggle [trying to determine whether or not to become a celibate monk], I used to keep a small notebook with me, to jot down my passing thoughts and feelings, in the hope that somehow it would help me to organize my thinking.* (Somei, 1993, p. 128)

In his brief remark about keeping a diary, Somei does not say that he recorded his decisions or his achievements, since the remark was in the context of describing his multilevel struggle, nor does Dabrowski state explicitly that diaries are valuable for recording thoughts and feelings and organizing thinking, but I think we can infer from Dabrowski's comment that keeping a diary is useful as an aid to development, for more reasons than the one he explicitly states. The goal of the various aids to development is of course the transformation of personality, and part of this process is restructuring through mystical experiences.

Mystical Experience

The term that Dabrowski uses for mystical experience is "ecstasy," which he defines as "extreme absorption of attention resulting in a semi-trance as a consequence of intense contemplation of a limited field; a state characteristic of mystical experiences" (1972, p. 294). Mystical experience, or ecstasy, in Dabrowski's understanding, has a number of functions (both disintegrative and integrative), depending on the personality level of the one experiencing the ecstasy (Nixon, 1983). Here I will mention only two. One effect of these states of consciousness is as follows: "Ever more frequent and deeper ecstatic states fill a man with increasingly greater energy, thus enabling him to win ever stronger control over his instinctive nature" (Dabrowski, 1967, p. 34). This effect can be seen in a passage from 19th-century Hasidic mystic Isaac Eizik of Komarno (1806-1874).

> *I separated myself entirely from the world. It happened in the year 5583 (1823) at the beginning of winter. It was my habit to sleep only two hours a day, spending the rest of the time studying Torah, the Talmud, the [Law] Codes, the Zohar, the writings of our Master (Isaac Luria) and the works of Rabbi Moses Cordovero* [the last three are mystical texts]. *But I fell away from all these stages for three months and was in a state of immense smallness of soul. Many harsh and demonic forces (kelippot) rose against me to dissuade me from studying the Torah. Worse than all was a state of melancholy into which I was hurled. Yet my heart was as firm as a rock. During this time, the only pleasure I allowed myself was to drink a little water and eat a morsel of bread daily. I had no delight whatever in the Torah I studied or the prayers I recited. The cold was very severe and the demonic forces extremely powerful so that I actually stood equally balanced between two paths, depending on how I would choose. Much bitterness passed over my head as a result of these blandishments, really more bitter than a thousand times death. But once I had overcome these blandishments, suddenly, in the midst of the day... a great light fell upon me.... From that time onwards I began to serve the Creator of all with a marvelous,*

> *unvarying illumination. The blandishments had power over me no longer. Afterwards, I fell once again for a time so I came to realize that I must journey to the saints who would draw down His light...upon me since I already had a refined vessel wherewith to receive the light.* (Jacobs, 1978/1976, pp. 240-241)

In this passage, there is a reference to the meditative study of mystical texts, asceticism, and finally to a mystical experience and its effect—to use Dabrowski's words, of "increasingly greater energy, thus enabling him to win ever stronger control over his instinctive nature."

Dabrowski also speaks about the relationship between mystical experience and the personality ideal in his discussion of the reality function at the level of secondary integration.

> *Personality ideal acts as a force of transposition to ideal reality, which one achieves only by way of true empathy, mystical contemplation, and ecstasy, a reality which is free from selfishness and from temperamental egocentric actions and concerns. This is the reality of [the] ideal, of creativity and self-perfection on the borderline of transcendence. The center of gravity is transposed to the world of higher values and ideals which represent the objective and the subjective reality equally, and which endow transcendence with concreteness.* (Dabrowski, 1996a, p. 64)

An example of someone who had a mystical experience that revealed to her a transcendent ideal of personality is a 20th-century North American practitioner of Zen Buddhism, Flora Courtois. Here is her description:

> *Feeling myself centered as never before, at the same time I knew the whole universe to be centered at every point. Having plunged to the center of emptiness, having lost all purposefulness in the old sense, I had never felt so one-pointed, so clear and decisive. Freed from separateness, feeling one with the universe, everything including myself had become at once unique and equal. If God was the word for this Presence in which I was absorbed, then everything was either holy or nothing; no distinction was possible. All was meaningful, complete as it was, each bird, bud, midge, mole, atom, crystal, of total importance in itself. As in the notes of a great symphony, nothing was large or small, nothing of more or*

> *less importance to the whole. I now saw that wholeness and holiness are one.* (Courtois, 1986, p. 51)

The Value of Studying Mystical Autobiographies

I have found that the application of the theory of positive disintegration to mystical lives has made it possible to better understand those lives in terms of personality development. Specifically, I have found the theory useful in identifying common predispositional characteristics, both temperamental and environmental, in the lives of mystics from different historical periods and religious cultures; and useful in identifying and understanding the role of aids to mystical development at the various stages of personality. However, the value of the comparison between the theory of positive disintegration and mystical development is not just a one-way affair. On the one hand, the comparison between the theory and mystical lives allows for a better understanding of the phenomenon of mysticism in general and mystical growth in particular, but on the other hand, the correspondences also show that mystical autobiographies can provide additional data for a better understanding of personality development, as described by Kazimierz Dabrowski.

It is interesting how the psychospiritual development described in these autobiographies so closely parallels Dabrowski's levels. It is also interesting how, in his discussions of aids to personality development, Dabrowski has referred to almost every aid to development mentioned in mystical autobiographies from the various religious traditions in the world. On the other hand, he has not elaborated upon the variety of expressions that these aids can take. Furthermore, it is one thing to refer to an aid to development; it is another thing to see it in practice cross-culturally. Doing so enriches our understanding about the way any given aid to development functions in specific historical and cultural settings. If a researcher can bracket the particular religious world views assumed in mystical autobiographies, I believe that the study of these works can add to our understanding of the disintegration and reintegration of personality, as well as our understanding of the way some of the aids to development function in that process.

Chapter 12
Emotion Management and Emotional Development: A Sociological Perspective

Nancy B. Miller, Ph.D.[1]

"Emotion has come of age as a legitimate domain of study," declared Michael Lewis and Jeannette Haviland in 1993 in the Preface of the *Handbook of Emotions* (p. ix). After years of being considered little more than base impulse or irrational feeling, the 1980s saw emotion reintroduced into the social sciences as a viable, even necessary, complement to the study of human processes such as cognition, learning, and perception in psychology, and identity, attitudes, and interaction in sociology. The inclusion of emotion as a worthy area of study in these and other social science disciplines (e.g., philosophy, history, cultural studies) has been attributed to the development of new models, new measurement techniques, and new conceptions of emotion (Lewis & Haviland, 1993).

In this chapter, we will look at emotional development through a sociological lens. Sociologists' views of emotions and their management will be related to Kazimierz Dabrowski's (1977) levels of emotional development. Cathryn Johnson's (1992) framework for the analysis of emotions is presented as a developmental perspective of the emotional self. Next, two basic emotions, anger and joy, are used to distinguish emotional expression

---

1 Nancy B. Miller, Ph.D., Associate Editor, *Advanced Development*; Psycho-educational Examiner, Gifted Development Center, Denver, Colorodo; Executive Officer, Sociologists for Women in Society (Retired); Associate Professor, University of Akron (Retired).

at the five levels of Dabrowski's theory. Finally, the assessment of levels of development is chronicled from the original Canada Council grant to Dabrowski in 1969 for the empirical testing of the theory (Dabrowski, 1977) to the development of the Definition Response Instrument (Gage et al., 1981), the Miller Assessment Coding System (1985), and Bouchet's (2004) dictionary of phase groups for assessing moral emotional development. Both quantitative and qualitative studies assessing levels of emotional development are included.

Sociology of Emotion

Sociologists engaged in the study of emotion have focused primarily on how emotions are expressed or inhibited in face-to-face interaction, as well as how the expression varies with regard to a person's group membership, position in society, or social category—for example social class, gender, or race. Two factors in particular—power and status—have been shown to affect emotional expression (Kemper, 1993). A person's emotional response to a disagreement with the boss will differ from his or her response to disputes with co-workers or subordinates. This illustrates the way structural situations influence how we feel and respond. Other sociologists view emotion as more cultural in nature; they believe that emotions are "socially constructed, culturally prescribed features of social life" (Wisecup, Robinson, & Smith-Lovin, 2006). In their view, cultural norms are used to interpret our experiences as self-affirming and therefore positive, or disconfirming and negative. Positive assessment leads to pride and happiness; negative appraisal can lead to feelings of shame, guilt, and anxiety.

Sociologists believe that social interaction and social relations create emotions; therefore, emotional expression can be socialized, regulated, and even managed. Arlie Hochschild's groundbreaking research (1983) of flight attendants working for Delta Air Lines brought to light the struggle involved in putting on a public face that masks a person's true feelings. Her study focused on the requirement of flight attendants to display the appropriate feeling on the job. The attempt to manage a person's emotions in general is referred to as "emotion work," and the control of emotions required for success in an occupation is called "emotional labor." These emotion processes require the individual to perform surface acting as well as deep acting. Surface acting occurs when a person smiles although he or she feels angry or sad; deep acting requires one to attempt to change the feeling itself by reappraising the situation that led to the inappropriate emotion. Hochschild's work also revealed the unfortunate effects of emotional suppression, or "emotional numbing," that occurs when emotional restraint spills over into off-work hours. Researchers who followed in her footsteps have investigated emotion management and its consequences in other venues, such as classrooms, organizational settings, and therapeutic sites (Erickson & Cuthbertson-Johnson, 1997).

Sociology and Emotional Development

George Herbert Mead, an early philosopher and social psychologist, identified emotion as the inception of an act—an impulse or feeling whose expression is socialized by cultural prescription (Mead, 1934). Interaction with significant others, especially parents and caregivers, teaches us to alter, inhibit, or suppress certain responses in favor of other more appropriate replies in the situation. A child who is challenged by another may be cautioned to respond with kindness rather than malice, thus inhibiting and redirecting what may have been an initial negative emotional reaction. For Mead, the ability to delay action in favor of a thoughtful response represented self-conscious, minded behavior, or reflective intelligence.

One of Mead's major contributions was the specification:

> *. . . of a processual theory of how people develop minds and acquire selves through social interaction. He gives primacy to the universe of discourse (referential symbols) and specifies a set of stages of development which describes how infants transform into mindful and self-reflexive social beings.* (Johnson, 1992, p. 183)

According to Mead, the self emerges as we learn to take an objective, impersonal attitude toward ourselves. This allows self-consciousness to develop, and a person is able to respond to him- or herself as others would. This development takes place in four stages involving: (1) meaningless imitation, (2) role-playing, (3) assuming the attitude of others toward oneself, and finally, (4) the internalization of shared attitudes, definitions, and expectations (Charon, 1995).

Yet as important as Mead was in the study of the self and its reflexive nature (Falk & Miller, 1998), it is Charles Horton Cooley who has been credited by sociologists with drawing our attention to the affective domain of the self (Turner & Stets, 2006). Cooley (1964/1902) described the self as a looking glass. We see ourselves in the reactions of others, imagine their evaluation, and experience a feeling (i.e., pride or shame) about their judgment. For Cooley, the feeling component is crucial in the formation of the self, because it involves "taking the perspective of the other" (Charon, 1995, p. 105). This indicates an ability to take the role of another toward oneself. Both Mead and Cooley laid the groundwork for sociological research in the area of self-development.

In her article "The Emergence of the Emotional Self: A Developmental Theory," Cathryn Johnson (1992) extends Mead's five stages of socialization by focusing on emotional development, which she argues is closely aligned with the development of mind and self. For Johnson, "emotions are viewed as processes of an experiencing self that originate and develop in social relations" (p. 184). In her seven-stage theory of emotional development, she presents an experienced-based progression that represents a "hierarchy of emotional experiences from simple to more complex" (p. 184). In stages one through five, the child experiences basic emotions and moves from mere response to stimuli to the sharing of emotions with others and the identification of one's own emotions, as well as those of others. It is only in stage six that a child begins to experience more complex emotions, such as empathy and guilt. This is possible when the child can adopt the standpoint of others toward him- or herself (reflexive role-taking, in Mead's terms) and acquires a consciousness of relationships—i.e., the attitude of role-taking has generalized to the group or community and has been internalized. The child is now able to act with a certain amount of consistency in accordance with a generalized set of expectations and definitions that have been internalized. "At this point, children acquire a more sophisticated understanding of the separation between what is felt and what can be displayed.... They also learn appropriate times to express various emotions" (p. 197).

At stage seven, children learn how to "manage" their emotions, changing inappropriate feelings to those more appropriate to the situation, discussed as "emotion work" in the preceding section. At times, this requires that children or adults mask their true or authentic feelings to adhere to social customs. The ability to evoke, shape, and suppress one's emotions is built on the "feeling rules" learned from significant others. This occurs through modeling and direction, such as "no fooling around in church."

Managing one's emotions and actions in accordance with one's values, rather than social convention, can be associated with the characteristics of Dabrowski's (1977) advanced levels of emotional development (Levels III through V), to be discussed in the following section. In Dabrowski's higher levels, personal standards of ethics and morality guide emotional development, and processes such as self-control and self-direction facilitate emotional expression.

Dabrowski, Piechowski, and Emotions

In the mid 1970s, Kazimierz Dabrowski (1977; Dabrowski & Piechowski, 1977) and Michael Piechowski (1975b) published research on human development in which emotion and feeling take center stage. What we feel, as well as what we think, is essential to understanding personality development. In the theory, the role of emotions equals, or surpasses, that of cognition in the transformation of the individual from lower to higher levels of development.

Dabrowski reflects on formulating the theory: "The world of external and internal phenomena began to form itself in my experience as a world of values arranged in a hierarchy of levels" (Dabrowski, 1977, p. xii). The theory is unique in that values are distinguished at each level of emotional, moral, and social development. Recently, Mróz (2002b) presented what she sees as two distinct meanings of values as used in the theory:

> *On the one hand, values are defined as all the needs of an individual perceived as significant or even motivating his or her actions. They may be determined in a variety of factors, including impulses, the influence of social environment or autonomous factors dependant on the level of development of the given individual (which determines the multilevel character of values). On the other hand... Dabrowski...assumes the existence of absolute values prior to their experience by the individual. These values are only discovered in the process of disintegration and the discovery is associated with the achievement of advanced levels of development (the third, fourth and fifth level, namely)....The values consciously selected and adopted by the individual...become the building material for the personality ideal formed at these levels....* (p. 141-142)

Using values in the sense of both a motivator of behavior and the building blocks for advanced development, the following exercise shows how two basic emotions differ at Levels I through V. This is not to be considered a well-studied description of levels of development or a comprehensive treatment of these two emotions; rather, examples are provided that show possible distinctions between the levels of development. Beyond that, the exercise shows how efforts to work with theoretical concepts lead to greater understanding of the overall theory.

Examining Source, Expression, and Inhibitor

At a summer workshop on emotional development and giftedness at the University of Wisconsin in the late 1990s, a colleague (Frank Falk) and I began a group session by asking participants how we could distinguish the expression of emotions at various levels of development. We explained prior attempts to present a developmental view of concepts, such as friendship and play (Mos & Boodt, 1991), perfectionism (Silverman, 1990), and the ego (Loevinger, 1976). We briefly discussed Dabrowski's (1977) description of the most basic emotions. Then we asked the group to identify dimensions that could be used to examine the levels of emotions. Based on the ensuing conversation and our own research on the topic, three areas were selected: (1) the source of the emotion, (2) the manner of expression, and (3) the inhibitor.

The concepts are defined in the following way. The *source* is the stimulus or eliciting agent of an emotion. It may come from the external environment or from internal processes, such as self-blame. The *expression* refers to the way the emotion is displayed, and it may include both the direction and frequency. The *inhibitor* indicates possible controls on emotional expression and perhaps even the experiencing of the emotion itself. Using "anger" and "joy," identified by Izard (1971), Ekman (1984), and others (e.g., Dabrowski, 1977) as two of the basic emotions, the group proposed examples that illustrate the source, expression, and inhibitor at the five levels of development described by Dabrowski (1977). Tables 12.1 and 12.2 represent a brief outline of the workshop results. I have supplemented where information was insufficient or missing. I summarize below the distinguishing features across levels.

Table 12.1: The Expression of Anger

Level	Source	Expression	Inhibitors
I	Obstacles in the realization of basic drives; status loss	Spontaneous, immediate and outward; may be brutal	Fear of reprisal
II	Personal confrontation; opposing tendencies in oneself	Less automatic and aggressive	Social standards; sympathy with others and oneself
III	Discrepancies between one's own intentions and actions	Less anger toward others; more anger toward oneself for personal shortcomings	Personal standards of behavior
IV	Injustice; unfairness	Controlled; somewhat diminished	Respect and empathy for others
V	Moral, ethical, and social wrongs	Calm resistance to transgression	Universal love and understanding

Table 12.2: The Expression of Joy

Level	Source	Expression	Inhibitors
I	Satisfaction of basic needs	Uncontrolled displays of pleasure	Failure; losses; powerlessness
II	Support and kindness of others; security	Enthusiasm but with reservations	Self-doubt; ambivalence
III	Self-discovery; overcoming inner conflicts; unselfish actions	Passion for ideals	Negative traits in oneself
IV	Inner strength; service to others	Controlled pleasure	Slowness in reaching out to others and in reaching one's personality ideal
V	Authentic self; all-encompassing love; realization of ideals	Contentment	Injustice; inequality; exploitation and suffering of others

Expressing Anger

Anger in its milder form is annoyance or impatience, in its stronger form rage or fury. Individuals in Level I usually respond with angry outbursts whenever they are provoked. For example, an angry employee may actually strike the boss but will be deterred, in most cases, by fear of losing his job. A girlfriend's or boyfriend's attraction to another can lead to overt or repressed anger and attempts to get even. Consider the female astronaut who was charged with trying to kidnap and assault a romantic competitor (NASA, 2007). Strong social and moral prohibitions did not deter her plans.

Anger at Level II comes from personal confrontation around the issues of power, prestige, and privilege, but it is less automatic and usually less aggressive. An angry employee may verbally express anger to the boss and to others but will not hit the boss, no matter how great the anger.

At Level III, anger directed toward others may be caused by violations of expectations, such as trust, or infractions of the rules. Anger directed toward the self, the primary object of anger at this level, occurs because of discrepancies between a person's intentions and his or her actions. Anger toward others is less outward, less frequent, and less automatic. Self-recrimination, however, is likely to follow any displays of anger toward others. The display of anger is inhibited, most of the time, by personal standards of behavior.

Although the group tried to discriminate at the two highest levels, we found similar sources, expression, and inhibitors. Injustice and any discrepancies between one's behavior and one's moral concerns can cause a person to feel anger at Level IV, but the anger is controlled, subtle, and diminished in its experience and expression. Self-recrimination for shortcomings subsides. Respect and empathy for others along with the conscious containment of tension and conflict act as inhibitors. At Level V, moral, ethical, and social offenses can lead to calm resistance, but there is no anger toward others or oneself. Universal love and understanding prevent any experience or expression of anger.

Expressing Joy

Joy is the feeling of elation that accompanies conquest or attainment. It may also be the happiness and satisfaction that come with success, security, self-discovery, inner strength, and the realization of a person's ideals. At Level I, joy is having one's needs met—for example, good food, drink, and pleasure of the senses. Uncontrolled displays of pleasure and pride are its expression. Failure, loss, and powerlessness lead to unhappiness.

In contrast, joy for those at Level II comes from the support and kindness of others and the security of predictable relationships. Enthusiasm, appreciation, and eagerness are common expressions of joy; self-doubt and uncertainty are what usually prevent happiness.

Self-discovery can lead to joy for those at Level III, as can the resolution of inner conflicts. Passion for one's ideals is the hallmark at this level. One's faults and negative traits can cause shame, guilt, anger, and unhappiness.

At Level IV, inner strength and service are the sources of joy. Happiness is expressed as controlled pleasure. A person may be unhappy because of slowness in reaching out to others or in attaining one's own personality ideal.

Finally, at Level V, joy comes from an all encompassing love for others and attaining the authentic self. These feelings lead to genuine pleasure and contentment. Deterrents to happiness are injustices, exploitation, or the suffering of others.

From the exercise, two crucial aspects of the theory were recognized: (1) "differences between levels of an emotional expression are greater and more significant than differences between particular emotions" (Dabrowski, 1977, p. 119), and (2) "differences between lower levels of development are much sharper than differences between higher levels" (Dabrowski, 1977, p. 102). Discovering these important differences through group discussion provided insight into the levels that reading alone had not done. Because participants pursued the task diligently, they demonstrated the ability to guide their own learning; understanding of important features of the levels of emotional development was achieved.

Assessing Levels of Emotional Development

Empirical testing of levels of emotional development began in 1969 with a research grant from the Canada Council to Kazimierz Dabrowski. Researchers on the project at the University of Alberta used several methods of data collection to construct developmental profiles. These included neurological examinations, autobiographical essays, responses to verbal stimuli (e.g., great joy and great sadness), clinical interviews (inquiry and initial assessment), and the Wechsler Adult Intelligence Scale (Dabrowski & Piechowski, 1977). Although hundreds of subjects were screened, the final numbers for different tests ranged from 81 to 950.

This early research was successful in its main goals: determining methods, developing procedures, establishing the relation between theoretical concepts and individual responses, and generally providing support for the theory. However, the rating process turned out to be "a rather complex and uneconomical task" (Dabrowski & Piechowski, 1977, p. 224). Further, very few individuals were found at higher levels in the general population—the average person scored at the intersection of Level 1 and 2. Details on methods and research results are reported in "A Theoretical and Empirical Approach to the Study of Development" (Piechowski, 1975b).

In 1981, researchers David Gage, Philip Morse, and Michael Piechowski designed and tested an open-ended questionnaire to assess levels of emotional development. The questionnaire, called the Definition Response Instrument (DRI), was intended to elicit responses that could be coded for developmental dynamisms, reflecting level of emotional development. The DRI consists of six thought-provoking questions, each directing attention to an important developmental dynamism (see Table 12.3). They include: (1) susceptibility to the influence of others, (2) internal conflict, (3) feelings of inferiority, (4) dissatisfaction with oneself, (5) self-reflection and evaluation, and (6) the personality ideal. By comparing five different methods of measuring levels, important theoretical evidence for the structure of levels, including convergent and discriminant validity, was demonstrated (Gage et al., 1981). Inter-rater reliability was reported to be .8. Based on their empirical study, these researchers were able to recommend the DRI as a reliable, valid, and efficient means of assessing levels.

Table 12.3: Definition Response Instrument

Open-Ended Items
1. Think of times when you have been strongly affected by what others think of you or when you have compared yourself in some way to others.
2. Think of those questions that cause strong doubts within you, that frustrate you, and perhaps result in anxiety or depression. The problems should be limited to struggles that are internal (for example, philosophical, sexual, and emotional), not struggles which are primarily external (for example, a purely economic problem).
3. Recall times when you have felt inadequate, unworthy, not good enough. Possibly, you felt frustrated with what may have been lacking in yourself (abilities, skills, talents, personal qualities, etc.).

Open-Ended Items
4. Consider those situations that have caused you to feel frustration or anger toward yourself. They may have been over something you did and later regretted, as well as over something you feel you should have done but did not do. Likewise, you could have become angered with yourself for having felt a certain way or believing something you no longer feel is true. Describe these situations and your feelings.
5. Think if there have been any times when you have tried to stand back and look at yourself objectively. Upon what specific things did you reflect, if you did so?
6. Think of your "ideal self" and those qualities that you think are best for an ideal life. What attributes have you most dreamed of having?

Note: From "Measuring levels of emotional development" by D. F. Gage, P. A. Morse, & M. M. Piechowski, (1981), *Genetic Psychology Monographs*, *103*, 150. Copyright 1981 by *The Journal Press*. Adapted with permission.

During the 1970s and '80s, Michael Piechowski, at the University of Illinois and then Northwestern University, directed three dissertations and three theses based on Dabrowski's theory that included assessment of levels of emotional development. They are summarized as follows.

1. Margaret Schmidt, M.A., 1977, investigated primary integration in several developmental theories, including those of Kohlberg, Loevinger, and Dabrowski. She found individuals at Dabrowski's Level I to be products of their social environment, "limited and narrow and truly alienated in Marx's sense" (p. 75)—alienated from themselves and others. Her research offers implications for counseling individuals with primary integrated personality structure.

2. Katherine Lysy, Ph.D., 1979, studied personal growth in graduate students, some who were in counseling psychology and some who were in other fields. She used Jung's and Dabrowski's models of personal growth but found that concepts did not differentiate between the two groups of students. However, concepts from both theories, Jung's intuition function and Dabrowski's emotional and intellectual overexcitability (OE), were associated with developmental level as assessed by the DRI. In her work, she distinguished two types of growth: conserving and transforming. Conserving growth operates at Dabrowski's Levels II and III,

while characteristics of transforming growth are necessary for higher levels of development.

3. Cynthia Tyska, M.A., 1980, compared self-actualization in Eleanor Roosevelt to that of Antoine de Saint-Exupéry (Piechowski, 1978). She found similar patterns of personality traits in their biographies. Her analysis confirmed Eleanor Roosevelt as a nontranscender, or "doer," in Maslow's terms, while Antoine de Saint-Exupéry was a transgender, or "seer." These distinctions do not change the fact that both were self-actualizing persons.

4. Lorel Greene, M.A., 1982, compared Dabrowski's theory of emotional development and Loevinger's theory of ego development. She found some overlap at the lower and middle levels. However, she discovered that "Loevinger's theory offers a detailed description of the lower spectrum of development, where the bulk of the population is found, and of the stages involved in 'normal' development…[while] Dabrowski's theory offers a conceptual order of five broad personality structures and an elaborate vision of higher levels of development rarely found in a normal population" (pp. 60-61).

5. Judith Robert, Ph.D., 1984, developed typologies of personal growth that distinguish conserving and transforming subjects. Transforming subjects, compared to conserving subjects, had higher scores on the following emotional variables: "hierarchy" (feeling of higher and lower guiding principles), self-evaluation, and sense of self. They had lower scores on negative reactions toward self based on the responses of others. Transforming subjects also had higher scores on some intellectual variables: problem solving, introspecting, and curiosity. They had average scores on thinking and probing questions. Conserving subjects scored in the reverse on these variables. Her research identifies personality characteristics that are necessary for higher-level development.

6. Thomas Brennan, Ph.D., 1987, conducted in-depth case studies of three individuals who met the criteria of advanced, multilevel development—Level IV in Dabrowski's terms, or self-actualizers in Maslow's terms. An additional subject provided a comparison between multilevel potential, in her case, and its attainment in the

other three. He used real life examples of individuals with self-actualizing characteristics as exemplars of advanced personality development.

During the same time, another dissertation using Dabrowski's model of advanced development was completed by Berdena Beach (1980) at the University of Iowa. Beach examined women's profiles of development and self-actualization, comparing self-defined lesbians and heterosexually-oriented women. She found that lesbians had higher scores on the DRI index of developmental level and on intellectual, imaginational, sensual, and psychomotor OE, but not on emotional OE.

In the mid-1980s Clive Hazell, who completed his graduate work at Northwestern University, continued research on his dissertation topic—the experience of emptiness (1982). Using two different student samples, he examined the relationships among emptiness, existential concern, levels of emotional development, and values (1984; 1989). In research with his gifted clients, he drew on insights from Dabrowski's theory and its relation to experiences of emptiness "to explain the dynamics of counseling strategies" (Hazell, 1999, p. 31).

Studies such as these, directly influenced by Piechowski, as well as his own research during the time (Piechowski, 1975b; 1978; 1979b) expanded the study of levels of emotional development into promising new areas. They led to numerous conference presentations and to publications in several psychology journals (Brennan & Piechowski, 1991; Lysy & Piechowski, 1983; Piechowski, 1975b; 1978; Piechowski & Tyska, 1982). Further, they had the effect of widening interest in emotional development to other disciplines—for example gifted education, higher education, religious studies, and sociology.

As a graduate student, my interest in Dabrowski's theory was sparked by a group of researchers at the University of Denver, which included Linda Silverman and Frank Falk. I was interested in personality development and content analysis, and they were involved in coding open-ended responses to DRI items and the *Overexcitability Questionnaire* (OEQ), a 21-item measure of OE (Lysy & Piechowski, 1983). It was a perfect match, and a dissertation project was born. Michael Piechowski came to Denver on several occasions to train coders; I was fortunate to have learned the techniques of analysis from him. However, having had trouble coding the DRI, I proposed to develop a standardized technique to analyze responses to the DRI, which became known as the Miller Assessment Coding System (MACS) (Miller, 1985; Miller & Silverman, 1987). In the MACS, categories reflect a cognitive perspective of motivation that holds that introspection, self-evaluations, judgments, social comparisons, and other thought processes are the determinants of individuals' behavior. Motivation toward the world, oneself, and others is reflected in themes concerning values, self-feeling, and relations with others. Table 12.4 shows the subcategories at each level.

Table 12.4: Miller Assessment Coding System

Level	Values	Self	Others
I	Self-serving	Egocentric	Superficial
II	Stereotypical	Ambivalent	Adaptive
III	Individual	Inner conflict	Interdependent
IV	Universal	Self-directed	Democratic
V	Transcendent	Inner peace	Communionistic

Note: From "Levels of personality development," by N. B. Miller & L. K. Silverman, (1987), *Roeper Review*, *9*, 223. Adapted with permission.

In the new coding system, each paragraph is rated separately. Coders identify themes in a paragraph that reflect one of the three categories (values, self, others) and then find its correct level or subcategory. In comparison with the previous method of scoring, in which coders have to keep in mind all 32 dynamisms, the new system is considered superior in several ways: (1) ease of coding, (2) less time-consuming and therefore less costly, (3) consistent across categories, and (4) most importantly, increased inter-rater reliability (.73 vs. .40).

Research using the MACS coding system has proceeded from establishing increased systemization, objectivity, and reliability (Miller & Silverman, 1987) to examining predictors of level scores (Miller et al., 1994; Bouchet, 2004). In a study of intellectually gifted adults, emotional and imaginational OE were strong predictors of developmental level; the addition of intellectual, psychomotor, and sensual OE added little (Miller et al., 1994). These findings replicated results of a study conducted 10 years earlier with a graduate student sample (Lysy & Piechowski, 1983). In both cases, emotional OE had the highest correlation with developmental level (.47 in the gifted adult sample, .59 in the graduate student sample) and therefore was the major predictor of level. The addition of sensual and psychomotor OE was negligible in both studies.

The only difference between findings was that in the graduate sample, intellectual OE, rather than imaginational OE, contributed significantly to explaining level. This difference can be understood by the fact that a moderate degree of correlation usually exists among these three variables: emotional OE, intellectual OE, and imaginational OE. Consistent with the theory, all three tend to have a rather high association with level scores. This creates a problem for regression analysis, because only independent variance is considered. The result is that, in the case of gifted adults, emotional and imaginational OE are found to predict level, while among graduate students, it is emotional and intellectual OE.

In gifted education at the University of Denver, Samuel Ammirato (1987), under the direction of Linda K. Silverman, completed a dissertation in which he compared instruments used to measure several of the concepts in Dabrowski's theory. His first comparisons were between the two existing questionnaires (OEQ and DRI) and very similar versions that had been revised for clarity and grammatical correctness. Results showed the revised versions were comparable to the originals; thus, researchers were free to use the revised instruments, knowing that the slight changes would not affect responses. Additional comparisons were made between the open-ended questionnaires and a multiple-choice instrument that had been developed by a University of Denver research group composed of educators and social scientists. Results showed that OE and developmental level scores on the multiple-choice format were not equivalent to those on the open-ended questionnaires. As far as I know, no further work has been done to design multiple-choice measures of these concepts.

Mark Wagstaff, a student at Oklahoma State University in the late 1990s, used the DRI and the *Personal Orientation Inventory* (POI), based on Maslow's (1970) concept of self-actualization, to examine leadership skills. He was interested primarily in self-awareness, a component of co-leader rapport. In his dissertation, Mark explored the relationship between self-awareness and instructors' perceptions of interpersonal influence. Results showed positive, but weak, correlations between level of emotional development and interpersonal influence, and moderate correlations with certain POI scales. However, Wagstaff's use of these concepts has important implications for future research—understanding how emotional development correlates with other variables of interest and identifying new research questions. For example, he asked, "Are self-directed individuals more likely to be perceived as experts?" In his conclusions, Wagstaff suggests additional ways that information from the theory may be used in his area of specialization. He writes:

> *Emotional development, as operationalized by the DRI, provides rich information as a way of analyzing behaviors and value orientation.... [I]f self-awareness is defined within the context of emotional development...trainers of outdoor leaders have a reference to formulate specific goals for "soft skill" improvement based on the developmental level of the trainees.* (1997, p. 91)

In addition to facilitating research, another valuable function of the assessment of levels has been to provide insight and counseling for personal growth. In one such case, Linda Silverman (1996) asked a young man who came to her specifically for Dabrowski-based counseling to complete both the OEQ and DRI. His responses to the DRI showed clear indications of Dabrowski's Level III dynamisms. For instance, he severely chastised himself for not living up to his own convictions. In answer to question #4, he wrote:

> *I feel anger towards myself when I catch myself feeling anger towards others. I despise the thought of doing wrong, acting in a cruel manner, or becoming angry towards anyone/anything besides myself....Along similar lines, it bothers me greatly when I notice myself passing up an opportunity to do good.* (p. 6)

In another case, Piechowski (1992b) invited a professor and mother of two who was struggling with personal issues to respond to the DRI. She willingly did so over a three-year period. Transforming growth was obvious in her answers. From an obsession with "how flawed I am," she advanced to see that the way ahead for her lay in perfecting her weaknesses: "The important point is to take stock, to be thankful for what I already have and to try to pick up what I do not have.... Every effort that I make now toward more tolerance, more patience, etc., will produce fruit down the road" (p. 200). Her mantra became, "To live impeccably, to practice harmlessness, to serve humanity" (p. 200).

One of the more recent projects to focus on Dabrowski's model of advanced development was Nicole Bouchet's (2004) dissertation, directed by Frank Falk at the University of Akron. Nicole's primary objective was to answer the question: "What social factors influence the development of moral emotions?" Using a computer-aided content analysis program to measure her variables, Bouchet found positive and significant correlations between Dabrowski's level of emotional development and emotional OE (.31), imaginational OE (.18), and intellectual OE (.25). In addition, several new variables she created also correlated with developmental level:

chaos (.62), moral imperatives (.25), positive states (.34), sadness (.35), and aspirations (.21). Eight variables in her analysis were not correlated with level: psychomotor OE, sensual OE, gender, age, education, dependents, intimate relations, and abuse. In comparing the computer-assisted ratings for developmental level with previous consensus ratings of the same material, she reported that the computer scores were slightly higher. In both cases, the average person's score was between Level 2 and 2.5.

The most significant contribution of the research, in Bouchet's own words, was "the establishment of the phrase groups constructed by the researcher that represent the five levels of development of moral emotions that range from the most self-serving and egocentric feelings at level one to the most altruistic feelings at level five" (2004, p. 11). These phrase groups are actually word chains contained in prior responses to the DRI and scored using the MACS categories—values, self, and others. Examples of some of the "phrase groups" from the Self Category are shown in Table 12.5. Phase groups from this study are provided in the Bouchet dictionary for assessing the development of moral emotions, an appendix to her dissertation. The dictionary may be enlarged or further refined in future research with DRI questionnaires.

Table 12.5: Excerpts from the *Bouchet Dictionary* for Assessing Moral Emotions

Level	Self Subcategory Phrase Groups
I	**Egocentric**: a great deal of money, a terrible temper, afraid of being caught, afraid of losing, avoid self-analysis, I am crude, I can be cruel, I am not attractive enough, little willpower, make my mark on, my looks, pick the right boyfriend, self-conscious, wish I was very thin
II	**Ambivalence**: always felt inadequate, be more assertive, cannot be alone, compared to others, courage which I lack, doubt myself, dream of accepting myself, embarrassed, emphasize my limitations, fear of doing it wrong, I am oversensitive to, I do what the majority does, I feel that I'm a failure, I don't measure up, I worry about what people think, my doubts, my insecurities, need for approval, not good enough
III	**Inner Conflict**: angry at myself for doing less, become painfully aware, conscience-stricken, directing my life in the right direction, disappointed in myself, extremely angry at myself, higher standards for myself, I fail so miserably, I feel terrible afterwards, I want to be better than I am at, I want to do more than, more critical of myself, my failure to, not as patient as I should be, things I could have done

Level	Self Subcategory Phrase Groups
IV	**Self-Direction**: a time of deep reflection for me, accept myself, always did what I thought was right, aware of myself, easier now to accept the fact, have tried to reach buried feelings, my self-control, personal discipline, personal growth, personally confident now, personally satisfied, reflect upon my life, self-aware, self-discipline, self-knowledge with, self-reflection, valuing of self
V	**Inner Peace**: accept responsibility, am secure, autonomous, basic moral values, confidence in the direction of, free from social pressure, fulfilled, harmonious, humanitarian, inner strength, intuitive synthesis, live my ideals, merciful, sacrifice all, so strong in my own essence

Qualitative Analysis

In addition to the questionnaire format to assess level, Michael Piechowski and Kathleen Spaltro have used textual analysis of historical cases to illustrate higher-level development according to Dabrowski's theory. Piechowski's subjects include: Antoine de Saint-Exupéry (Piechowski, 1978), Eleanor Roosevelt (Piechowski, 1990; Piechowski & Tyska, 1982), Etty Hillesum (Piechowski, 1991a; 1992a), and Peace Pilgrim (Piechowski, 1991b). The cases of Eleanor Roosevelt and Etty Hillesum are important, because they show the growth processes at Levels III and IV, or higher. The significance of Peace Pilgrim is that she is the only case of Level V (M. M. Piechowski, personal communication, March 20, 2007), although Kathleen Spaltro's (1991) analysis of Etty Hillesum also places her at Level V toward the end of her life. Spaltro documents Hillesum's multilevel growth leading up to secondary integration as follows:

> *[Etty] wrote diaries and letters from 1941 to 1943 that document a remarkable spiritual progression amid devastating circumstances. Intense emotional and intellectual growth crystallized in her free decision to work in the hospital of the transit camp Westerbork, the last stop on the way to Auschwitz. If one views Etty's diaries through the prism of Kazimierz Dabrowski's theory of moral development, they show her progression through the confusion and mal-adjustment that characterize Dabrowski's Level III to her embodiment of her ideals in daily service that signifies her attainment of Level IV. Her letters from Westerbork illuminate how a human being might feel, think, and live at Level V.* (p. 61)

Two additional analyses of historical cases that demonstrate higher-level development are those of Laurence Nixon (1994a) and Anne-Marie Morrissey (1996). Nixon examined the biographies of ancient spiritual leaders and proposed that "the inner struggles reported by many mystics [including Buddhist, Christian, Islamic, and Neo-Confucian] correspond to Kazimierz Dabrowski's psychological account of the higher levels of personality disintegration" (p. 57). Morrissey's research focused on the structure and methods supporting higher-level development in two cultures: Aboriginal Australians and Sufis in Moorish Spain. She concluded that, "By acknowledging the universality of this human potential, we can access their wisdom across time and place, looking past the distractions of superficial differences to the unity of their essential message, a message that is always relevant to the here and now" (p. 114). Her analysis shows that the message is one of enlightenment borne of a spiritually supportive environment.

Other investigators have used interviews as case study material. Barry Grant (1988) interviewed four remarkable individuals for his dissertation research. In his study, he uses "theories [of moral development] to illustrate lives and uses lives to criticize theories" (pp. 85-86). This approach empowers individuals as interpreters of their own development and offers new perspectives on theory. Excerpts from two subjects are used in an article in the journal *Advanced Development* (Grant, 1990), in which individuals' views on their own lives and morality act as examples of, and corrections to, the theories of Kohlberg and Dabrowski. Rich interview material from a third subject, a divorced mother of three (Grant, 1996), demonstrates what some may consider an anomaly—the coexistence of moral relativism and moral commitment. According to Grant's analysis, this woman's thinking offers a challenge to the theories of Kohlberg (1981; 1984), Gilligan (1982), and Dabrowski (1977), who see relativistic views as inconsistent with advanced moral development.

The studies cited thus far were all conducted in North America. A few years ago, a remarkable dissertation was completed by Anna Mróz (2002a) at the Catholic University of Lublin in Poland. Mróz's research involved extensive biographical narrative interviews with seven subjects. Her study, reported at the Fifth International Conference on the Theory of Positive Disintegration, is unique in that she used the DRI for selection of subjects, then used their autobiographies for analysis of the developmental process. The emotional level scores of her subjects ranged from 3.3 to 3.8. Mróz's research shows that universal human values and emotional relations with others play a positive role in the process of advanced development. Her findings support the basic tenets of Dabrowski's theory. In particular, she stresses the importance of therapists and counselors holding a positive view of the disintegration process in personality development. (For more information on methods and findings in her dissertation, see Chapter 3 in this book.)

Taken together, these theses, dissertations, and articles represent a significant body of research on Dabrowski's levels of emotional development. Both quantitative and qualitative analysis has contributed to this compilation of assessment of levels. I did not include the many conference presentations and workshops conducted on the topic.

Conclusion

Sociologists describe emotion management as the process of controlling the expression or display of our emotions. Emotion management can even include control of the experience of feeling itself. When we manage our emotions, we present ourselves in a manner appropriate for the role we play (e.g., mother or widow) or the occupation we engage in (e.g., nurse or teacher). Through emotion socialization, modeling, and acculturation, we learn that the "rules of social order prescribe feelings as well as actions" (Wisecup et al., 2006, p. 107). From this perspective, emotion is more than physiological arousal or individual response; it is a characteristic of social life, and its expression follows cultural expectations. When there is disparity between cultural standards, behavior, and a person's identity, he or she will go to great lengths to bring these perceptions into line (Turner & Stets, 2006).

Recently, a few sociologists have begun to argue for the inclusion of physiological explanations of emotion in social research (Turner & Stets, 2006; Wisecup et al., 2006). They assert, "It is time to engage in a more meaningful discussion of the role of physiology in the production of emotions and the implications of physiological bases of emotions" (Wisecup et al., 2006, p. 113). These researchers argue that measures of physiological features could and should be incorporated into sociological investigations of emotion. Specifically, physiological measures corresponding to those currently used to test hypotheses in theories of identify, self, mental health, and emotion would enhance our understanding and explanation of processes in these areas. Measures such as "cortisol levels, heart rate, blood pressure, and vagal tone" could inform researchers in the sociology of emotion (Wisecup et al., 2006, p. 113).

Just as important, I would argue, are individual explanations—such as a person's level of emotional development—in understanding emotional processes such as emotional expression and impression management in sociology. Including this specific variable, along with other individual measures, ensures a more complete representation of social processes, because such a model recognizes the contribution of biological (or physiological), psychological (individual), and social factors. The interplay of life science, personality, and society provide more predictive power and greater understanding of emotion in everyday life.

The contribution that sociological insights can make to understanding emotional development also should be recognized by theorists and students of Dabrowski's theory of positive disintegration. Emotion socialization and emotional development occur within the social environment, with all its complexity and variability. The effect of "the profoundly interactive nature of self-society relations," which Dale Dannefer (1984, p. 100) alludes to in his critique of adult developmental models, is one we should not ignore. Social structure (e.g., education, occupation) as well as social relations (e.g., face-to-face interactions, social networks) not only influence the climate of the environment in which emotion is experienced, they influence how, when, and in what manner emotion is experienced.

Dannefer identified:

> *. . . three types of sociological principles that are crucial to an adequate understanding of human development: (1) the malleability of the human organism in relation to environments; (2) the structural complexity and diversity of the social environment; [and] (3) the role of the symbolic—of social knowledge and human intentionality—as factors mediating development"* (1984, p. 106-107).

Consideration of these factors would enrich our conception of levels of emotional development. For example, a child growing up in worn-torn Iraq today faces fear and anxiety, as does the boy or girl who grows up in a dangerous neighborhood in any large city throughout the world. Though these children may have loving families, their future is uncertain, and they live disrupted lives of pain, loss, and suffering. How does this affect their emotional expression? How does this environment affect their values, their identity and self-feeling, and their relationships with others? Sociologists encourage us to consider the macro environmental effect on our personality, as well as the more evident community, family, and peer effect.

Although I have documented numerous projects assessing levels of emotional development, much more research is needed. Additional predictors, more comparisons with other measures, and research with unique populations will expand our understanding of emotional development. A student in the field of transpersonal psychology recently proposed dissertation research that would explore the specific features of emotional development that characterize spiritually developed persons. Her plans are to use the MACS *Manual for Rating Levels of Emotional Development* (Miller, 1985) in coding responses to the DRI (Apablaza, personal communication, March 23, 2007). More pioneering projects such as this are called for.

As new scholars tackle the difficulty of conceptualization, measurement, and analysis, new techniques will ensue in both quantitative and qualitative research. The combination of physiological, psychological, and sociological variables will enable greater insights into emotions and their relations to cognition in human development.

Further refinements of current instruments and elaboration of the links between emotional development and roles such as parenting and teacher would be a valuable contribution. Future research on Dabrowski's theory, as well as application of its concepts, could benefit from insights offered by sociologists. Likewise, sociologists have much to gain by taking into account biology and personality variables in their research on emotion.

Chapter 13
The Theory of Positive Disintegration (TPD) and Other Approaches to Personality

Sal Mendaglio, Ph.D.[1]

In planning to write this chapter, I had to decide to which approaches should I compare TPD. An obvious criterion was that the approaches had to be well known; it would not be useful to compare TPD, a theory unknown in American personology, to an accepted but little known personality theory. I perused classic and recent theories of personality texts for ideas. Some of the texts (e.g., Corsini, 1977; Walters, 2004) organize their texts similar to the presentation by Hall and Lindzey (1970)—that is, the theories are presented in more or less chronological order of their publication. Other authors categorize personality theories by a theme—for example, depth psychology and humanism (Massey, 1981). Some depart from the chronological or thematic approach and organize their presentation according to issues (e.g., Magnivita, 2002).

Dissatisfied with the way theories were commonly presented, Maddi (1989) created a unique approach to organizing his text on theories of personality. Unlike other schemes, he classified theories to "capture the essential pattern or overall meaning behind…the theories concerning the

1 Sal Mendaglio, Ph.D., Associate Professor, Division of Teacher Preparation, Graduate Division of Educational Research and Research Associate, Centre for Gifted Education, Faculty of Education, University of Calgary, Calgary, Alberta, Canada.

nature of human life" (p. 41), and he devised a three-category solution—conflict model, fulfillment model, and consistency model.

Conflict model includes theories that postulate two forces, which interact to produce conflict within individuals. Typically, the two forces are nature and nurture or person and society. For theorists in this category, conflict is universally experienced, and life is seen as a compromise. Individuals either strike a balance between the two forces or deny one of them.

Fulfillment model includes theories that postulate only one force. Development in these theories is premised on the progressive unfolding of one force within an individual. Life is driven by a sole motivation—actualization of inherited potentials. Society may facilitate or impede the spontaneous unfolding of the inherited force.

Consistency model includes theories that postulate no forces resident within individuals. The theories in this category focus on individuals' responses to feedback received from the social environment in daily living. The prime motivation of individuals is to maintain consistency. Self-referent information that is consistent with individuals' expectations produces no change or discomfort. Feedback that is inconsistent with expectations creates tension and, under some circumstances, leads to change.

Maddi's approach made sense to me, and I decided to use the categories to select theories for my purpose. My first task was to decide in which model category TPD should fit. Given its unique approach to personality, I wasn't surprised when I couldn't fit TPD into any one category (Maddi did warn readers that they may find some theories that did not fit any of his models, though he himself had not encountered any).

TPD postulates the existence of two forces, biology and environment, which Dabrowski called the first factor and second factor, respectively (Dabrowski, 1970). In addition, conflict is a hallmark of the theory, and so it is a conflict model theory. However, Dabrowski also postulated the existence of a third factor of development, representing a powerful autonomous inner force which is rooted in the biological endowment of individuals (Dabrowski, 1973). With this additional force, TPD has elements of the progressive unfolding of a force within individuals, characteristic of Maddi's fulfillment model. After considering the consistency model criteria, I concluded that TPD did not match the main criterion of the consistency model. Theories, in this model, emphasize the role of feedback from the social environment for personality development. In TPD, although developing individuals certainly note the inconsistencies within themselves and society, personality is achieved, in large measure, by the individuals' transcending the influence of the social environment (Dabrowski, 1967). It seemed to me that TPD has fundamental elements in common with both conflict model and fulfillment model theories of personality.

Having established the categories where TPD fits, my next task was to select a theory from each model as contrasts. In the conflict model category, Maddi included Freud (1970/1924) and other theorists such as Murray (1959). Rogers (1959) and Maslow (1968) were theorists that fit the fulfillment model category. Using my popularity criterion, I selected Freud over other conflict theorists such as Murray. Deciding between Rogers and Maslow was more difficult. Given the overlap between Rogers and Maslow, I decided that I needed an additional criterion for my decision making; psychotherapy emerged as a new criterion. Dabrowski not only had extensive psychotherapeutic experience that influenced his theorizing, but also, like Freud and Rogers, had a theory of psychotherapy related to his personality theory. Therefore, I decided to compare TPD to Freud's psychoanalysis and Rogers' self theory.

I could also have considered existential approaches to personality, because they are part of Maddi's fulfillment model. They were not included for two reasons: first, they are not popular approaches, but more importantly, they do not represent a unified theory. However, there is a great deal of similarity between existential psychology and the theory of positive disintegration. Both emphasize similar key concepts such as values, autonomy, authenticity, and existential emotions such as anxiety and depression. A more fundamental similarity is seen in the philosophical underpinnings of TPD, which is in large measure existentialism. Dabrowski was influenced significantly by the works of Kierkegaard (see Chapters 1 and 5 in this volume). The theory of positive disintegration could serve as an effective conceptual framework to systematize the contributions made by existential psychologists such as Binswanger (1963), Boss (1963), May (1958), and Yalom (1980; 1985). A discussion of this is beyond the scope of this chapter.

While Freud's and Rogers' theories are well known, they are not currently the most popular approaches to personality in psychology. The Big Five, also known as the Five Factor Model (John & Scrivastava, 1999), is the most popular current approach to personality (e.g., Ekehammar & Akrami, 2007). Although the Big Five is not a theory of personality, because of its current influence in the field, I decided to also include this approach to personality. Therefore, in this chapter, I contrast some core elements of psychoanalysis, self theory, the Big Five, and TPD. I discuss the three theories under the headings of biological force, social force, personality structure, and stages of development. After a brief introductory note for each topic, my discussion of the theories proceeds in the following order: psychoanalysis, self theory, and positive disintegration. I contrast the Big Five and TPD in a final, separate section.

Psychoanalysis, Self Theory, and Theory of Positive Disintegration

Biological Force: Instincts

Psychoanalysis, self theory, and the theory of positive disintegration postulate the existence of a biological force that influences personality development. Instincts are a manifestation of this force. Freud, Dabrowski, and Rogers differ in their representation of instincts. Of the three theorists, Freud presents the most detailed account of the nature of instincts and their function. Dabrowski recognized the same instincts as Freud, but Dabrowski interprets them differently and adds some of his own. Rogers' account of the biological force underlying his theory is rather brief. He did not use the term instinct, but his biological force, in my view, is tantamount to an instinct. While their presentation varies, all three theories view a biological force as a *sine qua non* of personality development.

Psychoanalysis

In psychoanalysis, (Freud, 1970/1924; Maddi, 1989; Hall & Lindzey, 1970) instincts are part of the biological makeup of all individuals and dictate daily behavior throughout life. Gratification of instincts is *the* motivator of human behavior. According to this view, if it weren't for societal prescriptions and prohibitions, individuals would act impulsively, gratifying each biological need as it arises. Freud, in a detailed account of his view of instincts, noted that their source lies in the in somatic process. Energy of the instincts emanates from the organism's experience of a deprivation in some system—both the source and energy of instincts are internal to the organism. Instincts are mental representations of bodily processes. When the body lacks something, a state of tension is created, and there is internal pressure on the individual to act to reduce the tension by eliminating the deprivation. States of bodily deprivation are presumed to occur constantly within organisms, and so instincts are continually influencing individuals' behavior in daily life.

An important aspect of instincts in psychoanalysis is the object needed for gratification. While the source and energy aspects of instincts are constant, objects are variable. For example, when bodily processes result in a lowering of blood-sugar levels, tension is created—interpreted as hunger—and the individual is motivated to seek food, the object that would gratify the need. The type of food used, however, varies and is influenced by other factors such as learning and cultural contexts. An important element in the notion of object is the idea of substitution. In some cases, for example, when the bodily tension called hunger emerges, an individual may not seek out solid food but may have a cup of coffee or seek distraction instead. Such substitutions, of course, have their limitations and potential problems.

Freud proposed three types of instincts: life instinct, sexual instinct, and death instinct. Of the three instincts, he gave the most prominent position in his theory to the sexual instinct. Gratification of the sexual instinct provides the greatest opportunity for individuals to encounter difficulties with societal mores and expectations. Behaviors driven by the life (self-preservation) instinct—that is, seeking food, water, and air for survival—are governed by fewer societal regulations and taboos. Further, food, water, and air are essential for life. Sexual gratification, on the other hand, while essential for the survival of the species, is not essential for the survival of an individual. In addition, mature gratification of the sexual instinct brings individuals into intimate contact with other members of society.

Freud included the death instinct later in his life (Maddi, 1989). It seems that the death instinct is an extension of the organism's need to be at rest, to be in homeostatic balance. Drives and needs create tension—a disruption of homeostasis—and the individual is motivated to engage in activities to reduce tension and restore balance. The death instinct represents the individual's desire to achieve the ultimate reduction of tension. Of the three instincts, it seems logical that Freud gave the sexual instinct *the* influential role in personality development (Maddi, 1989).

The instincts are subsumed in Freud's structure of personality; they constitute the id. The id is the repository of the instincts, and it is the innate part of the personality—the constitutional endowment of all individuals. There are neither controls nor consciousness in this part of the personality. Organismic tensions rise, and individuals automatically respond to reduce the tension, to gratify a need. The primary function of individuals is the gratification of instinctual drives and needs—to respond to their ids. When this cannot be done, individuals experience negative emotions such as frustration and anger. The primary reason this cannot be done is civilized society, which is ultimately responsible for the experiencing of such negative emotions—and the emergence of the other components of personality.

Self Theory

Self theory (Rogers, 1959; 1961) postulates a universal biological tendency of all living things to actualize their inherited potentialities. This *actualizing tendency* is the "inherent tendency of the organism to develop all its capacities in ways which serve to maintain or enhance the organism" (1959, p. 196). In addition to satisfying biological needs associated with self-preservation, the actualizing tendency includes a movement away from external, social control toward autonomy. Further, actualizing one's potentialities is consistent with, and not in conflict with, others' actualizing their potentials. In self theory, the actualizing tendency is the only motivation, and the organism as a whole exhibits it. While Rogers does not use the word *instinct*, the actualizing tendency, with its biological nature and universality, could also be called the actualizing instinct. The actualizing tendency is guided by the organismic valuing process, which selects stimuli and behaviors that serve to enhance the organism. Unlike Freud, Rogers did not elaborate on the biologically-based concepts that are of critical importance to his theory of personality.

Rogers also stipulated that individuals have a need for unconditional positive regard. That is, individuals need to be accepted, or prized, for who they are without judgment; they should not be valued based on the quality of their behaviors. It is unclear whether this need is inherited or learned, though for Rogers (1959), this is irrelevant. Unconditional positive regard, or the lack of it, is of paramount importance for personality development in self theory.

Positive Disintegration

Biological endowment also occupies a central role in positive disintegration (Dabrowski, 1964a; 1967; 1970; 1973). There are countless references to instincts in positive disintegration (e.g., Dabrowski, 1970). The theory includes a number of instincts: self-preservation, sexual, developmental, death, creative, and self-perfection. Unlike Freud's analysis of the self-preservation and sexual instincts, Dabrowski believed that, if personality is to develop, these instincts need to be transformed, not simply gratified. Self-preservation instinct transforms to include the preservation of the integrity of the person, not simple biological survival; sexual instinct moves from an indiscriminant drive for gratification to an exclusive loving relationship with another. While psychoanalysis also speaks of transformation of instincts, the process is unconscious, and the motivation is ego defensive. For example, sublimation of the sexual instinct occurs to protect individuals from the anxiety associated with acknowledging socially tabooed sexual impulses into awareness. For Dabrowski, it is clear that the transformation of instincts is a conscious process motivated by individuals' values; individuals intentionally reject the lower expression of the instincts for a higher form.

In addition to the two basic instincts, Dabrowski proposed several others. The developmental instinct is the repository of all forces of development and is endowed differentially among individuals. From the developmental instinct, *developmental potential* is differentiated. Dabrowski included overexcitability, dynamisms, and special abilities and talents in his concept of developmental potential. Overexcitability, a property of the central nervous system, has five forms: psychomotor, sensual, imaginational, intellectual, and emotional. Dynamisms are autonomous inner forces which direct the process of personality development. Dabrowski proposed that developmental potential is manifested early in life in various forms of special abilities and talents. As an outgrowth of the developmental instinct, level of development also varies among individuals.

Similar to Freud, Dabrowski included a death instinct, which he depicted as having two directions: external and internal. Externally focused death instinct includes aggression, hatred, and the desire to inflict pain on others. The internally focused form may result in suicide or in the destruction of primitive aspects of mental organization. The latter form, termed "partial death instinct," is positive and contributes to the development of personality.

The instincts of creativity and self-perfection are not instincts in the usual sense of the word. They are not universally endowed, only appearing in some individuals when they are on the path of advanced development. Dabrowski noted that the creative instinct "discovers and molds new forms of reality" (1973, p. 27). Similarly, the self-perfection instinct appears in the course of advanced development and is described as "the highest instinct of a human being" (1973, p. 32). Both instincts are anchored to biology—that is, their seeds are evident early in life in those individuals endowed with favorable developmental potential. When combined, creative and self-perfection instincts play an essential role in personality development; their combination results not only in novel mental structures, but also in structures characterized by higher values.

There is some similarity between Dabrowski's and Rogers' theorizing regarding biological forces. Left to their own devices, developmental instinct and actualizing tendency will unfold, revealing individuals' natures. When individuals are favorably endowed with the Dabrowskian instincts—developmental potential, creative instincts, and self-perfection—the result is movement toward autonomy and authenticity similar to the unimpeded evolution of the actualizing tendency. However, there is major difference: Rogers assumed that all living organisms are equally endowed with an actualizing tendency, while Dabrowski spoke of variable endowment of his instincts.

Social Force: Socialization

Psychoanalysis and the theory of positive disintegration postulate a social force which interacts with the biological force, producing conflict in individuals. However, Freud and Dabrowski conceptualized the nature of the conflict and its role in personality development in dramatically different ways. Self theory does not postulate a social force that is in opposition with the biological force. In self theory, conflict occurs, but it is not inevitable nor necessary for personality development. However, all three theories do emphasize the importance of the socialization process in personality development.

Psychoanalysis

For Freud, there is a double-edged quality to civilized society—it is essential for human functioning, and it causes problems. A world in which individuals are continuously and automatically responding to id impulses is untenable. Instinctual needs are never permanently sated; instincts have a continual, moment-to-moment influence on the organism. A primary purpose of society is to create order out of an otherwise chaotic and dangerous world of self-gratifications. Societies specify acceptable and unacceptable modes of gratification with enforcement of these prescriptions, ranging from inducing feelings of embarrassment and guilt to physical punishment and death. This instilling of inhibition of impulses is achieved through the socialization process in the first few years of life. Society, through parents as primary agents of socialization, teaches inhibition through direct instruction and punishment or the threat of it. Through parental instructions, admonishments, criticism, and punishment, children learn self-regulation.

Self Theory

Unlike Freud and Dabrowski, Rogers did not postulate society as one of two antagonistic forces. An individual's actualizing tendency—the instinct of maintaining and enhancing the organism—does not, in and of itself, run counter to others' actualizing their inherited potentials. In Rogers' approach, actualizing one's potentials is not only good for the individual, it is good for others as well; what's good for an individual is good for society. However, the social environment has a significant influence on the actualizing tendency and on personality development.

The social environment may facilitate or impede the operation of the actualizing tendency. If individuals' need for unconditional positive regard from significant others such as parents is met, then individuals' *organismic valuing process* occurs, in which "the organism experiences satisfaction in those stimuli or behaviors which maintain and enhance the organism and the self both in the immediate present and in the long range" (Rogers, 1959, p. 210). This process works in concert with the actualizing tendency of the organism. Problems arise if socialization interferes with the organismic valuing process and if young children begin to shift their focus for guiding their actions and experiencing away from the internal to the external world. In essence, problems arise when the need for unconditional positive regard is not met and children are not valued for themselves but rather for the quality of their actions. In this way, individuals learn to evaluate their experiences and actions based on the values and expectations of others rather than their actualizing tendency. Rogers noted that his analysis did not mean that children should not be socialized, but rather that significant others need to do this in a way that communicates acceptance and respect for the personhood of the child.

Positive Disintegration

Dabrowski proposed that the two forces—nature and nurture—may or may not produce conflict for individuals. For highly socialized individuals, there may be little conflict experienced as they live their lives in robotic compliance with societal demands. When conflict is experienced, it is not simply of the psychoanalytic type. Some individuals experience conflict caused by their exclusive focus on gratification of biological needs, which conflicts with the strictures of society. Other individuals may experience conflict that stems from the discrepancy they experience between the way society ought to be and the way it is. Whether or not conflict is experienced, and its type, depends largely on constitutional endowment. The greater the developmental potential, the more likely individuals are to experience conflict stemming from the discrepancy they perceive between universal values and the actual workings of society.

In positive disintegration, the social environment is also discussed in terms of its role in development. At the extreme levels of developmental potential, high or low levels, the environment has virtually no influence. Those with very high levels will develop psychologically, while those at the other extreme will not, regardless of the quality of the social environment. For levels of developmental potential in between, a nurturing environment will facilitate development; a neglectful or abusive social environment will impede development.

The theory of positive disintegration notes, as does self theory, that socialization of children should be conducted in a sensitive manner. Adults are to accept children's expression of overexcitabilities and nurture their special abilities and talents. However, the goal is not to have highly socialized individuals who are adjusted to society. For Dabrowski, adjustment to societal expectations did not indicate mental health. Instead, living life by one's constructed system of values, which would at times be in conflict with society, was an important feature of mental health.

Personality Structure

Both psychoanalysis and self theory discuss the structure of personality in varying detail, with Freud's account being more elaborate than Rogers. With his unique approach to personality, Dabrowski (not surprisingly) does not specify a structure, but rather describes its nature in terms of traits that comprise it.

Psychoanalysis

The structure of personality includes the id, ego, and superego. The id, as previously noted, is part of the universal constitutional endowment of individuals and is the repository of all instincts. Were it not for societal demands, the id would form the entirety of Freudian personality; it is the socialization process that necessitates the Freudian personality structure. Young children learn that when they do what comes naturally, they are likely to experience harsh consequences from significant others. To deal with this eventuality, psychoanalysis postulates the differentiation of the ego from the id. It is important to note that the ego is in the service of the id.

The ego is a mental function that becomes conscious of societal rules and expectations, with its aim being the gratification of id impulses in the external, social world. In order to accomplish this, the ego guides an individual's intelligence and muscles in such as way as to minimizing punishment and defend the individual against anxiety and guilt (Maddi, 1989). The ebb and flow of tension created by instincts and their gratification continually puts the individual at odds with societal rules. Because of the ubiquitousness of the action of instincts, individuals regularly experience conflict with society. They learn to avoid punishment by inhibition of impulses or by using socially prescribed objects for instinctual gratification.

However, whenever these processes cannot be followed or when the intensity of an instinct is too strong, individuals experience anxiety and guilt, and they anticipate punishment. The well-known ego defenses (e.g., denial, sublimation, and projection) spontaneously engage to deal with the conflict and prevent anxiety from coming into awareness. By definition, the defenses are unconscious, and so the process of transforming an original prohibited impulse into an acceptable desire or behavior is not available to individuals. If it were, the individual would experience dire psychological consequences, such as a loss of integrity—disintegration of the personality. According to Freud, we can't handle the truth! Defenses protect us from it.

The superego is a mental process that is differentiated from the ego. Societal rules and expectations are incorporated by children into a set of values, which are used to classify behaviors or thoughts into either "right" or "wrong." With the emergence of the superego, individuals begin to feel guilt. Whereas punishment controls individuals from the outside, guilt is an internal regulator of behavior. Guilt produces tension in individuals equal to that produced by punishment. The superego, as a result, affects ego functioning; the ego now has to include guilt reduction as well as prevention of punishment as factors to manage while it engages in instinctual gratification.

Self Theory

In self theory, the organism is the biological substrate of personality; it is the "locus of experience" (Hall & Lindzey, 1970, p. 528). For Rogers, experiencing is the *sine qua non* of personality, which consists of the phenomenal field and self-concept (Rogers, 1951). The phenomenal field "includes all that is experienced by the organism…whether or not these experiences are consciously perceived" (p. 483). The phenomenal field, also termed the "perceptual field," is dynamic and fluid, representing the variability of moment-to-moment experiencing of the individual. Specific sensations and perceptions continuously move from background to figure in the phenomenal field. Rogers contended that only a small portion of the phenomenal field is consciously experienced at any particular time, though a large portion of it is available to conscious awareness.

Rogers used the term "experience" both as a noun and a verb. Experience, the noun, referred to all the here-and-now processes within the organism that are available to awareness. As such, experience does not refer to the accumulation of an organism's history. Experience as a verb referred to "symboliz[ing] in some accurate form at the conscious level the impact of...sensory or visceral events" (1959, p. 197). Symbolization, awareness, and consciousness were used synonymously by Rogers. Awareness or consciousness is the symbolic representation of one's experience. Symbolizing experience may be accurate or inaccurate. Accurate symbolization results when the symbols we use to represent a sensation accurately reflect external reality. Determination of accuracy for Rogers rests on the individual's use of hypothesis testing of inwardnesses. Inaccurate symbolization of experiences is presumed to create psychological difficulties for individuals.

From a portion of the individual's total experiences emerges an awareness of one's being that Rogers termed "self-experience" (1959, p. 223), and it is from this self-experience that self-concept is constructed. Self-experience, shaped by interaction with significant adults, becomes the self or self-concept—a perceptual object in one's phenomenal field. The self-perceptions that comprise self-concept are not necessarily conscious, though they are available to consciousness. Rogers described self-concept as a gestalt of perceptions that are related to "I" or "me," including any values associated with these perceptions (1959). Self-experiences include an evaluative dimension which is emotionally laden and "may arise directly from organismic responses to experiences, or they may be introjected or borrowed from others, so that the individuals claim them as his or her own, but is really distorting personal experience by imposing another's interpretation on it" (Massey, 1981, p. 310). Rogers also included an ideal self—what the person would like to be—in addition to the self as it is.

Positive Disintegration

Dabrowski proposed a conception of personality that difffers significantly from Freud's and Rogers.' While Freud and Rogers obviously differ in their respective approaches to personality, there is a common element in their theories: universality of personality. All individuals possess an id, ego, and superego, or a phenomenal field and a self-concept. In contrast, positive disintegration views personality as an achievement—and a rare one at that. Personality is a coherent and harmonized mental organization characterized by the most positive of human values. It represents the highest level of human development. Individuals who achieve personality are highly self-aware, autonomous, authentic, and responsible for self and others. They are capable of guiding their own learning and, when confronted with difficulties, can act as their own therapists. Personality consists of a constellation of traits, many of which are encountered in humanistic theories of personality, such as self theory. Dabrowski's view of personality has some features in common with Rogers' fully functioning person (discussed below); a major difference is that Dabrowski reserved the term "personality" to denote the highest level of human functioning and not as an attribute of all humanity. Though personality is an organized and harmonized mental organization, it is not static; self-improvement continues, though it is consciously guided by the individual and his or her system of values (Dabrowski, 1967).

Stages of Personality Development

Both Freud and Dabrowski articulated stages of personality development. While their thinking on this issue is dramatically different, there is at least one similarity: not all individuals progress through all of the stages. Rogers does not specify stages, but I see a progression, an evolution, in his articulation of self theory, and so I have included that description in this section as well.

Psychoanalysis

As noted earlier, Freud focused his theory of personality on the sexual instinct, because compared with the self-preservation instinct, individuals will experience more conflict in the course of sexual gratification than the other instincts; society simply has more rules and regulations surrounding this area of human nature. The main stages of development are identified by "concrete form[s] of the sexual instinct" (Maddi, 1989, p. 274) and, as such, can be described as particular instances of the general conflict between society and the sexual instinct. Psychoanalysis postulates four major psychosexual stages associated with so-called erogenous—pleasure-producing—zones of the body: oral, anal, phallic, and genital. Stages are associated with physical maturation, ranging from infancy to adolescence, but "*the first few years of life are decisive for the formation of personality*" (italics in original, Hall & Lindzey, 1970, p. 51).

In the oral stage, which is associated with the first year of life, pleasure is primarily associated with the mouth and eating. With the eruption of teeth comes chewing of food and biting. Incorporating of food and biting are said to be prototypical of later traits. Incorporation of food is later transformed, for example, into *taking in* knowledge—that is, learning. Biting may later be expressed in sarcasm.

In the anal stage, associated with the second year of life, the primary source of pleasure is bowel movements, which eliminate the source of discomfort brought on by the digestive process. Toilet training is the child's first experience with a societally-imposed control over an instinctual impulse. In essence, the child is required to delay gratification of the elimination impulse and the pleasure associated with it. How toilet training is implemented is said to have significant consequences for the development of personality traits. Approached in a strict, punitive manner, this training may result in a child's withholding elimination. Later in life, this may lead to a retentive characteristic, which may express itself in miserliness and stubbornness. Alternatively, if the training is conducted in a supportive manner including praise, creativity and productivity may ensue in later life.

In the phallic stage, ages three to five, the sex organs are the primary source of pleasure. It is in this phase that the child experiences the Oedipus complex, for males, and the Electra complex, for females. Children want to possess parents of the opposite sex, displacing parents of the same sex. As children resolve these conflicts through such processes as identification with the same-sex parent, they long to be adults.

If individuals' development is not arrested or fixated at any of the first three stages of development, they progress to the genital stage, the apex of personality development. While the erogenous zone is not different from the phallic stage, the genital stage is characterized by complete physical sexual maturation and full adult expression of the sexual instinct. However, the genital stage is not conflict-free; individuals still need to contend with societal taboos.

In psychoanalysis, the pregenital stages represent immaturity; the genital stage represents maturity. Psychological maturity is defined in terms of how successful individuals are in coming to terms with the inevitable conflict stemming from the sexual instinct bumping up against the taboos of society at each stage of development.

Self Theory

Self theory does not include any stages of personality development. However, Rogers did describe a progression beginning with the differentiation of self-concept from the phenomenal field, the development of the needs for positive self-regard, the development of maladjustment and its remediation, and culminating in his pinnacle of development—the fully functioning person.

With the emergence of self-concept, the needs for positive regard from others and positive self-regard appear. These needs, which are considered universal and persistent, refer to needing attitudes such as respect, liking, and warmth from other people. However, for Rogers, to facilitate an individual's growth, the positive regard should be given without conditions. *Unconditional positive regard*, a key concept in his theory, is synonymous with acceptance and prizing; in this form of positive regard, there is literally no judgment or evaluation of the person or his or her behaviors. As a result of receiving unconditional positive regard, all self-experience is equal and allowed into awareness. The need for positive self-regard is an extension of the need for positive regard by others and is presumed to be learned through the incorporation of positive regard from others. As with positive regard from others, the highest form of positive self-regard is the unconditional type.

Rogers postulated that problems develop when the need for positive regard from significant others overrides the organismic valuing process, which is anchored to experiencing and the actualizing tendency. When children, for example, do not receive unconditional positive regard, they become conditioned to focus their behavior and selectively attend to their experiences that do receive positive regard from parents. This process subverts the naturally occurring organismic valuing process by which the organism attends to stimuli and engages in behaviors that maintain and enhance both the organism and the self—in concert with the actualizing tendency. To illustrate this, Rogers provided an example of an "infant who at one moment values food, and when satiated, is disgusted with it; at one moment values stimulation, and soon after, values only rest; who finds satisfying that diet which in the long run most enhances its development" (1959, p. 210). This example also illustrates the related notion of locus of evaluation. In self theory, this could either be internal or external. The example illustrates internal locus of evaluation. Left to his or her own devices, the infant is the center of the valuing process; what is of importance is determined by sensory experience. When the locus of evaluation is external, the judgment of others becomes the criterion determining the value of an event or object.

Related to external locus of evaluation is the concept of *conditions of worth*, italicized to indicate its importance in self theory. Conditions of worth are created when positive regard, dispensed by significant others, is contingent on what those significant others perceive to be worthy based on their standards and values. Over time, such feedback from significant others is incorporated into individuals' self-concepts. Assimilated conditions of worth serve to impose values on experiences, not because of their intrinsic value, but because certain experiences and behaviors have satisfied the need for positive regard from significant others. In this way, the locus of evaluation shifts from internal to external—to society—meaning that values are not created by the organismic valuing process but rather by the opinions of others. In the process, conditions of worth interfere with accurate symbolization of experience. Individuals decide upon the value of experiences as positive or negative as if they were applying the actualizing tendency, when they are actually using external criteria that have been introjected. With the valuing process disturbed, individuals' ability to function effectively and freely is reduced.

Conditions of worth, once incorporated into self-concept, produce selective perception of experience, which ultimately has negative psychological consequences for individuals. Experiences that are consistent with the conditions of worth are accurately symbolized; experiences that are inconsistent with the conditions of worth are distorted or denied awareness. What this means is that some of the experiences occurring in the organism are not allowed into awareness; the experiences are not recognized as self-experiences. In this fashion, the conditions of worth, by producing incongruence between self and experience, lead to psychological maladjustment. Incongruence is a state of tension and confusion. For Rogers, as conditions of worth increase, so does incongruence with proportionate increases in psychological maladjustment.

Rogers postulated that the source of maladjustment is internal conflict, because with the incorporation of the conditions of worth, the organism no longer acts as a whole. This fragmentation is reflected in behaviors. Some behaviors will be motivated by the conditions of worth; other behaviors by the actualizing tendency. For Rogers, when conditions of worth are involved, the tendency to self-actualize is a partial actualization of the organism's experiences—only those that have been symbolized as the self-concept will be actualized. Neurotic behavior, which is incomprehensible to the individual him- or herself, is one result of this conflict: "What is commonly called neurotic behavior is one example; the neurotic behavior is incomprehensible to the individual himself, since it is at variance with what he consciously 'wants' to do, which is to actualize a self no longer congruent with experience" (Rogers, 1959, p. 203). This conflict and the severity of the maladjustment intensify as conditions of worth become a greater influence on the self with the ensuing selective handling of one's experiencing.

Some experiences that are inconsistent with the self-concept are subceived—perceived as threatening without symbolizing into awareness (Rogers, 1959). If such experiences were symbolized for what they actually are, they would have a drastic effect on the self-concept. Awareness of such experiences would shatter the organization of the self-concept, because they run counter to the conditions of worth. A state of anxiety would ensue. To counter this eventuality, defenses are activated. For Rogers, defenses included selective perception, distortion, and denial. In the course of protecting the gestalt structure of the self, defensiveness produce rigidity in perception and inaccurate perception of reality.

The description of self theory to this point involves concepts and processes that are universal, but Rogers also included concepts and processes that occur only under certain circumstances. These include disorganization, reintegration, and the fully functioning person.

Disorganization is a rather serious state of distress caused by the failure of defenses. The integrity of self-concept is ruptured by the failure of the individual to deny or distort a threatening experience. The discrepancy between self-concept and the awareness of the experience produces intense anxiety. The state of disorganization manifests in fluctuations of behaviors; some behaviors are motivated by the experience newly admitted into awareness; other behaviors are motivated by the existing self-concept. Disorganization is an extreme form of "the basic estrangement" (Rogers, 1959, p. 226) of humanity, which has its origins in the conditions of worth. Severe maladjustment is associated with disorganization, and Rogers was not optimistic about the prognosis for individuals who experience it.

As one can see, in self theory, the conditions of worth are *the* cause of psychological maladjustment. The communication of these conditions causes infants to move away from their naturally occurring integrated state, thereby subverting the natural organismic valuing system. Seeking positive regard from others becomes the primary motivation. Attaining positive regard from others requires distortion and denying of experiences that are inconsistent with others' values. The need for positive regard gives rise to defensiveness. Defensiveness creates neurotic and psychotic behaviors. Unlike his view of disorganization representing a failure of defensiveness, Rogers stated that neurotic and some psychotic conditions brought about by defensiveness can be treated successfully. The process by which individuals may approximate the original organismic valuing process and actualizing tendency is reintegration.

Reintegration is a twofold process of elimination of defensiveness and assimilation of a previously threatening experience into the self-structure. For Rogers, reintegration rests on individuals' experiencing an increase of unconditional positive regard with the concomitant reduction in conditions of worth. Empathic understanding is the way that unconditional positive regard is communicated. Through empathic understanding, individuals' perception of threat is reduced, with the concomitant reduction in the need for defense. With a lessening of perception of threat, individuals allow awareness of experience and integrate it into the self-concept. Rogers noted that this process of reintegration rests squarely on feedback from other people:

> *[T]he reintegration or restoration of personality occurs always and only...in the presence of certain definable conditions [unconditional positive regard and empathic communication]. These are essentially the same whether we are speaking of formal psychotherapy continued over a considerable period, in which rather drastic personality changes may occur, or whether we are speaking of the minor constructive changes which may be brought about by contact with an understanding friend or family member* (1959, p. 231).

Reintegration cannot be accomplished through individual effort. This restorative process occurs within a relationship in which an individual experiences unconditional positive regard from a significant other. With ongoing receipt of this acceptance and prizing by another, a series of events is triggered that are necessary for reaching the pinnacle of human development. With the empathically communicated unconditional positive regard, individuals dramatically reduce the perception of threat in their experiences. They significantly reduce the need for defensives, and self and experience become more congruent. Positive regard for others increases with increase in self-regard. In the reintegration process, the person becomes fully functioning.

Rogers used various terms to describe the fully functioning person, including "the goal of social evolution" and "the end point of optimal psychotherapy;" however, I think that the best phrase, congruent with his theory, is "the ultimate in the actualization of the human organism" (1959, p. 234). The fully functioning person is attuned to the actualizing tendency and organismic valuing system. The self-structure is consistent with the individual's experiencing. Such individuals are also open to experience; all experiences are allowed into awareness. With no need for external regard, the individual experiences unconditional positive self-regard, which is also extended to others. Rogers' depiction of optimal psychological adjustment and maturity is not static—that is, the fully functioning person is a "person-in-process" (1959, p. 235). There are certain factors that are absent in the fully functioning person. These include conditions of worth, incongruence, and external locus of evaluation.

Positive Disintegration

Dabrowski proposed five levels of development representing different forms of integration and disintegration. Progression through the levels is neither universal nor linear. In psychoanalysis, individuals are presumed to experience the three pregenital stages unless fixation occurs, though not everyone reaches the genital stage—the psychoanalytical pinnacle of development. Reaching the genital stage is premised on one's handling of the societal prescriptions; presumably, the less restrictive the social environment is regarding sexual gratification, the better it is for individual development. An environment with fewer taboos seemingly facilitates individuals' achievement of the genital stage and psychological maturity. In self theory, only those who experience sufficient unconditional positive regard by significant others, communicated empathically, will become fully functioning. In both of these theories, advanced development is largely dependent on the social environment. In positive disintegration, advanced development is premised on favorable constitutional endowment. Such endowment, reflected in developmental potential, spurs individuals into the process of development. Personality is achieved through the internal process of positive disintegration, which is responsible for the destruction of an individual's original primitive mental organization, and a reintegration at a higher level of functioning culminating in secondary integration.

The primitive or primary integration, Level I, is not considered healthy, because at this level, individuals are motivated by their biological need and the need to comply with societal norms. Dabrowski proposed two subgroups of individuals who are at the first level: highly socialized individuals, and sociopaths. Many of the primitively integrated individuals, though potentially successful materially, lead an unexamined life. Such individuals are not considered unworthy or evil by Dabrowski; in fact, they may be perceived as "the salt of the earth" types. They simply are prisoners either of their biological drives and/or the need to unquestionably conform to societal standards.

The other subgroup, however, is more notorious and dangerous. Such individuals typically use their personal resources, such as intelligence, to take advantage of others to gratify their egocentric needs and, in extreme cases, to gratify their needs regardless of the consequences to others and themselves. Individuals' integrated mental organization is at the service of biological needs and/or compliance with society.

Dabrowski's view of integration is different from other theorists' (such as Rogers') use of the term. Integration has traditionally been thought of as a positive psychological quality. In positive disintegration, only secondary integration, the final level of development, is seen as positive in terms of psychological health.

The mental organization associated with primary integration needs to be loosened before an individual can move to the next level. The process of undoing and ultimately destroying the existing mental organization is performed by dynamisms, autonomous forces that are part of developmental potential. Initially, dynamisms are triggered by developmental milestones, such as puberty, or crises in the social environment. Such experiences serve to disrupt mental equilibrium, creating a state of ambiguity where structure and predictability once existed. Level II, unilevel disintegration, is in essence a transition level; because of the high anxiety associated with it, individuals either return to primary integration or move to Level III, spontaneous multilevel disintegration.

In contrast to the ambivalences experienced in unilevel disintegration in Level II, disintegration is multilevel and spontaneous in Level III. It is called multilevel because individuals begin to experience phenomena in a hierarchical way: some feelings, attitudes, and behaviors are perceived to be more valuable than others. It is in this phase of development that individuals experience the internal conflict arising from their experiencing the discrepancy between how the world ought to be and the way it actually is. It is called spontaneous because it is not under the direction of the person. A variety of dynamisms operate at this level—including feelings of shame and guilt, astonishment with oneself, and dissatisfaction with self—to extend the loosening of the mental organization begun in Level II and form the disintegration process.

In contrast to the spontaneous quality of the disintegration in Level III, disintegration in Level IV is organized and multilevel—that is, it is under the deliberate control of the individual. At this level, human functioning is driven by dynamisms of empathy, autonomy, authenticity, and the third factor, which coordinates the operation of the dynamisms. In addition, the dynamisms of self-education and autopsychotherapy appear, motivating individuals to identify areas of improvement and to develop their own strategies to meet those needs. Dynamisms at this level begin the reintegration process.

Level V completes the reintegration process with the achievement of personality. The only novel dynamism at this final level is one's personality ideal, which individuals use to guide their daily behaviors. Individuals at Level V have achieved personality and represent the epitome of humanity.

The levels of development represent the process of positive disintegration. Positive disintegration is a combination of disintegration and reintegration at a higher level. It is defined by the positive outcome of the process. In Dabrowski's theory, there is also negative disintegration—that is, a disintegrative process that ends in negative outcomes, such as suicide. In both cases, however, "disintegration" is different from its use by Freud or Rogers. In both psychoanalysis and self theory, disintegration is always negative, representing a failure of defensiveness. In both of those theories, defensiveness is seen as necessary for psychological adjustment. Implicit in Freud's and Rogers' views is that unconsciousness or lack of awareness is associated with adjustment. With ideal environmental conditions, this would not be the case, but because of societal taboos regarding sex or because of the conditions of worth present in the social environment, a certain amount of unconsciousness is required.

On the other hand, Dabrowski's disintegration is not the product of a breakdown of defenses, but rather the result of a disruption of mental equilibrium brought about primarily by autonomous inner forces, specifically the dynamisms. Although Dabrowski uses defensive terms such as "sublimation," their use lacks the unconscious quality associated with their use by Freud or Rogers. In fact, for Dabrowski, psychological development is a progression from an unconscious approach to life to an increasingly conscious appreciation of self and society. Awareness of one's nature, including self-preservation and sexual instincts, enables its transformation from an animal-like state to one of being truly human.

Similarly, Rogers' use of reintegration is different from Dabrowski's. For Rogers, reintegration refers to assimilation of a previously threatening experience into the self-structure by the elimination of defensiveness. Reintegration can only occur when individuals experience unconditional positive regard. For Dabrowski, reintegration, as part of positive disintegration, occurs within an individual and is equated with the acquisition of a higher level of human functioning.

Similar contrasts can be seen in the terminology used by both Rogers and Dabrowski. "Consistency" or "congruence" appears in both theories. However, Rogers spoke of congruence between self-concept and phenomenal field of experiencing, whereas Dabrowski referred to consistency of behavior and values. Both use terms such as "autonomy" and "authenticity," and there is some overlap between Dabrowski's view of personality and Rogers' fully functioning person. However, the process by which these arise and their role in personality development is explained by Dabrowski and, largely, simply proclaimed by Rogers.

A related difference between positive disintegration and the other theories rests in how it sees psychopathology. This difference is particularly evident in the area of neuroses. What Freud and Rogers saw as something to be remedied, Dabrowski saw as indicative of the potential for advanced development. To be precise, Dabrowski spoke of psychoneuroses, which referred to mental processes, rather than neuroses, which he equated with psychosomatic conditions (Dabrowski, 1972). The disintegration part of positive disintegration—the dynamisms such as shame, guilt, and dissatisfaction with oneself—are psychoneurotic symptoms serving the essential purpose of destroying the existing primitive mental structures. Not only are psychoneuroses not illnesses, they are essential for personality development. Psychoneurotic individuals are not to be treated with the intention of "curing" them; such individuals need to understand the essential contribution of their suffering to their development.

On a final note, unlike psychoanalysis, positive disintegration does not view values and morals as factors to be coped with or denied. They are to be lived. The contents of the superego are not to be rejected because the moral standards may be too high; they are to be scrutinized, and those inconsistent with an individual's hierarchy of values are discarded. Further, the pinnacle of human development is not the satisfaction of sexual instincts in all of its erogenous zones in mature relationships with others, but rather consciously living one's life consistent with one's ideals autonomously, authentically, and altruistically.

The Big Five and Positive Disintegration

The Big Five is a trait approach to personality that has immense popularity among those conducting psychological research in personality. Traits are also mentioned in the theory of positive disintegration, though Dabrowski typically used "psychological types" to refer to them.

The Big Five

Also known as the Five Factor Model, the Big Five approach has its origin in the lexical approach to personality traits used by Allport and Odbert (1936). In their seminal work, they perused dictionaries to identify words that they deemed to have relevance for describing people. They amassed about 18,000 words, which they presented alphabetically and in four categories: (1) personality traits; (2) states, moods, and activities; (3) judgments of personality conduct and reputation; and (4) physical characteristics, capacities, and talents (John & Scrivastava, 1999). Of relevance to the development of the Big Five are those words categorized as personality traits, which Allport and Odbert defined as "generalized and personalized determining tendencies—consistent and stable modes of an individual's adjustment to his environment"(p. 26). As predicted by Allport and Odbert, their compilation of words did keep researchers busy for many years. Researchers working with the personality traits category ultimately discovered the Big Five trait taxonomy.

Cattell (1959) made a significant contribution to the development of the taxonomy of traits. Using a subset of 4,500 trait terms drawn from Allport and Odbert's list, Cattell extracted 35 variables, and in so doing, eliminated 99% of the terms on the original list (John & Scrivastava, 1999). From his factor analytic research with the variables, Cattell identified 12 personality factors that he included in his Sixteen Personality Factor Questionnaire (Cattell, Eber, & Tatsuoka, 1970). The discovery and clarification of the Big Five were accomplished by several researchers (e.g., Borgatta, 1964; Digman & Takemotto-Chock, 1981; Fiske, 1949, Norman, 1963; Tupes & Christal, 1992) working with Cattell's variable list.

The Big Five taxonomy consists of five higher-order personality traits or factors: Neuroticism, Extroversion, Openness to Experience, Agreeableness, and Conscientiousness (Chamorro-Premuzic, 2005). These factors have been found consistently, regardless of measurement technique used [e.g., self-report or expert rating (McCrae & Costa, 1999)] or specific scales [e.g., California Psychological Inventory (Gough, 1987), *Adjective Check List* (Gough & Heilbrun, 1983), NEO Personality Inventory Revised (Costa & McCrae, 1992; John & Scrivastava, 1999)].

The best validated measure of the Big Five (John & Scrivastava, 1999), the NEO Personality Inventory Revised (NEO-PI-R) (Costa & McCrae, 1992) operationally defines the five factors with facets. *Neuroticism* consists of the following facets: anxiety, hostility, depression, self-consciousness, impulsiveness, and vulnerability; *Extroversion*: warmth, gregariousness, assertiveness, activity, excitement-seeking, and positive emotions; *Openness*: fantasy, aesthetics, feelings, actions, ideas, and values; *Agreeableness*: trust, straightforwardness, altruism, compliance, modesty, and tender-mindedness; *Conscientiousness*: competence, order, dutifulness, achievement-striving, self-discipline, and deliberation.

The Five Factor Model of personality is not a theory of personality (McCrae & Costa, 1999), a fact that has led to some criticism of this approach to personality (e.g. Pervin, 1994). Instead, it is empirically derived and has its origins in words that the general population uses, rather than in the work of experts in psychology and psychiatry. There is a degree of overlap, however, between the terminology of the Big Five and personality theorists. For example, extroversion is part of Jung's (1933) elaborate framework of psychological types; openness to experience is one of Rogers' (1961) characteristics of fully functioning persons.

Positive Disintegration and Traits

For Dabrowski, traits were inherited, molded by the environment, and included both temperamental qualities and qualities of character. Dabrowski (1973) recognized others' approaches to traits and specifically referred to Jung's (1933) introversion and extroversion, Kretschmer's cylothymes and schiothymes (Roeckelein, 1998), and Sheldon's somatotypes (Sheldon & Stevens, 1942). Both Kretschmer and Sheldon were interested in relating constitutional types of psychiatric disorders. Jung proposed an elaborate typology that was founded on introversion and extroversion but also included functional modes. Jung's introversion and extroversion were not mutually exclusive categories. For example, when we describe a person as extroverted, in Jungian terms, it means that extroversion is dominant and conscious within that person, and introversion is nondominant but active at the unconscious level (Maddi, 1989). Jung constructed his psychological types by adding four styles of experiencing, termed "functional modes": thinking, feeling, sensing, and intuiting. As a result, Jung described eight major types by combining the dominant factor with the functional modes.

Apparently borrowing Jung's phrase, Dabrowski used *psychological types* to refer to all traits, including his own five forms of overexcitability. However, Dabrowski was not interested in psychological types *per se*; he was not interested in distinguishing introverts from extroverts, associating body types and psychiatric disorders or body types and temperament. When it came to psychological types, *the* question for him related to transformation: "Is there any possibility of transformation of such psychological types as introverted and extraverted, cyclothymic and schizothymic; types of various kinds of mental hyperexcitability, such as emotional, imaginational, sensual, psychomotor or intellectual?" (Dabrowski, 1973, p. 136). Transformation referred to both processes of sublimation and the acquiring of other traits, at times polar opposite to the pre-existing ones. Dabrowski argued that such transformations of psychological types are possible and particularly evident in individuals' possessing favorable constitutional endowment—that is, in individuals who are endowed with the potential for accelerated or advanced development. Hereditary forces, then, provide the substrate for development of traits and, in some cases, the power to change their expression to higher forms (sublimation) and to add traits that are not there and not part of the original endowment (e.g., conscious introverts become both conscious extroverts as well as introverts).

Various facets of the Big Five are similar to concepts used in the theory of positive disintegration—for example, the facets of trust, altruism, tender-mindedness, and straightforwardness of Agreeableness; and the warmth of Extroversion. Other traits would be descriptive of some forms of overexcitability—for example, activity and excitement-seeking of the psychomotor form; fantasy and aesthetics of imaginational; ideas of intellectual; and positive emotions, trust, and values of emotional overexcitability. However, value placed on some of the traits would likely differ from the interpretation of the Big Five. Neuroticism, with the exception of the facet of hostility, would be viewed as positive in positive disintegration. Anxiety, depression, self-consciousness, impulsiveness, and vulnerability are viewed as indicators of positive disintegration and as such are reframed as signifying development.

Conclusion

Positive disintegration includes many of the same components as the other approaches to personality, but the components are reframed. The basic instincts are to be transformed, not sated. The prescriptions of the social environment are to be transcended, not complied with. Conflict is rooted in individuals' values, not the product of frustration of needs. Ideals are to be lived, not attenuated. Neurotic symptoms are not to be remedied, but celebrated. Traits are not to be static, but dynamic. Unlike the other approaches, positive disintegration places values and morality front and center. Thoughts, feelings, and behaviors are viewed hierarchically, and development occurs as individuals move from their primitive forms to the more refined ones.

Dabrowski proposed a distinctive theory of personality. The uniqueness of positive disintegration compels its students to become more aware of their taken-for-granted assumptions regarding personality and its development. Whether one becomes a devotee or not, examination of one's assumption and viewing concepts from a different perspective enhances the prospect of creativity. It may very well be that the process would include the destruction of rigidly held beliefs, causing distress in the reader, with a reintegration at a higher level of thinking about personality.

References

Ackerman, C. M. (1993). *Investigating an alternate method of identifying gifted students.* Unpublished master's thesis, University of Calgary, Calgary, Alberta.

Ackerman, C. M. (1996). The interrater reliability of the Overexcitability Questionnaire. *The Dabrowski Newsletter, 2*(3), 5-6.

Ackerman, C. M. (1997a). Identifying gifted adolescents using personality characteristics: Dabrowski's overexcitabilities. *Roeper Review, 19*, 229-236.

Ackerman, C. M. (1997b). *A secondary analysis of research using the Overexcitability Questionnaire.* Unpublished doctoral dissertation, Texas A & M University, College Station, TX.

Ackerman, C. M., & Miller, N. B. (1997, November). *Exploring a shortened version of the Overexcitability Questionnaire.* Paper presented at the annual convention of the National Association for Gifted Children, Little Rock, AR.

Adorno, T. W., Fraenkel-Brunswick, E., Levinson, D. J., & Sanford, R. N. (1950). *The authoritarian personality.* New York: Harper.

Allport, G. W. (1937). *Personality: A psychological interpretation.* New York: Holt, Rhinehart, & Winston.

Allport, G. W., & Odbert, H. S. (1936). Trait-names: A psycho-lexical study. *Psychological Monographs, 47*(211).

American Psychiatric Association. (1994). *Diagnostic and statistical manual of mental disorders* (4th ed.) Washington, DC: Author.

Ammirato, S. P. (1987). *Comparison study of instruments used to measure developmental potential according to Dabrowski's theory of emotional development.* Unpublished doctoral dissertation, University of Denver, Denver, CO.

Amuli, S. H. (1989). *Inner secrets of the path.* Longmead: Element Books. (Available online at: http://al-islam.org/innersecretsofthepath/).

Andreasen, N. C. (2007). DSM and the death of phenomenology in America: An example of unintended consequences. *Schizophrenia Bulletin,* 33(1). Retrieved July 3, 2007, from www.oxfordjournals.org/schbul/about.html

Aronson, J. (1964). Introduction. In K. Dabrowski, *Positive disintegration* (pp. ix-xxviii). Boston: Little, Brown.

Babiak, P., & Hare, R. D. (2006). *Snakes in suits: When psychopaths go to work.* New York: HarperCollins.

Barrow, J. C., & Moore, C. A. (1983). Group interventions with perfectionistic thinking. *Personnel and Guidance Journal, 61*, 612-615.

Battaglia, M. M. (2002). *A hermeneutic historical study of Kazimierz Dabrowski and his theory of positive disintegration.* Unpublished doctoral dissertation. Virginia Polytechnic Institute and State University, Blacksburg, Virginia. (Available online at: http://scholar.lib.vt.edu/theses/available/etd-04082002-204054/unrestricted/Dissertation.pdf).

Baum, S. M., Olenchak, F. R., & Owen, S. V. (1998). Gifted students with attention deficits: Fact and/or fiction? Or, can we see the forest for the trees? *Gifted Child Quarterly, 42,* 92-104.

Beach, B. J. (1980). *Lesbian and nonlesbian women: Profiles of development and self-actualization.* Unpublished doctoral dissertation, The University of Iowa, Iowa City, IA.

Belenky, M. F., Clinchy, B. M., Goldberger, N. R., & Tarule, J. M. (1986). *Women's ways of knowing: The development of self, voice, and mind.* New York: Basic Books.

Benet, W. R. (Ed.). (1948). *The readers' encyclopedia.* New York: Thomas Y. Crowell.

Bergson, H. (1935). *The two sources of morality and religion.* New York: Henry Holt.

Bergson, H. (1944). *Creative evolution.* New York: The Modern Library.

Berling, J. A. (1980). *The syncretic religion of Lin Chao-en.* New York: Columbia University.

Binswanger, L. (1963). *Being-in-the-world: Selected papers of Ludwig Binswanger.* New York: Basic Books.

Borgatta, E. F. (1964). The structure of personality characteristics. *Behavioral Science, 9*, 8-17.

Boss, M. (1963). *Psychoanalysis and daseinanalysis.* New York: Basic Books.

Bouchard, L. L. (2004). An instrument for the measure of Dabrowskian overexcitabilities to identify gifted elementary students. *Gifted Child Quarterly, 48*, 339-350.

Bouchet, N. M. (1998). *Social structure and personality: Explicating the second factor from Dabrowski's theory of emotional development.* Unpublished master's thesis, The University of Akron, Akron, OH.

Bouchet, N. M. (2004). *To give or to take: Assessing five levels of moral emotional development.* Unpublished doctoral dissertation, University of Akron, Akron, OH.

Bouchet, N. M., & Falk, R. F. (2001). The relationship among giftedness, gender, and overexcitability. *Gifted Child Quarterly, 45*, 260-267.

Bowlby, J. (1969). *Attachment.* New York: Basic Books.

Brandstatter, H., & Eliaz, A. (2001). *Persons, situations, and emotions: An ecological approach.* New York: Oxford University Press.

Bransky, T., Jenkins-Friedman, R., & Murphy, D. (1987). Identifying and working with gifted students "at risk" for disabling perfectionism. In R. Jenkins-Friedman & A. Robinson (Eds.), *Research briefs: A collection of research-based papers presented at the annual convention, New Orleans, November 1987* (pp. 14-16). Circle Pines, MN: National Association for Gifted Children.

Breard, N. S. (1994). *Exploring a different way to identify gifted African-American students.* Unpublished doctoral dissertation, University of Georgia, Athens, GA.

Brennan, T. P. (1987). *Case studies of multilevel development.* Unpublished doctoral dissertation, Northwestern University, Evanston, IL.

Brennan, T. P., & Piechowski, M. M. (1991). A developmental framework for self-actualization: Evidence from case studies. *Journal of Humanistic Psychology, 31*(3), 43-64.

Buerschen, T. (1995). *Researching an alternative assessment in the identification of gifted and talented students.* Unpublished research project, Miami University, Oxford, OH.

Burns, D. D. (1980, November). The perfectionist's script for self-defeat. *Psychology Today,* 34-52.

Calic, S. (1994). *Heightened sensitivities as an indicator of creative potential in visual and performing arts.* Unpublished doctoral dissertation, University of Georgia, Athens, GA.

Carlisle, C. (2005). *Kierkegaard's philosophy of becoming: Movements and positions.* Albany, NY: State University of New York Press.

Cattell, R. B. (1959). Personality theory growing from multivariate quantitative research. In S. Koch (Ed.), *Psychology: A study of a science* (Vol. 3, pp. 257-327). New York: McGraw-Hill.

Cattell, R. B., Eber, H. W., & Tatsuoka, M. M. (1970). *Handbook for the sixteen personality factor questionnaire (16PF).* Champaign, IL: IPAT.

Cavalier, R. (1990). *Plato for beginners.* New York: Writers & Readers.

Chagdud, T. R. (1992). *Lord of the dance: The autobiography of a Tibetan lama.* Junction City, CA: Padma.

Chamorro-Premuzic, T. (2005). *Personality and intellectual competence.* Mahwah, NJ: Erlbaum.

Chang, H. J. (2001). *A research on the overexcitability traits of gifted and talented students in Taiwan.* Unpublished master thesis, National Taiwan Normal University, Taipei.

Charon, J. M. (1995). *Symbolic interactionism: An introduction, an interpretation, an integration.* Englewood Cliffs, NJ: Prentice Hall.

Chavez, R. A. (2004). *Evaluación Integral de la personalidad creativa: Fenomenología clínica y genética [Integral evaluation of the creative personality: Phenomenology, clinical, and genetics].* Unpublished doctoral dissertation, National Autonomous University of Mexico, UNAM, Mexico City.

Cienin, P. (Pseudonym of K. Dabrowski). (1972a). *Existential thoughts and aphorisms.* London: Gryf Publications.

Cienin, P. (Pseudonym of K. Dabrowski). (1972b). *Fragments from the diary of a madman.* London: Gryf Publications.

Clark, B. (1988). *Growing up gifted* (3rd ed). Columbus, OH: Merrill.

Cohen, J. (1988). *Statistical power analysis for the behavioral sciences* (2nd ed.). Hillsdale, NJ: Erlbaum.

Colangelo, N., & Zaffrann, R. T. (Eds.). (1979). *New voices in counseling the gifted.* Dubuque, IA: Kendall/Hunt.

Colby, A., & Damon, W. (1992). *Some do care: Contemporary lives of moral commitment.* New York: Free Press.

Cooley, C. H. (1964). *Human nature and the social order.* New York: Schocken. (Original work published 1902).

Corsini, R. J. (Ed.). (1977). *Current theories of personality.* Itasca, IL: Peacock.

Costa, P. T., Jr., & McCrae, R. R. (1992). *Revised NEO Personality Inventory and NEO Five Inventory professional manual.* Odessa, FL: Psychological Assessment Resources.

Courtois, F. (1986). *An experience of enlightenment.* Wheaton, IL: The Theosophical Publishing House.

Dabrowski, K. (1929). *Les conditions psychologique du suicide [The psychological conditions of suicide].* Geneva: Imprimerie du Commerce.

Dabrowski, K. (1934a). *Behawioryzm i kierunki pokrewne w psychologii [Behaviorism and related schools in psychology].* Warszawa: Lekarz Polski.

Dabrowski, K. (1934b). *Podstawy psychologiczne samodreczenia (automutylacji) [Psychological bases of self-torture].* Warszawa: Przyszlosc.

Dabrowski, K. (1935). *Nerwowosc dzieci i mlodziezy [The nervousness of children and youth].* Warszawa: Nasza Ksiegarnia.

Dabrowski, K. (1937). Psychological bases of self-mutilation (W. Thau, Trans.). *Genetic Psychology Monographs, 19,* 1-104.

Dabrowski, K. (1938). Typy wzmozonej pobudliwosci psychicznej [Types of increased psychic excitability]. *Biuletyn Instytutu Higieny Psychicznej, 1*(3-4), 3-26.

Dabrowski, K. (1964a). *Positive disintegration.* Boston: Little, Brown.

Dabrowski, K. (1964b). *0 dezyntegracji pozytywnej [On positive disintegration].* Warszawa: Panstwowy Zaklad Wydawnictw Lekarskich.

Dabrowski, K. (1964c). *Spoleczno-wychowawcza psychiatria dziecieca [Socio-educational child psychiatry]* (2nd ed.). Warszawa: Panstwowy Zaklad Wydawnictw Szkolnych. (Original work published 1959).

Dabrowski, K. (1966). The theory of positive disintegration. *International Journal of Psychiatry, 2*(2), 229-244.

Dabrowski, K. (1967). *Personality-shaping through positive disintegration.* Boston: Little, Brown.

Dabrowski, K. (1968). Le milieu psychique interne [The inner psychic milieu]. *Annales Médico-Psychologiques, 126, t. 2*(4), 457-485.

Dabrowski, K. (with Kawczak, A., & Piechowski, M. M.). (1970). *Mental growth through positive disintegration.* London: Gryf.

Dabrowski, K. (1972). *Psychoneurosis is not an illness.* London: Gryf.

Dabrowski, K. (with Kawczak, A., & Sochanska, J.). (1973). *The dynamics of concepts.* London: Gryf.

Dabrowski, K. (1975). Foreword. In M. M. Piechowski, A theoretical and empirical approach to the study of development. *Genetic Psychology Monographs, 92,* 233-237.

Dabrowski, K. (with Piechowski, M. M.). (1977). *Theory of levels of emotional development: Multilevelness and positive disintegration* (Vol. 1). Oceanside, NY: Dabor Science.

Dabrowski, K. (1979a). *Nothing can be changed here.* (Mazurkiewicz, E., Trans.; Rolland, P., Ed.). Unpublished play.

Dabrowski, K. (1979b). *Wprowadzenie do higieny psychicznej [Introduction to mental hygiene].* Warszawa: Wydawnictwa Szkolne i Pedagogiczne.

Dabrowski, K. (1986). *Trud istnienia [The toil of existence].* Warszawa: Wiedza Powszechna.

Dabrowski, K. (1996a). *Multilevelness of emotional and instinctive functions. Part 1: Theory and description of levels of behavior.* Lublin, Poland: Towarzystwo Naukowe Katolickiego Uniwersytetu Lubelskiego.

Dabrowski, K. (1996b). *W poszukiwaniu zdrowia psychicznego [In search of mental health].* Warszawa: Wydawnictwo Naukowe PWN.

Dabrowski, K., & Amend, D. R. (1972). *Differences in nervous activity as indicators of development.* Paper presented at the Second International Congress of Positive Disintegration, Montreal, Canada.

Dabrowski, K., & Piechowski, M. M. (1969). Les émotions supérieures et l'objectivité d'évaluation *[Higher emotions and objectivity of values]. Annales Médico-Psychologiques, 127, t. 2*(5), 589-613.

Dabrowski, K., & Piechowski, M. M. (1977). *Theory of levels of emotional development: From primary integration to self-actualization* (Vol. 2). Oceanside, NY: Dabor Science.

Dabrowski, K., & Piechowski, M. M. (with Rankel M., & Amend, D. R.). (1996). *Multilevelness of emotional and instinctive functions. Part 2: Types and levels of development.* Lublin, Poland: Towarzystwo Naukowe Katolickiego Uniwersytetu Lubelskiego.

Dabrowski, K. (with Rankel, M.). (n.d. 1). *Authentic education.* Unpublished manuscript.

Dabrowski, K. (n.d. 2). *Normality, mental health and mental illness.* Unpublished manuscript.

Daniels, S., Falk, R. F., & Piechowski, M. M. (in preparation). Measuring overexcitabilities in young children. In S. Daniels & M. M. Piechowski (Eds.), *Living with intensity: Understanding sensitivity, excitability, and emotional development in gifted children, adolescents, and adults.* Scottsdale, AZ: Great Potential Press.

Dannefer, D. (1984). Adult development and social theory: A paradigmatic reappraisal. *American Sociological Review, 49,* 100-116.

Darwin, C. R. (1965). *The expression of the emotions in man and animals.* Chicago: University of Chicago Press. (Original work published 1872).

Delisle, J. R. (1986). Death with honors: Suicide and the gifted adolescent. *Journal of Counseling and Development, 64,* 558-560.

Delisle, J. R. (1990). The gifted adolescent at risk: Strategies and resources for suicide prevention among gifted youth. *Journal for the Education of the Gifted, 13,* 212-228.

Domroese, C. (1993). *Investigating an alternate method for identifying gifted students.* Research project, Oak Park Elementary School District #97, Oak Park, IL.

Digman, J. M., & Takemotto-Chock, N. K. (1981). Factors in the natural language of personality: Reanalysis and comparison of six major studies. *Multivariate Behavioral Research, 16,* 149-170.

Ebner, M. (1993). *Margaret Ebner: Major works.* (Translated and edited by Leonard P. Hindsley). New York: Paulist.

Eisenberg, N., Fabes, R. A., Guthrie, I. K., & Reiser, M. (2002). The role of emotionality and regulation in children's social competence and adjustment. In L. Pulkkinen (Ed.), P*aths to successful development: Personality in the life course* (pp. 46-72). West Nyack, NY: Cambridge University Press.

Ekehammar, B., & Akrami, N. (2007). Personality and prejudice: From big five personality factors to facets. *Journal of Personality, 75*(5), 1-27.

Ekman, P. (1984). Expression and the nature of emotion. In K. R. Scherer & P. Ekman (Eds.), *Approaches to emotion* (pp. 319-343). Hillsdale, NJ: Erlbaum.

Elkind, D. (1984). *All grown up & no place to go: Teenagers in crisis.* Reading, MA: Addison-Wesley.

Ely, E. I. (1995). *The Overexcitability Questionnaire: An alternative method for identifying creative giftedness in seventh grade junior high school students.* Unpublished doctoral dissertation, Kent State University, Kent, OH.

Erickson, R. J., & Cuthbertson-Johnson. (Eds.). (1997). *Social perspectives on emotion.* (D. D. Franks, Series Ed.). Greenwich, CT: JAI Press.

Erikson, E. H. (1950). *Childhood and society.* New York: Norton.

Falk, R. F., & Lind, S. (1998, July). *Developing and testing a new Overexcitability Questionnaire (OEQ-II).* Paper presented at the 3rd International Symposium on Dabrowski's Theory, Evanston, IL.

Falk, R. F., Lind, S., Miller, N. B., Piechowski, M. M., & Silverman, L. K. (1999a). *The Overexcitability Inventory for Parents* (adapted by H. Dudeney). Denver, CO: Institute for the Study of Advanced Development.

Falk, R. F., Lind, S., Miller, N. B., Piechowski, M. M., & Silverman, L. K. (1999b). *The Overexcitability Questionnaire – Two (OEQ-II): Manual, scoring system, and questionnaire.* Denver, CO: Institute for the Study of Advanced Development.

Falk, R. F., Manzanero, J. B., & Miller, N. B. (1997). Developmental potential in Venezuelan and American artists: A cross-cultural validity study. *Creativity Research Journal, 10*, 201-206.

Falk, R. F., & Miller, N. B. (1998). The reflexive self: A sociological perspective. *Roeper Review, 20*(3), 150-153.

Falk, R. F., Piechowski, M. M., & Lind, S. (1994). *Criteria for rating the intensity of overexcitabilities.* Unpublished manuscript, Department of Sociology, University of Akron. (Available from the Institute for the Study of Advanced Development, 1452 Marion Street, Denver, CO).

Felder, R. F. (1982, October). *Developmental potential of chemical engineering and gifted education graduate students.* Paper presented at the National Association for Gifted Children Conference, New Orleans, LA.

Fiedler, E. D. (1998). Denial of anger/denial of self: Dealing with the dilemmas. *Roeper Review, 20*,158-161.

Fiske, D. W. (1949). Consistency of the factorial structures of personality ratings from different sources. *Journal of Abnormal and Social Psychology, 44*, 329-344.

Frank, J. (2006). *Portrait of an inspirational teacher of the gifted.* Unpublished doctoral dissertation, University of Calgary, Calgary, Alberta.

Freud, S. (1970). *A general introduction to psychoanalysis.* New York: Pocket Books. (Original work published 1924).

Gage, D. F., Morse, P. A., & Piechowski, M. M. (1981). Measuring levels of emotional development. *Genetic Psychology Monographs, 103,* 120-152.

Gallagher, S. A. (1983). *A comparison of Dabrowski's concept of overexcitabilities with measures of creativity and school achievement in sixth grade students.* Unpublished master's thesis, University of Arizona, Tucson, AZ.

Gallagher, S. A. (1985). A comparison of the concept of overexcitabilities with measures of creativity and school achievement in sixth grade students. *Roeper Review, 8,* 115-119.

Gardner, H. G. (1983). *Frames of mind: The theory of multiple intelligences.* New York: Basic Books.

Gatto-Walden, P. (1999). Counseling gifted females with eating disorders. *Advanced Development, 8,* 113-130.

Gaudet, L. (1981). The theory of positive disintegration in the light of developmental psychology. In N. Duda (Ed.), *Theory of positive disintegration: Proceedings of the Third International Conference* (pp.241-248). Miami, FL: University of Miami.

Gendlin, E. P. (1981). *Focusing* (2nd ed.). New York: Bantam.

Ghosh, S. L. (1980). *Mejda: The family and early life of Paramahansa Yogananda.* Los Angeles: Self Realization Fellowship.

Gilligan, C. (1982). *In a different voice.* Cambridge, MA: Harvard University Press.

Goleman, D. (1995). *Emotional intelligence: Why it can matter more than IQ.* New York: Bantam Books.

Gottfried, A. W., Gottfried, A. E., Bathurst, K., & Guerin, D. W. (1994). *Gifted IQ: Early developmental aspects. The Fullerton longitudinal study.* New York: Plenum.

Gough, H. G. (1987). *The California Psychological Inventory administrator's guide.* Palo Alto, CA: Consulting Psychologists Press.

Gough, H. G., & Heilbrun, A. B., Jr. (1983). *The Adjective Check List manual.* Palo Alto, CA: Consulting Psychologists Press.

Grant, B. (1988). *Four voices: Life history studies of moral development.* Unpublished doctoral dissertation, Northwestern University, Evanston, IL.

Grant, B. (1990). Moral development: Theories and lives. *Advanced Development, 2,* 85-91.

Grant, B. (1996). "There are exceptions to everything": Moral relativism and moral commitment in the life of Hope Weiss. *Advanced Development, 7,* 119-128.

Grant, B., & Piechowski, M. M. (1999). Theories and the good: Toward a child-centered gifted education. *Gifted Child Quarterly, 43,* 4-12.

Greene, L. A. (1982). *Dabrowski's theory of emotional development and Loevinger's theory of ego development: A direct comparison.* Unpublished master's thesis, Northwestern University, Evanston, IL.

Gross, M., Rinn, A. N., & Jamieson, K. M. (2007). Gifted adolescents' overexcitabilities and self-concepts: An analysis of gender and grade level. *Roeper Review, 29,* 240-248.

Hague, W. J. (1986). *New perspectives on religious and moral development.* Alberta, Canada: University of Alberta.

Hakuin, E. (1971). Orategama III. In P. B. Yampolsky (Ed.), *The Zen master Hakuin: Selected writings.* New York: Columbia University.

Hall, C. S., & Lindzey, G. (1970). *Theories of personality* (2nd ed.). New York: Wiley.

Hamachek, D. E. (1978). Psychodynamics of normal and neurotic perfectionism. *Psychology, 15,* 27-33.

Hammarskjöld, D. (1964). *Markings.* New York: Knopf.

Hazell, C. G. (1982). *An empirical study of the experience of emptiness.* Unpublished doctoral dissertation, Northwestern University, Evanston, IL.

Hazell, C. G. (1984). Experienced levels of emptiness and existential concern with different levels of emotional development and profiles of values. *Psychological Reports, 55,* 967-976.

Hazell, C. G. (1989). Levels of emotional development with experienced levels of emptiness and existential concern. *Psychological Reports, 64,* 835-838.

Hazell, C. G. (1999). The experience of emptiness and the use of Dabrowski's theory in counseling gifted clients: Clinical case examples. *Advanced Development: A Journal on Adult Giftedness, 8,* 31-46.

Hillesum, E. (1985). *An interrupted life: Diaries of Etty Hillesum, 1941-43.* New York: Washington Square Press.

Hochschild, A. R. (1983). *The managed heart: The commercialization of human feeling.* Berkeley, CA: University of California Press.

Hollingworth, L. S. (1942). *Children above 180 IQ.* New York: World Book.

Ibn Ajiba, A. (1999). *The autobiography of the Moroccan Sufi, Ibn Ajiba.* (Translation and commentary in French by Jean-Louis Michon. Translated into English by David Streight). Louisville, KY: Fons Vitae.

Izard, C. E. (1971). *The face of emotion.* New York: Appleton-Century-Crofts.

Izard, C. E. (1977). *Human emotions*. New York: Plenum.

Izard, C. E., & Ackerman, B. P. (2000). Motivation, organizational, and regulatory functions of discrete emotions. In M. Lewis & J. Heviland-Jones (Eds.), *Handbook of emotions* (2nd ed., pp. 253-264). New York: Guilford.

Jackson, J. H. (1884). Croonian lectures on the evolution and dissolution in the nervous system. Delivered at the Royal College of Physicians. (In three parts). Lecture 1: *The Lancet, 123*(3161), 555-558 (29 March); Lecture 2: *The Lancet, 123*(3163), 649-652 (12 April); Lecture 3: *The Lancet, 123*(3165), 739-744 (26 April).

Jackson, S. (1995). *Bright star: Black sky origins and manifestations of the depressed state in the lived experience of the gifted adolescent.* Unpublished master's thesis, Vermont College of Norwich University, Northfield, VT.

Jackson, S., Moyle, V., & Piechowski, M. M. (in press). Emotional life and psychotherapy of the gifted in light of Dabrowski's theory. In L. Shavinina (Ed.), *Handbook of giftedness.* New York: Springer.

Jacobs, L. (1978). *Jewish mystical testimonies.* New York: Schocken. (Original work published 1976).

Jacobsen, M. E. (1999). *Liberating everyday genius.* New York: Ballantine.

Jahoda, M. (1958). *Current concepts of positive mental health.* New York: Basic Books.

James, W. (1990). *The principles of psychology.* New York: Dover. (Original work published 1890).

John, O. P., & Scrivastava, S. (1999). The big five trait taxonomy: History, measurement, and theoretical perspectives. In L. A. Pervin & O. P. John (Eds.), *Handbook of personality: Theory and research* (2nd ed., pp. 102-138). New York: Guilford Press.

Johnson, C. (1992). The emergence of the emotional self: A developmental theory. *Symbolic Interaction, 15*(2), 183-202.

Jones, W. T. (1969). *A history of Western philosophy: Kant to Wittgenstein and Sartre* (2nd ed., pp. 262-281). New York: Harcourt.

Jung, C. G. (1933). *Psychological types.* New York: Harcourt, Brace, & World.

Kaufmann, W. (1969). *Existentialism from Dostoevsky to Sartre.* New York: Meridian Books.

Kawczak, A. (1970). Introduction—The methodological structure of the theory of positive disintegration. In K. Dabrowski (with A. Kawczak & M.M. Piechowski), *Mental growth through positive disintegration* (pp. 1-16). London: Gryf.

Kawczak, A. (2002). Abraham Lincoln's personality development seen through the theory of positive disintegration. Part II. In N. Duda (Ed.), *Proceedings of the Fifth International Conference on the Theory of Positive Disintegration* (pp. 59-62). Ft. Lauderdale, FL: Institute for Positive Disintegration in Human Development.

Kemper, T. D. (1993). Sociological models in the explanation of emotions. In M. Lewis & J. M. Haviland (Eds.), *Handbook of emotions* (pp. 41-51). New York: Guilford Press.

Kerr, B. A. (1991). *A handbook for counseling the gifted and talented.* Alexandria, VA: American Counseling Association.

Keyes, C. L. M. (2002). The mental health continuum: From languishing to flourishing in life. *Journal of Health and Social Behavior, 43,* 207-222.

Kobierzycki, T. (2002). Creativity and mental health in the process of positive disintegration. In N. Duda (Ed.), *Proceedings of the Fifth International Conference on the Theory of Positive Disintegration* (pp. 395-407). Ft. Lauderdale, FL: Institute for Positive Disintegration in Human Development.

Kohlberg, L. (1969). Stage and sequence: A cognitive-developmental approach to socialization. In D. A. Goslin (Ed.), *Handbook of socialization theory and research* (pp. 347-480). Chicago: Rand McNally.

Kohlberg, L. (1981). *Essays on moral development: The psychology of moral development* (Vol. I). San Francisco: Harper & Row.

Kohlberg, L. (1984). *Essays on moral development: The psychology of moral development* (Vol. II). San Francisco: Harper & Row.

Kokoszka, A. (2007). *States of consciousness: Models for psychology and psychotherapy.* New York: Springer.

Kort-Butler, L., & Falk, R. F. (1999, April). *Replicating factor structure: The art of factor analysis.* Paper presented at the meeting of the North Central Sociological Association, Troy, MI.

Krishna, G. (1993). *Living with kundalini: The autobiography of Gopi Krishna.* (L. Shepherd, Ed.). Boston: Shambhala.

Lewis, M., & Haviland, J. M. (1993). Preface. In M. Lewis & J. M. Haviland (Eds.), *Handbook of emotions* (pp. ix-x). New York: Guilford Press.

Lewis, R. B., Kitano, M. K., & Lynch, E. W. (1992). Psychological intensities in gifted adults. *Roeper Review, 15,* 25-31.

Lifton, B. J. (1997). *The king of children: The life and death of Janusz Korczak.* New York: St. Martin's Griffin.

Lisieux, T. (1976). *The story of a soul: The autobiography of St. Thérèse of Lisieux.* (Translated by John Clarke). Washington, DC: Institute of Carmelite Studies. (Original work published 1975).

Loevinger, J. (1976). *Ego development: Conceptions and theories.* San Francisco: Jossey-Bass.

Lynn, A. B. (2002). The *emotional intelligence activity book: 50 activities for developing EQ at work.* New York: HRD Press.

Lysy, K. Z. (1979). *Personal growth in counselors and noncounselors: A Jungian and Dabrowskian approach.* Unpublished doctoral dissertation, University of Illinois, Champaign-Urbana, IL.

Lysy, K. Z., & Piechowski, M. M. (1983). Personal growth: An empirical study using Jungian and Dabrowskian measures. *Genetic Psychology Monographs, 108,* 267-320.

Maddi, S. R. (1989). *Personality theories: A conceptual analysis.* Pacific Grove, CA: Brooks/Cole.

Magnavita, J. (2002). *Theories of personality: Contemporary approaches to the science of personality.* New York: Wiley.

Maj, P. (2002). The creative instinct of Kazimierz Dabrowski in relation to the creative evolution of Henri Bergson. In N. Duda (Ed.), *Proceedings of the Fifth International Conference on the Theory of Positive Disintegration* (pp. 373-381). Ft. Lauderdale: FL: Institute for Positive Disintegration in Human Development.

Manzanero, J. (1985). *A cross-cultural comparison of overexcitability profiles and levels of emotional development between American and Venezuelan artists.* Unpublished master's thesis, University of Denver, Denver, CO.

Marsh, C. S., & Colangelo. N. (1983). The application of Dabrowski's concept of multilevelness to Allport's concept of unity. *Counseling and Values, 27,* 213-228.

Marsh, H. W. (1990). *Self-Description Questionnaire (SDQ) II: Manual.* New South Wales, Australia: University of Western Sydney.

Maslow, A. H. (1968). *Toward a psychology of being.* Princeton, NJ: Van Nostrand.

Maslow, A. H. (1970). *Motivation and personality* (2nd ed.). New York: Harper & Row.

Maslow, A. H. (1971). *The farther reaches of human nature.* New York: Viking.

Massey, R. F. (1981). *Personality theories: Comparisons and syntheses.* New York: Van Nostrand.

Maxwell, P., & Tschudin, V. (1990). *Seeing the invisible: Modern religious and other transcendent experiences.* London: Penguin.

May, R. (1958). Contributions of existential pyschotherapy. In R. May, E. Angel, & H. F. Ellenberger (Eds.), *Existence: A new dimension in psychiatry and psychology.* New York: Basic Books.

McCrae, R. R., & Costa, P., Jr. (1999). A five factor theory of personality. In L. A. Pervin & O. P. John (Eds.), *Handbook of personality: Theory and research* (2nd ed., pp. 139-153). New York: Guilford Press.

McDonald, W. (2006). Søren Kierkegaard. In E. N. Zalta (Ed.), *The Stanford encyclopedia of philosophy.* Retrieved February 21, 2007, from http://plato.stanford.edu/archives/sum2006/entries/kierkegaard

McGraw, J. G. (1986). Personality and its ideal in K. Dabrowski's theory of positive disintegration: A philosophical interpretation. *Dialectics and Humanism, 13*, 211-237.

McGraw, J. G. (2002). Personality in Nietzsche and Dabrowski: A conceptual comparison. In N. Duda (Ed.), *Positive disintegration: The theory of the future. Proceedings of the 100th Dabrowski anniversary program on the man, the theory, the application, and the future* (pp. 187-228). Ft. Lauderdale, FL: Fidlar Doubleday.

McPherson, I. (2001). Kierkegaard as an educational thinker: Communication through and across ways of being. *Journal of Philosophy of Education, 35*(2), 157-174.

Mead, G. H. (1934). *Mind, self, and society*. Chicago: University of Chicago Press.

Meckstroth, E. (1991, December). *Coping with sensitivities of gifted children.* Paper presented at the Illinois Gifted Education Conference, Chicago, IL.

Mendaglio, S. (1998). Counseling gifted students: Issues and recommendations for teachers and counselors. *AGATE, 12*, 18-25.

Mendaglio, S. (1999, Fall). A few guidelines for counseling the gifted arising from Dabrowski's theory. *Dabrowski Newsletter*, 3-4.

Mendaglio, S., & Pyryt, M. C. (1995). Self-concept of gifted students: Assessment-based intervention. *Teaching Exceptional Children, 27*(3), 40-45.

Mendaglio, S., & Pyryt, M. C. (2003). Self-concept and giftedness: A multi-theoretical perspective. *Gifted and Talented International, 18*, 76-82.

Mendaglio, S., & Pyryt, M. C. (2004). The role of intelligence in TPD. In B. Tillier (Ed.), *Proceedings of the Sixth International Congress of the Institute for Positive Disintegration.* Calgary, AB: Institute for Positive Disintegration.

Mendaglio, S., & Tillier, W. (2006). Dabrowski's theory of positive disintegration and giftedness: Overexcitability research findings. *Journal for the Education of the Gifted, 30*, 68-87.

Mika, E. (2004). *Ecce homo: Adam Chmielowski's growth through positive disintegration.* Paper presented at The Sixth International Congress of the Institute for Positive Disintegration in Human Development, Calgary, Alberta.

Mika, E. (2005, Fall). Theory of positive disintegration as a model of personality development for exceptional individuals. In N. L. Hafenstein, B. Kutrumbos, & J. Delisle (Eds.), *Perspectives in gifted education* (Vol. 3, pp. 4-32). Denver, CO: University of Denver.

Miller, N. B. (1985). *A content analysis coding system for assessing adult emotional development.* Unpublished doctoral dissertation, University of Denver, Denver, CO.

Miller, N. B., & Silverman, L. K. (1987). Levels of personality development. *Roeper Review, 9*(4), 221-225.

Miller, N. B., Silverman, L. K., & Falk, R. F. (1994). Emotional development, intellectual ability, and gender. *Journal for the Education of the Gifted, 18*(1), 20-38.

Morrissey, A. M. (1996). Intellect as prelude: The potential for higher-level development in the gifted. *Advanced Development: A Journal on Adult Giftedness, 7*, 101-116.

Mos, L. P., & Boodt, C. P. (1991). Friendship and play: An evolutionary-developmental view. *Theory and Psychology, 1*(1), 132-144.

Mowrer, O. H. (1967). Introduction. In K. Dabrowski, *Personality-shaping through positive disintegration.* Boston: Little, Brown.

Mróz, A. (2002a). *Rozwoj osoby wedlug teorii dezyntegracji pozytywnej Kazimierza Dabrowskiego [Individual development according to Dabrowski's theory of positive disintegration].* Doctoral dissertation, Catholic University of Lublin, Lublin, Poland.

Mróz, A. (2002b). The significance of religious, esthetic, and other-oriented moral values in the process of personality development is the model of positive disintegration. In N. Duda (Ed.), *Proceedings of the Fifth International Conference on the Theory of Positive Disintegration* (pp. 141-150). Ft. Lauderdale, FL: Institute for Positive Disintegration in Human Development.

Murray, H. A. (1959). Preparations for the scaffold of a comprehensive system. In S. Koch (Ed.), *Psychology: A study of a science* (Vol. 3, pp. 7-54). New York: McGraw-Hill.

Myodo, S. (1987). *Passionate journey: The spiritual autobiography of Satomi Myodo.* (Translated and annotated by Sallie B. King). Boston: Shambhala.

NASA jettisons astronaut accused of kidnap attempt. (2007, March 8). *The Denver Post*, p. A2.

National Institute of Mental Health. (2007). *NIMH mission statement.* Retrieved July 2, 2007, from www.nimh.nih.gov/about/nimh.cfm

Nietzsche, F. (1961). *Thus spoke Zarathustra.* (Hollingdale, R. J., Trans.). New York: Penguin.

Nietzsche, F. (1968). *The will to power.* (Kaufmann, W., Ed.; Kaufmann, W., & Hollingdale, R. J., Trans.). New York: Vintage Books.

Nietzsche, F. (1974). *The gay science.* (Kaufmann, W., Trans.). New York: Vintage Books.

Nietzsche, F. (1989). *Beyond good and evil.* (Kaufmann, W., Trans.). New York: Vintage Books.

Nixon, L. (1983). *Meditation as a means of actualizing the religious personality ideal: A review of empirical research from the perspective of Kazimierz Dabrowski's TPD.* Unpublished master's thesis, Concordia University, Montreal, QC.

(Available online at: http://members.shaw.ca/positivedisintegration/DRIBiblio.htm#l-o).

Nixon, L. (1989). Maladjustment and self-actualization in the life of Teresa of Avila. *Studies in Religion, 18*, 283-295.

Nixon, L. (1990). *The mystical struggle: A psychological analysis.* Unpublished doctoral dissertation, Concordia University, Montreal, QC. (Available online at: http://members.shaw.ca/positivedisintegration/DRIBiblio.htm#l-o).

Nixon, L. (1994a). Multilevel disintegration in the lives of religious mystics. *Advanced Development, 6*, 57-74. (Available online at: http://members.shaw.ca/positivedisintegration/DRIBiblio.htm#l-o).

Nixon, L. (1994b, June 10). *Mystical stages and personality development.* Paper presented at the Dabrowski Symposium, Keystone, CO. (Available online at: http://members.shaw.ca/positivedisintegration/DRIBiblio.htm#l-o).

Nixon, L. (1995a, October). A Hindu swami's description of his experience at Level V. *The Dabrowski Newsletter, 2*(1) 1-2. (Available online at: http://members.shaw.ca/positivedisintegration/DRIBiblio.htm#l-o).

Nixon, L. (1995b, June 4). *Personal loss and emotional support in the lives of four hindu mystics.* Paper presented at the Annual Conference of the South Asia Council of the Canadian Asian Studies Association, Montreal, QC.

Nixon, L. (1996a). A Dabrowskian perspective on the practice of meditation. In W. Tillier (Ed.), *Perspectives on the self: Proceedings of the Second Biennial Conference on Dabrowski's Theory of Positive Disintegration* (pp. 174-198), Calgary, AB. (Available online at: http://members.shaw.ca/positivedisintegration/DRIBiblio.htm#lo).

Nixon, L. (1996b). Factors predispositional of creativity and mysticism: A comparative study of Charles Darwin and Thérèse of Lisieux. *Advanced Development, 7*, 81-100.

Nixon, L. (1998, April 17-18). *The significance of loss in Buddhist lives.* Paper presented at the American Academy of Religion Eastern International Region Annual Meeting, Toronto, ON.

Nixon, L. (1999). Intellectual overexcitability in mystical lives. *The Dabrowski Newsletter, 5*(3) 1-4. (Available online at: http://members.shaw.ca/positivedisintegration/DRIBiblio.htm#l-o).

Nixon, L. (2000). A Dabrowskian analysis of a Japanese Buddhist nun. *The Dabrowski Newsletter, 6*(2) 3-6. (Available online at: http://members.shaw.ca/positivedisintegration/DRIBiblio.htm#l-o).

Nixon, L. (2005). Potential for positive disintegration and IQ. *The Dabrowski Newsletter, 10*(2), 1-5.

Norman, W. T. (1963). Toward an adequate taxonomy of personality attributes: Replicated factor structure in peer nomination personality ratings. *Journal of Abnormal and Social Psychology, 66*, 574-583.

Ogburn-Colangelo, M. K. (1979). Giftedness as multilevel potential: A clinical example. In N. Colangelo & R. T. Zaffrann (Eds.), *New voices in counseling the gifted* (pp. 165-187). Dubuque, IA: Kendall/Hunt.

Ogburn-Colangelo, M. K. (1989). Giftedness as multilevel potential: A clinical example. *Advanced Development: A Journal on Adult Giftedness, 1*, 187-200.

Pacht, A. R. (1984). Reflections on perfectionism. *American Psychologist, 39*, 386-390.

Palmer, D. D. (1996). *Kierkegaard for beginners.* New York: Writers & Readers.

Pardo de Santayana Sanz, R. (2006). *El alumno superdotado y sus problemas de aprendizaje: Validación del OEQ-II como prueba de diagnóstico [The gifted student and learning disabilities: Validation of the OEQ-II as a diagnosis test].* Madrid, Spain: Universidad Complutense de Madrid.

Parker, W. (2000). Healthy perfectionism in the gifted. *Journal for Secondary Gifted Education, 11*, 173-182.

Parker, W. D., & Mills, C. (1996). The incidence of perfectionism in gifted students. *Gifted Child Quarterly, 40*, 194-199.

Payne, C. (1987). *A psychobiographical study of the emotional development of a controversial protest leader.* Unpublished doctoral dissertation, Northwestern University, Evanston, IL.

Peace Pilgrim. (1982). *Peace Pilgrim: Her life and work in her own words.* Sante Fe, NM: Ocean Tree.

Peck, R. F., & Havighurst, R. J. (1960). *The psychology of character development.* New York: Wiley.

Pervin, L. A. (1994). A critical analysis of current trait theory. *Psychological Inquiry, 5*, 103-113.

Piaget, J. (1948). *The moral judgment of the child.* Glencoe, IL: Free Press.

Piechowski, M. M. (1974). Two developmental concepts: Multilevelness and developmental potential. *Counseling and Values, 18*, 86-93.

Piechowski. M. M. (1975a). *Formless forms: The conceptual structure of theories of counseling and psychotherapy.* Unpublished doctoral dissertation, University of Wisconsin-Madison, Madison, WI.

Piechowski, M. M. (1975b). A theoretical and empirical approach to the study of development. *Genetic Psychology Monographs, 92*, 231-297.

Piechowski, M. M. (1978). Self-actualization as a developmental structure: The profile of Antoine de Saint-Exupéry. *Genetic Psychology Monographs, 97*, 181-242.

Piechowski, M. M. (1979a). Developmental potential. In N. Colangelo & R. T. Zaffrann (Eds.), *New voices in counseling the gifted* (pp. 25-57). Dubuque, IA: Kendall/Hunt.

Piechowski, M. M. (1979b, Jan/Feb). Levels of emotional development. *Illinois Teacher,* 134-139.

Piechowski, M. M. (1986). The concept of developmental potential. *Roeper Review, 8*(3), 190-197.

Piechowski, M. M. (1990). Inner growth and transformation in the life of Eleanor Roosevelt. *Advanced Development, 2,* 35-53.

Piechowski, M. M. (1991a). Emotional development and emotional giftedness. In N. Colangelo & G. A. Davis (Eds.), *Handbook of gifted education* (pp. 285-306). Boston: Allyn & Bacon.

Piechowski, M. M. (1991b). Giftedness for all seasons: Inner Peach in time of war. In N. Colangelo, S. G. Assouline, & D. L. Ambroson (Eds.), *Proceedings of the 1991 Jocelyn Wallace National Research Symposium on Talent Development* (pp. 180-203). Unionville, NY: Trillium Press.

Piechowski, M. M. (1992a). Etty Hillesum: "The thinking heart of the barracks." *Advanced Development, 4,* 105-118.

Piechowski, M. M. (1992b). Giftedness for all seasons: Inner peace in time of war. In N. Colangelo, S. G. Assouline, & D. L. Ambroson (Eds.), *Talent development. Proceedings of the Henry B. and Jocelyn Wallace National Research Symposium on Talent Development* (pp. 180-203). Unionville, NY: Trillium.

Piechowski, M. M. (1995). OE origins. *The Dabrowski Newsletter, 1*(4), 2-4.

Piechowski, M. M. (1997). Emotional giftedness: The measure of intrapersonal intelligence. In N. Colangelo & G. A. Davis (Eds.), *Handbook of gifted education* (2nd ed., pp. 366-381). Boston: Allyn & Bacon.

Piechowski, M. M. (1998). The self victorious: Personal strengths, chance, and co-incidence. *Roeper Review, 20,* 191-198.

Piechowski, M. M. (1999). Overexcitabilities. In M. Runco, & S. Pritzker (Eds.), *Encyclopedia of creativity* (Vol. 2, pp. 325-334). San Diego, CA: Academic Press.

Piechowski, M. M. (2003). From William James to Maslow and Dabrowski: Excitability of character and self-actualization. In D. Ambrose, L. Cohen, & A. J. Tannenbaum (Eds.), *Creative intelligence: Toward a theoretic integration* (pp. 283-322). Cresskill, NJ: Hampton Press.

Piechowski, M. M. (2006). *"Mellow Out," they say. If I only could: Intensities and sensitivities of the young and bright.* Madison, WI: Yunasa Books.

Piechowski, M. M. (2008). Peace Pilgrim, exemplar of Level V. *Roeper Review,* in press.

Piechowski, M. M., & Colangelo, N. (1984). Developmental potential of the gifted. *Gifted Child Quarterly, 28,* 80-88.

Piechowski, M. M., & Cunningham, K. (1985). Patterns of overexcitability in a group of artists. *Journal of Creative Behavior, 19*(3), 153-174.

Piechowski, M. M., & Miller, N. B. (1995). Assessing developmental potential in gifted children: A comparison of methods. *Roeper Review, 17*, 176-180.

Piechowski, M. M., Silverman, L. K., & Falk, R. F. (1985). Comparison of intellectually and artistically gifted on five dimensions of mental functioning. *Perceptual and Motor Skills, 60,* 539-549.

Piechowski, M. M., & Tyska, C. (1982). Self-actualization profile of Eleanor Roosevelt. *Genetic Psychology Monographs, 105*, 95-153.

Piirto, J. (1998). *Understanding those who create* (2nd ed.). Scottsdale, AZ: Great Potential Press.

Piirto, J. (2004). *Understanding creativity*. Scottsdale, AZ.: Great Potential Press.

Piirto, J., & Cassone, G. (1994). *Overexcitabilities in creative adolescents.* Paper presented at the 41st annual National Association for Gifted Children convention, Salt Lake City, UT.

Piirto, J., Cassone, G., Ackerman, C. M., & Fraas, J. (1996). *An international study of intensity in talented teenagers using the Overexcitability Questionnaire (OEQ).* Unpublished manuscript, Ashland University, Ashland, OH.

Purohit. (1992). The autobiography of an Indian monk. New Delhi, India: Munshiram Manoharlal. (Original work published 1932).

Pyryt, M. C., & Mendaglio, S. (1994). The multidimensional self-concept: A comparison of gifted and average-ability adolescents. *Journal for the Education of the Gifted, 17,* 299-305.

Pyryt, M. C., & Mendaglio, S. (1996/1997). The many facets of self-concept: Insights from the Pyryt Mendaglio Self-Perception Survey. *Exceptionality Education Canada, 6*(2), 75-83.

Pyryt, M. C., & Mendaglio, S. (2001, April). *Intelligence and moral development: A meta-analytic review*. Paper presented at the meeting of the American Educational Research Association, Seattle, WA.

Ram Chandra (1980). *The autobiography of Ram Chandra.* Shajahanpur, India: Shri Ram Chandra Mission. (Original work published 1974).

Ramdas, S. (1994). *In quest of God: The saga of an extraordinary pilgrimage.* San Diego, CA: Blue Dove.

Real, T. (1997). *I don't want to talk about it. Overcoming the secret legacy of male depression.* New York: Fireside.

Renzulli, J. S., Smith, L. H., White, A. J., Callahan, C. M., & Hartman, R. K. (1976). *Scales for rating the behavioral characteristics of superior students.* Mansfield Center, CT: Creative Learning Press.

Rest, J. R. (1979). *Revised manual for the Defining Issues Test.* Minneapolis, MN: Moral Research Projects.

Robert, J. A. (1984). *A study of typologies of personal growth.* Unpublished doctoral dissertation, Northwestern University, Evanston, IL.

Robert, J. A., & Piechowski, M. M. (1981). Two types of emotional overexcitability: Conserving and transforming. In N. Duda (Ed.). *Theory of positive disintegration: Proceedings of the Third International Conference* (pp. 159-178). Miami, FL: University of Miami.

Robinson, E. (1978). *Living the questions.* Oxford, England: The Religious Experience Research Unit.

Robinson, E. (2002). Abraham Lincoln's personality development seen through the theory of positive disintegration, Part I. In N. Duda (Ed.), *Proceedings of the Fifth International Conference on the Theory of Positive Disintegration* (pp. 53-57). Ft. Lauderdale, FL: Institute for Positive Disintegration in Human Development.

Roeckelein, J. E. (1998). *Dictionary of theories, laws & concepts in psychology.* Westport, CT: Greenwood.

Rogers, C. R. (1951). *Client centered therapy: Its current practice, implications, and theory.* Boston: Houghton Mifflin.

Rogers, C. R. (1959). A theory of therapy, personality, and interpersonal relationships. In S. Koch (Ed.), *Psychology: A study of a science* (Vol. 3, pp. 184-256). New York: McGraw-Hill.

Rogers, C. R. (1961). *On becoming a person.* Boston: Houghton Mifflin.

Rogers, C. R. (1980). *A way of being.* Boston: Houghton Mifflin.

Roid, G. (2003). *Stanford-Binet Intelligence Scales, Fifth Edition: Technical manual.* Itasca, IL: Riverside.

Roland, P. (1981). Nothing can be changed here—A modern miracle play. In N. Duda (Ed.), *Theory of positive disintegration: Proceedings of the Third International Conference* (pp. 486-500). Miami, FL: University of Miami.

Rush, A., & Rush, J. (1992). Peace Pilgrim: An extraordinary life. *Advanced Development, 4*, 61-74.

Salovey, P., & Mayer, J. D. (1990). Emotional intelligence. *Imagination, Cognition, & Personality, 9*, 185-211.

Scelfo, J. (2007, February 26). Men and depression: Facing darkness. *Newsweek,* 43-49.

Schiever, S. W. (1983). *The relationship of Dabrowski's theory of emotional development to giftedness and creativity.* Unpublished doctoral dissertation, University of Arizona, Tucson, AZ.

Schiever, S. W. (1985). Creative personality characteristics and dimensions of mental functioning in gifted adolescents. *Roeper Review, 7*, 223-226.

Schmidt, M. L. (1977). *The pebble in song and legend: Primary integration in studies of personality and development.* Unpublished master's thesis, University of Illinois at Urbana-Champaign, Urbana, Illinois.

Second International Congress on Positive Disintegration. (1972). (Brochure). Edmonton, Alberta: D. R. Amend.

Seligman, M. E. P. (2002). *Authentic happiness: Using the new positive psychology to realize your potential for lasting fulfillment.* New York: Free Press.

Seligman, M. E. P., & Csikszentmihalyi, M. (2000). Positive psychology: An introduction. *American Psychologist, 55,* 5-14.

Sheldon, W. H., & Stevens, S. S. (1942). *The varieties of temperament: A psychology of constitutional differences.* New York: Harper.

Shostrom, E. L. (1963). *Personal Orientation Inventory.* San Diego, CA: Educational & Industrial Testing Service.

Silverman, L. K. (1983). Personality development: The pursuit of excellence. *Journal for the Education of the Gifted, 6*(1), 5-19.

Silverman, L. K. (1990). The crucible of perfectionism. In B. Holyst (Ed.), *Mental health in a changing world* (pp. 39-49). Warsaw: Polish Society for Mental Health.

Silverman, L. K. (1993). *Counseling the gifted and talented.* Denver, CO: Love.

Silverman, L. K. (1996). Sir Lancelot and Dabrowski: A case study. *The Dabrowski Newsletter, 2*(4), 5-6.

Silverman, L. K. (1998). Personality and learning styles of gifted children. In J. VanTassel-Baska (Ed.), *Excellence in educating gifted & talented learners* (3rd ed., pp. 29-65). Denver: Love.

Silverman, L. K., & Ellsworth, B. (1981). The theory of positive disintegration and its implications for giftedness. In N. Duda (Ed.), *Theory of positive disintegration: Proceedings of the Third International Conference* (pp. 179-194). Miami, FL: University of Miami.

Singer, T. (2006). The neuronal basis and ontogeny of empathy and mind reading: Review of literature and implications for future research. *Neuroscience and Biobehavioral Reviews, 30,* 855-863.

Smith, R. E. (1993). *Psychology.* New York: West.

Somei, T. (1993). Treading the way of Zen: The autobiography of Tsuji Somei. In T. Leggett (Ed.), *Three ages of Zen: Samurai, feudal, and modern* (pp. 91-141). Rutland, VT: Tuttle.

Sorell, G. T., & Silverman, L. K. (1983). *Emotional development of women in mid-life.* Unpublished raw data. Denver, CO: Gifted Development Center.

Sowa, J. (1984). *Kulturowe zalozenia pojecia normalnosci w psychiatrii [Cultural foundations of the concept of normalcy in psychiatry].* Warszawa: Panstwowe Wydawnictwo Naukowe.

Spaltro, K. (1991). "A symbol perfected in death": Etty Hillesum as moral exemplar. *Advanced Development, 3,* 61-73.

Spirit of Peace, The. (1995). *A Peace Pilgrim documentary*. Hemet, CA: Friends of Peace Pilgrim.

Sroufe, L. A. (1995). *Emotional development.* New York: Cambridge University Press.

Starr, I. (1991). *Eight rungs on the ladder: A personal passage*. Ojai, CA: The Pilgrim's Path. (Original work published 1981).

Sullivan, H. S. (1953). *The interpersonal theory of psychiatry*. New York: Norton.

Suzuki, D. T. (1986). Early memories. In M. Abe (Ed.), *A Zen life: D.T. Suzuki remembered* (pp. 3-12). New York: Weatherhill.

Tannenbaum, A. J. (2000). Giftedness: The ultimate instrument for good and evil. In K. A. Heller, F. J. Mönks, R. J. Sternberg, & R. F. Subotnik (Eds.), *International handbook of giftedness and talent* (2nd ed., pp. 447-465). Oxford, England: Elsevier.

Taylor, J. (1958). (Ed.). *Selected writings of John Hughlings Jackson* (two vols.). New York: Basic Books.

Taylor, R. L. (1978). *The cultivation of sagehood as a religious goal in Neo-Confucianism: A study of selected writings of Kao P'an Lung*. Missoula, MT: Scholars.

Terman, L. M. (1925). *Genetic studies of genius: Mental and physical traits of a thousand gifted children* (Vol. 1). Stanford, CA: Stanford University Press.

Thomas, A., Chess, S., & Birch, H. G. (1968). *Temperament and behavior disorders in children*. New York: New York University Press.

Tieso, C. L. (2007a). Overexcitabilities: A new way to think about talent? *Roeper Review, 29,* 232-239.

Tieso, C. L. (2007b). Patterns of overexcitabilities in identified gifted students and their parents: A hierarchical model. *Gifted Child Quarterly, 51,* 11-22.

Tillier, W. (2006, August 3-5). The philosophical foundation of Dabrowski's theory of positive disintegration, Part 3: Friedrich Nietzsche and Dabrowski. In W. Tillier (Ed.), *Proceedings from the Seventh International Congress of the Institute of Positive Disintegration in Human Development*, Calgary, AB.

Tucker, B., & Hafenstein, N. (1997). Psychological intensities in young gifted children. *Gifted Child Quarterly, 41,* 66-75.

Tupes, E. C., & Christal, R. C. (1992). Recurrent personality factors based on trait ratings. *Journal of Personality, 60*, 225-251.

Turner, J. H., & Stets, J. E. (2006). Sociological theories of human emotions. *Annual Review of Sociology, 32*, 25-52.

Tyska, C. A. (1980). *A comparative case study of self-actualization in Eleanor Roosevelt and Antoine de Saint-Exupéry.* Unpublished master's thesis, University of Illinois, Urbana-Champaign, IL.

Unamuno, M. D. (1921). *Tragic sense of life*. New York: Dover.

VanTassel-Baska, J. (1998). *Excellence in educating gifted and talented learners.* Denver, CO: Love.

Wagstaff, M. (1997). *Outdoor leader self-awareness and its relationship to co-leaders' perceptions of influence.* Unpublished doctoral dissertation, Oklahoma State University, Stillwater, OK.

Walters, G. D. (2004). *Personality theory in context.* Allentown, PA: Center for Lifestyle Studies.

Wechsler, D. (2003). *WISC-IV technical and interpretive manual.* San Antonio, TX: Psychological Corp.

Whitmore, J. R. (1980). *Giftedness, conflict, and underachievement.* Boston: Allyn & Bacon.

Wikipedia, The Free Encyclopedia. (2007). Plato. Retrieved February 24, 2007, from http://en.wikipedia.org/w/index.php?title=Plato&oldid=110516394

Wilson, D. L. (1998). *Honor's voice: The transformation of Abraham Lincoln.* New York: Knopf.

Wisecup, A., Robinson, D. T., & Smith-Lovin, L. (2006). The sociology of emotions. In C. D. Bryant & D. L. Peck (Eds.), *21st century sociology: A reference handbook* (pp. 106-115). Thousand Oaks, CA: Sage.

Witzel, J. E. (1991). *Lives of successful never-married women: Myths and realities.* Unpublished doctoral dissertation. Northwestern University, Evanston, IL.

Yakmaci-Guzel, B. (2002). *Ustun yeteneklilerin belirlenmesinde yardimci yeni bir yaklasim: Dabrowski'nin asiri dduyarlilik alanlari [A supplementary method in the identification of gifted individuals: Dabrowski's overexcitabilities].* Unpublished doctoral dissertation, University of Istanbul, Turkey.

Yakmaci-Guzel, B. (2003). A comparison study about overexcitabilities of Turkish 10th graders. In F. J. Mönks & H. Wagner (Eds.), *Development of human potential: Investment into our future. Proceedings of the 8th Conference of the European Council for High Ability* (pp. 82-85). Bad Honnef, Germany: Bock.

Yakmaci-Guzel, B., & Akarsu, F. (2006). Comparing overexcitabilities of gifted and non-gifted 10th grade students in Turkey. *High Abilities Studies, 17,* 43-56.

Yalom, I. D. (1980). *Existential psychotherapy.* New York: Basic Books

Yalom, I. D. (1985). *The theory and practice of group psychotherapy* (3rd ed.). New York: Basic Books.

Yogananda, P. (1973). *Autobiography of a yogi.* Los Angeles, CA: Self-Realization Fellowship. (Original work published 1943).

Name Index

N

O

P

Q

R

S

T

U

V

W

Y

Z

Topic Index

T

U